A
BRUSH
WITH
NATURE

To Roz

A BRUSH WITH NATURE

25 years of personal reflections
on the natural world

RICHARD MABEY

Published in 2010 by BBC Books, an imprint of Ebury Publishing.
A Random House Group Company

Text copyright © Richard Mabey 2010
Copyright © Woodlands Books 2010
Jacket artwork and design © Woodlands Books 2010
Illustrations © Woodlands Books 2010

The Random House Group Limited Reg. No. 954009

Addresses for companies within the Random House Group can be found at
www.randomhouse.co.uk

A CIP catalogue record for this book is available from the British Library.

ISBN 978 1 84 607913 9

The Random House Group Limited supports the Forest Stewardship
Council (FSC), the leading international forest certification organisation.
All our titles that are printed on Greenpeace approved FSC certified paper
carry the FSC logo. Our paper procurement policy can be found at
www.rbooks.co.uk/environment

Commissioning editor: Muna Reyal
Project editor: Caroline McArthur
Copy-editor: Wendy Smith
Illustrations: Aaron Blecha
Production: Bridget Fish

Typeset by Seagull Design, London

Printed and bound in Great Britain by Clays of St Ives PLC

To buy books by your favourite authors and register for offers, visit
www.rbooks.co.uk

CONTENTS

3. LEAVES

4. TRACKS

5. IMAGES

6. WORDS

7. ISSUES

PREFACE

When I started contributing a column to *BBC Wildlife* back in 1984, I had very modest ambitions for it. I called it 'Turning Over an Old Leaf', and hoped to remind readers of the great English language tradition of nature writing, which seemed to have died from neglect – and from an avalanche of soulless coffee table books. I hoped that by sharing some of the forgotten delights from my own shelves – Vaughan Cornish, Edward Thomas, Gilbert White, for example – I might make it clear what I felt was missing from contemporary writing.

But books being what they are (they have subjects, for a start), this singleness of purpose quickly began to fray at the edges. With the encouragement of a supremely tolerant editor, Roz Kidman Cox, I went on to explore what the dearth of nature literature symbolised on the larger stage, especially what it said about the breakdown of the links between specialist natural history and the arts, politics, morals and our culture as a whole. Soon, the column became free-form and tales from the home patch, expeditions abroad and moments of pure fantasy began to creep in. Yet all of them, I hope, are variations on that underlying theme – that the experience of the natural world is part and parcel of our ordinary lives, and that we sideline it as a mere hobby, or as the prerogative of specialised scientists, at our – and the planet's – peril. These other beings of what has been called 'the more than human world' are our neighbours, and we need to understand how to get along with them.

The column has evolved to have something in common with traditional personal columns in the press, except that it has a much larger range of characters, of all species. It has had different titles (it has been 'A Brush with Nature' since 2005), and a few rests – once because, frankly, I'd become stale and short of ideas; and once because of a long period of illness. And I've moved house and home territory during its lifetime. From the beginning until 2002, I was based in the Chilterns. Then I moved to the Waveney Valley in south Norfolk. The columns since then have become more like single-subject essays, and I'm grateful to the current editor, Sophie Stafford, and her colleague Fergus Collins, for continuing to allow me the freedom to be outspoken at times.

The selection of pieces for this collection is my own, and has no more rationale than that they are the ones I like best, and seem to me to have stood the test of time. One way of ordering them might have been chronologically, but at the risk of occasional and, I hope, not too disorientating leaps in time and space, I felt that grouping the pieces around broad themes such as Birds, and Nature and Art, would be more helpful. I've resisted the temptation to indulge in rewriting and updating, beyond the correction of factual errors and slipshod phrasing.

This perhaps needs an explanation. The column has always been a kind of journal for me. It's where hobby-horses get their first airing, where new places and books are tentatively explored, where I try to find words for unshaped feelings. Sometimes it is unashamedly experimental and I use it as a testing ground for ideas I want to write about more fully. A few of these columns eventually became the basis for chapters in books, so if they seem vaguely familiar, remember the column is where the ideas (and sometimes the language) were first fleshed out. This sense of being written at the coal-face, so to speak, is something I think worth preserving. Whatever their faults, I've tried to make the columns an honest response to topical events and to my own developing feelings (the original date of publication appears at the end of each column). Organisations, conservation priorities, bird populations all change, but these notes are at least a contemporary record of how things were.

And reading them through again with the benefit of hindsight, I've been intrigued by the way certain themes and issues recur. Some of this is a consequence of my own fascinations and bugbears – barn owls, urban wildlife and land art among the former, and conservation jargon and the brutishness of the 'nature management' business among the latter. Elsewhere it's because the problems caused by, say, invasive species and intensive farming, won't go away.

But there are two areas where there have been big changes. Climate change was scarcely an issue 25 years ago. Now it overshadows everything we do and think – sometimes to the point of obscuring the resilience and creativity of the natural world. But a growing celebration of that creativity has been the second great change. The central premise on which the column was begun is now obsolete, and over the past few years we've seen a renaissance in English nature writing, which is now on a par with the great American tradition stretching from Henry Thoreau to Aldo Leopold and Annie Dillard. Witnessing that revival – and exploring it in the column – has been one of the most gratifying things for me, and in a way brings the story in this collection full circle.

Richard Mabey

1. ROOTS

How the column began – and how I began:
home landscapes and childhood enthusiasms.

TURNING OVER A NEW LEAF

'Writing is not living,' wrote Henry Williamson in the dark days of 1941, explaining why he had left his literary eyrie in Devon to bury himself in working the thin soil of a rundown Norfolk farm. To which *'reading* is not like living' seems to have been the retort of the post-war world, which has cocked a snook at Williamson's vast, cryptic and – except for *Tarka* and *Salar* – almost completely forgotten natural history writings.

I have no great affection for Williamson myself. The extreme right-wing views which got him into such trouble, his belief in purification through sacrifice and bloodshed, and in the righteousness of strength, seep too much into his nature books for my taste. But I mourn the fact that the *kind* of books he wrote, books of parable and allegory and metaphor in which human predicaments were seen as inextricable from natural ones, are now regarded as irrelevant if not plain soppy. What modern publisher would contemplate a piece of adult fiction called *A Weed's Tale* (1921) unless the plants were dressed up as humans and engaged in some kind of back-garden gang warfare?

Two or three times during the past 10 years I have deliberately tried to step back from despair at the endlessly wallowing tide of Country Diaries and Granny's Tips to look objectively at the state of nature writing, at its losses and gains and sense of direction. And the overriding impression each time was that just as the increasing sophistication of close-up photography and colour printing brings the workings of the natural world ever closer, so the vision of its possible meanings for us gets narrower.

What is there beyond the repetitive, anonymous guidebooks and austerely scientific texts? A handful of writers who have managed to combine real scholarship with a gift for imaginative and accessible prose, but maybe no more than a couple of works of real literature – and this from an area of concern that has been part of the central core of English writing, indeed of our whole culture. Who is writing a body of intelligent fiction rooted in the rural experience that can compare with that of John Moore or H E Bates or the Powys brothers? Where are the essayists who can move between the worlds of nature and the arts as easily as W H Hudson, Edward Thomas and Richard Jefferies? Why does our increasingly lively company of amateur naturalists no longer produce master-pieces of vision like the Victorian stone-mason Hugh Miller's *The Old Red Sandstone* and *Testimony of the Rocks,* but confine themselves to minute studies and maddeningly restrained papers in 'the journals'?

Where is the poetry, the passion, the insights, the *breadth* of learning that is precisely what we value about our heritage of nature writing? We barely have, at this moment of deepening ecological crisis, the beginnings of some tough political writing here, and have to look for this to the supposedly philistine New World. The hard fact is that in the exploration and expression of our relationships with nature we have become monocultural. It could not be more ironic. In an area whose whole driving force is a celebration of the variety of life, we are bent on impoverishing the variety of our own responses. Even in television, ever more spectacular locations and feats of photography are offered as a substitute for imagination and feeling, as if gawping were the only possible response to this world.

But of course this trend cannot be explained away by techno-logical advance. Much of it is due to an understandable and univer-sal yearning to find some kind of solace or refuge in nature, to use it as a retreat from the increasingly terrifying experience of the man-made world (forgetting that the single most important fact about the former is its ever closer engagement with the latter). Unfortunately, this habit happens to coincide with other interests that would like to keep our exploration of this central experience as bland as possible – the publishing conglomerates that do not wish to risk upsetting their consumers, the vested interests that wish to 'keep politics out of the countryside', a scientific establish-ment that does not want its authority challenged by maverick and unquantifiable views.

It was not always so, even in science, and in this column over the next few months I want to try to disinter some of the rare and vanished species of English nature writing, to show what we have lost and what we (and I mean *all* creatures here) might gain by rejoining the tradition. Books with unusual origins, like the Blooms-bury aesthete Jocelyn Brooke's extraordinary guide to British orchids. Books that make what to us seem eccentric connections, like one I came across in the Bodleian Library a few weeks ago, *An Essay on the Application of Natural History to Poetry* (1777), by John Aikin (who, besides editing Gilbert White, published a collection of English folk-songs, a history of medicine and an edition of Spenser's *Faerie Queene*). And books like Vaughan Cornish's *The Churchyard Yew and Immortality* (1946) which I offer as my Easter Book of the Month.

Vaughan Cornish was an influential writer on landscape in the 1920s and 1930s, and has been rightly subject to some severe criti-cism recently for his remote aesthetic views. But this is an altogether more human book. It is a complete survey of all the venerable yew trees in parish churchyards, prefaced by an essay on their possible significance. What makes it special and a delight to read is Cornish's willingness to work right outside conventional strait-jackets.

He compares maps of the distribution of these yews, and finds that they tie in with patterns of Roman settlement. But he also finds some correlation with their natural distribution, and concludes that there were cases, especially in southern England, where the church was put by the tree, not vice versa (an almost heretical view still). Then he looks at the distribution of yews *inside* the churchyard (there are nearly always two, the second close by the gate where coffins entered the churchyard) and at the significance of yews in local mythology and history. As a result he was, to my knowledge, the first writer to dispute the conventional patriotic view that they were planted for the sake of English archers, and to suggest that, as immensely long-lived evergreens, they were symbols of immortality and, more directly, sources of green 'palm' for Eastertide.

But it is a tantalisingly short book, written out on a limb, and you cannot help feeling how much more exciting it could have been made today, combining Cornish's vision with the skills of, say, Oliver Rackham – if only our automatic reaction to such a notion and such a preposterous title, wasn't a dismissive snort.

1984

EASING THE SPRING

'Jan 3: 1903. Am writing an essay on the life-history of insects and have abandoned the idea of writing on "How Cats Spend their Time".' So W N P Barbellion began his classic *Journal of a Disappointed Man.* He was only 13 at the time, and I have heartfelt sympathy with his sense of not being quite in control of the rudder.

Fits of self-doubt are endemic to writers. I sometimes try to assuage mine by pretending that writing is a legitimate rural trade and prose a kind of alternative crop, yielding so many bushels of words to acres tramped. If so, I can report that there is no danger of a word mountain in this particular corner of the countryside. To tell the truth it seems more like hunter-gathering than farming. There is the same element of serendipity, of lucky finds and blank days; the same merging of roles, so that foraging, as it were, becomes part of everything that you do.

Which is why, in that balmy weather towards the end of February, I found myself walking down a familiar track in a mood in which it was impossible to disentangle childish excitement and professional curiosity. The evening before I had seen the glint of running water where no running water had been for decades, and I was off, chasing whole volumes of memories and possibilities.

I have walked these hills to the south of my home since I was a teenager, and the route has become almost a ritual beat, a survey of my own personal parish. It is an unexceptional landscape of run-down parkland and narrow commons, a Home Counties pastoral. But after 30 years you can come to love every fence-post. And in this unseasonable weather there was an extraordinary, wild *frisson* in the air – a thin gauze of green already in the hedges, rooks tossing over the copses and gale-wrecked trees in every field, already seeming as cryptic and anciently rooted as standing stones.

At the edge of Icedell Wood was the most awesome collapse I have seen following the 1987 hurricane: eight oak trees on a single root-plate 15 feet high and nearly 40 feet across. The branches on the two central trees had grown away from each other, forming a huge vaulted aisle now they were prostrate. I walked up and down this immense whale's gullet, counting my steps. It was 135 feet long.

I wriggled through the tangled branches into the wood. Drifts of tits and chaffinches, fellow foragers, rose and fell in front of me. Under the beeches by the old icehouse, the first green hellebores were in flower, only days behind the celandines and on the same site they were recorded in our first county flora in 1849.

I know their history. I rejoice in their continuity. But I barely glance at them. I realise I have been racing through the wood, drawn on by the lure of the water and by workaday anxieties that I haven't unwound from. Just a few hours before I had been listening to a radio reading of Henry Reed's famous war poem, *The Naming of Parts*, in which he contrasts the stripping down of a rifle with the first stirrings of a winter garden:

> And this you can see is the bolt. The purpose of this
> Is to open the breech, as you see. We can slide it
> Rapidly backwards and forwards: we call this
> Easing the spring. And rapidly backwards and forwards
> The early bees are assaulting and fumbling the flowers:
> They call it easing the Spring.

Not yet eased myself, I ponder that we write a good deal on the names of the parts of bees, on what we do to bees, but not on what bees do to us. Just a few hundred yards more and I am in the valley, barely able to stop running. That distant glint of silver had been no mirage. Our local winterbourne, the Woewater, is up and flowing for the first time in 15 years. The vast winter rains are bursting through the seams between clay and chalk and charging down the valley.

Within half a mile the stream is four feet wide and flowing as fast as I can walk. It has torrents and oxbows and eddies, and underneath them the young meadow grass is waving as silkily as waterweed. In one dip it has formed a pool by the edge of a wood, and bubbles rising from buried air-pockets look like summer midges settling on the surface. I am time-warped, and for a few seconds am seized by the conviction that a first precocious swallow will coast down the valley and begin hawking over the pool.

It doesn't, of course, but a mile or so further on I see something almost as wondrous. The stream has flooded the valley meadows, and flocks of fieldfares and redwings are feeding near the edge of the water. A snipe jinks in the distance and, much closer, a heron lopes up from a pond that has been a dry pit since I was a child. The water suddenly makes sense of the whole geography of the valley – the position of the farms, the ancient black poplar again standing with its roots in water. There is a legend here that the Woewater only flows in time of war and dire trouble, but it is hard to see how it could have brought anything but good to this dry chalk country.

Back home I check in my diary to see if I had recalled the last rising accurately. I noted it on 12 April 1975 – a year memorable more for its wonderful summer than any particular woe. I remember it chiefly for the fact that the fighting in Vietnam finally ended a fortnight later. I am not superstitious, but I think that is a better legend to cling to, and that the rising of water and sap, the easing of spring, is a sign of hope.

1988

NATURE STUDY

When I was about 11 years old, my father let me make a laboratory in the far end of his greenhouse. To tell the truth, it was more like an alchemist's den than a lab, a place where I could indulge a precocious fascination with the transformation of matter. I kept my chemicals in mum's old kitchen jars: iron filings, copper sulphate, magnesium ribbon, mercury (which you could then buy over the counter at Boots) and potassium permanganate, with which a gang of us later dyed the local girls' school swimming pool dark purple one night. I learned how to glass-blow my own thistle-funnels, and make the allotropes of sulphur – plastic and crystalline – in a candle-heated tin. But not a single living thing ever entered the lab to be poked about, cut up or peered at through a microscope.

This is even odder when I recall the siting of my research shack. On one side were dad's luxuriant tomatoes. On the other – just two yards away – was the tumbledown landscape park where we local kids spent our holidays. This was where I did a different kind of experimentation, gathering nuts, testing the tastes of leaves, walking my own songlines. And this was where I first watched barn owls, beating along the edges of the park, sharing our gang's territorial boundaries–creatures from another, luminous world. There was just a single thread of barbed wire separating this arcadia from the lab, but I took it for granted they were two entirely separate worlds. Nature and science.

I went on to do passably well at physics and chemistry and went to Oxford with the intention of studying biochemistry, never having done an hour's scientific biology in my life. I changed subjects after a fortnight, appalled at the animal experiments we were required to do. It wasn't that I disliked or mistrusted science – far from it. But when it came to living things, science seemed to me just one way of looking at them, and in no way adequate for catching their inner lives and relationships. When I first started writing about nature in the early 1970s it was the poets' and artists' visions of the natural world that fascinated me, the way nature had been taken into human culture. More objective, mechanistic information was there, but always in the background.

My stance on this was shifted dramatically last year, and again a barn owl was in the thick of it. It was spending the winter in an old farm building just a couple of hundred yards from our house in Norfolk. The first time I saw it (him, I think) I felt like a shaman. I'd planned a route for a walk near the house, and he swum into view almost immediately, an intensely pale bird, with a slight grey chequering on the back. For the next hour he languidly flew just 50 metres in front of me, on exactly the route I'd planned to follow before I set out.

For most of that winter I watched and followed him obsessively. I began to see the farming landscape through his eyes: the thin seams of unploughed grass, the tangled field dykes, his mysteriously favoured paddocks. I'd always been in thrall to barn owls, and had written about them as symbols of the dusk, talismans of 'good ground'. But I could no more reduce this intimate companion to the status of a symbol than I could regard him as an object. I wanted to get to know him. What happened to him in the rain? Why would he hunt the same beat at the same time for days on end, then suddenly go round it the opposite way? Was he really a male? Might he meet the female bird (or so I dubbed her) that lived in the next parish? If they did, whose roost would they nest in, if either? I was asking the same questions that scientists do, but for very different reasons. One afternoon, when he sailed lazily out of a tree right above me, he turned through 90 degrees and stared at me before flying away. I felt both chastised and recognised. He'd become, I suddenly realised, a *neighbour*. If I couldn't gossip with him, at least I could gossip about him.

He went away that spring, alas, and hasn't returned. But he's made a lasting impact on me. On the rebound, I'm flirting with lichens. I used to see these as distant beauties too, chiaroscuro patterns on dark trunks. Now I'm trying to get neighbourly with them. I'm learning the unfamiliar language of podetia and thallus. I've unearthed a brass Victorian microscope I was given 20 years ago, and have seen them in intimate close-up, the intricate forests of leaves and twigs that these symbiotic combinations of fungus and alga produce in working out their own neighbourly relations. The pursuit of neighbourliness requires the exact curiosity of science and the caringness of affection. That's not a bad combination for approaching our fellow organisms.

2007

* * *

Even before it was spruced up to become the location for *Middlemarch*, Stamford was one of England's most gracious towns. The River Welland's watermeadows form a valley right through the centre of the town, and you can see herons and kingfishers flying past the car parks. Ferns deck out the Barnack limestone walls of the ruined castle and the multitude of courtyards, churches and valleys.

Stamford also has its quota of antique shops – a relatively new diversion in my life – and in one of these I found an object that could have come straight from Mr Casaubon's study, as he laboured on his life's work *A Key to All Mythologies*. It was a small tin box, about the size of a pencil case, called 'The Requisite Box for Nature Study – Complete with Requisite Note Book'.

From the elaborate ornamentation on the lid, I would guess it was just a little post-*Middlemarch*, probably from the early years of this century. Inside was an odd but telling assortment of bits and pieces: a rosewood-handled scalpel, still razor-sharp; an impaling pin; a pair of tweezers; a botanist's magnifying glass (minus lens, alas); a microscope slide; a strip of cork, criss-crossed with deep cuts; and a few pieces of blackboard chalk. It was rather like a set of clues in a game of 'Whodunit' – and to what?

But the 'Requisite Note Book' told a rather different story. Inside its front cover is printed a set of salutary 'Hints for Beginners':

> **Remember.** *Order is Nature's first law, therefore keep your specimens and notebook tidy.*
> **Microscope.** *Use your microscope on every possible occasion, the small things of Nature being the most beautiful.*
> **Notebook.** *Write and draw everything possible in your notebook. You will be surprised how this improves the memory.*
> **Be careful!** *Do not destroy life, either vegetable or animal, wantonly. You are the Guardian of these things.*

Inside the book, the hand of one A. Leeds had written and sketched in pencil on the structure of maize seeds and beans and snowdrop bulbs. His or her other notes are in turgid botanical language, but produced with passion and meticulousness.

I hope the gashes on the cork board weren't breaches of 'rule four', and I'm not totally convinced about order and smallness being at the aesthetic heart of Nature. But I wouldn't be unhappy about these precepts being set up at the front of the environment section of the National Curriculum. I confess I have a soft spot for what always used to be called 'nature study', which I think is a friendlier and more accurate description than the more formal 'natural history', and the various cross-disciplinary 'environmental studies' that succeeded it. I guess the term became compromised by association with supposedly tweedy teachers in the Joyce Grenfell mould and too many anthropomorphised animals.

My own memories of nature study are very different. We had a brilliant local naturalist as our teacher, and she took us on field trips almost every week, out on fungus forays in autumn and pond-dipping in summer, to watch whirligig beetles spinning on the surface and search for the extraordinary diving-bell which the water spider spins for itself. I remember finding, on my way to school one morning, a freshly dead pipistrelle bat impaled on a car radiator. It was still warm, from the sun reflected off the chrome, and seemed completely undamaged. I was barely eight years old, moved in ways I scarcely understood by its look of composure, and stroked it distractedly all the way back to school, hoping I could coax it back to life. It ended up as an exhibit in a jar at the back of the class.

I regret all the collecting and bottling of those early years, but not the riveting attention I acquired for what William Cowper called nature's 'minute particulars'. In the sense of crisis in which all environmental science is taught today, I sometimes feel that real living things get lost in a vague green haze. Yet it is their particularity, and our fascination with this (that the 'Requisite Box' so vehemently urged) on which the future of the whole system rests. I also suspect – though this may seem paradoxical on the surface – that such attentiveness is a key to imaginative, and maybe even spiritual, understanding and writing about nature. Exactness of observation is inseparable from clarity of thinking and language; both imply that the subject deserves respect – which is the gateway to both affection and care.

1995

SECOND HOME

Almost exactly a year ago, when I was just surfacing after a long illness, a dear friend who'd helped rescue me, spied me cringing on the edge of a boat and said, 'If you're moving up to East Anglia, you'd bloody well better learn to cope with water.' Well, she'd be proud of me now. In a gale that would have kept me in bed if I'd known it would blow up, I've just taken the helm of an 18ft dinghy in the Broads, and sailed it for five whole minutes without capsizing or even making a fool of myself. We were on Hickling National Nature Reserve, and there was wildfire in the reedbeds. Marsh harriers were patrolling the fringes of the smoke cloud, looking for refugees, and awash with confidence, I tried to line up the sail with the dihedral in their wings, which carries them in that seeming miracle of moving against the wind. Then one did a 90° tack on a pinhead ... I know my limits, even though they're changing.

Water defines much of East Anglia, just as woodland defines my old stamping ground in the Chilterns, and over the past 12 months I've learnt to understand a little about Gerard Manley Hopkins' 'wildness and wet', and how it differs from the more measured gravitas of woodland wildness.

Even from the briefest encounters, you realise that environments touched by water are fleet-footed, opportunist, joined-up. This spring, I watched our house martins gather mud from the smallest possible wetlands in the chain – the little pools that had collected on the sugar-beet stand. The water was sticky from sugar, leached out of the stacked roots, and I'm surprised it didn't gum up the martins' beaks. Their nests must be unique in being made of rock-cake. But those puddles were partly topped-up by overflow from the field-ditch that runs alongside the lane, which in winter turns into a raging bourne, stained yellow by washed-out sand, and which joins up with the River Waveney and all its drains and tiny tributaries. These in turn water what remain of the valley fens and a host of unclassifiable damp patches – field-corner reed-stands, dykes, old clay-pits – driving a stew of living stuff, from moorhens to meadowsweet roots, through what amounts to a blood-vessel system.

Wetness here, for all its fabulous variety, is a great leveller. It conspires livelihoods in the new and the old, the natural and man-made alike. It fills the natural ponds formed by glacial ice lumps ('pingos') with cranberries, and the next-door parish peat-diggings with raft-spiders. It animates Broads, moats, cattle-wallows. You can sense this continuity, this quickening, whenever you step into the wet. Your pressure squeezes water from the peat, makes an efflorescence about your foot, and you can believe that yards, maybe miles, further on, it presses water out into a parched dyke, on to slumbering aquatic growths.

The fen hums around you. The wind passes on the sweet and sharp scents of valerian and watermint, and rocks the flower-spikes of marsh helleborines that are uncurling like swans' necks. Froglets seem an embodiment of the oozing mud. Dragonflies shoot past at eye-level, soundlessly I guess, but seeming to find a new sense in you between hearing and peripheral vision, to make some brittle crack in the air. You are not just *in* a habitat, you are part of a living membrane, pulsing with life, its scents and vibrations linked with your own. You leave your own mark, too, churning the mud, ferrying seeds, briefly opening the canopy. The wet, for all its underlying layers of ancestral peat, is about here, now, living in the moment, taking your chances.

The wood, by contrast, is about memory, about centuries of experience locked up in grain and forkings and the slow cycles of light and shade. It is a slow, resilient, reflective state. Between them, the wood and the water represent the complementary qualities of nature: the deep, accumulated wild-wisdom of evolution, the encoded experience; and that electric immediacy of growth, of spring and play. These are the two states that nature oscillates between. In a few special places in the Broads and fens, where the water level is high and there is no fussy management, you can see one such cycle in a human life-time. Tussocks rise above the pools, dry enough for alder and willows to take root. The developing trees shade out the fen vegetation and gradually weigh the tussocks down until their roots become unstable or waterlogged and they fall over. The water rises and the cycle begins again. All life exists between the wood and the water.

2003

I moved from the Chilterns to the Waveney Valley in the autumn of 2002, first to lodgings in a farmhouse on the Suffolk side, then 9 months later with Polly to a house on the Norfolk side (see p 22). [2009]

NEW NEIGHBOURS

It's been by turns intriguing and perplexing getting to know the plants of my new territory. I've seen a few species entirely fresh to me (cowbane in the Broadland dykes is a cracker), and more which have been renewed by their settings and companions. Down in the fen, for instance, I've seen some very familiar species in their ancestral habitats. Hops shoot out of the damp loams, often yards from any support, and twine up flag blades, tussocks, even each other. Wild redcurrants grow straight out of pools. Their leaf tops have a purple sheen, as if dabbed with wine, and the small tassels of yellow-green flowers, five-petalled, edged with purple, have the look of tiny medieval carvings.

But in the spring, I was quite foxed by the wetland flora. In all the dank and quaggy places, the peat sprouted bewitching tangles of spikes and tendrils and frills. I knew the bright green, beached-starfish leaves of butterwort, but were those clubby shoots poking out of the moss the beginnings of sundew? What about the purple crowns and viridian fern-tips that stood up like finials in the fen? As for sedges, they were luxuriantly incomprehensible. Most of my books, alas, were still in a storage container somewhere up the Great North Road, and I was rusty after two seasons out of the field, frustrated that I didn't know what was what.

But then an unfamiliar inner voice said to me: why bother? Why not simply relish the returning life (and your new life, for that matter) – its exquisite variegation, the subtle interplay of the yellow moss ground, the filigree sedges and the solid mass of tussocks, the intricate, pulsing wholeness of it all? Well, I can, I think, but I can't stop there. Some inner compulsion makes me want to *know who they are*. It may be just a hangover of whatever impulse made me repeatedly check my stamp collection against a Stanley Gibbons catalogue when I was a boy, but I'd still make a strong argument for the cultural importance of identification and naming. Some years ago, the writer John Fowles argued that 'the name of an object is like a pane of dirty glass between it and you.' I can't agree. It seems to me that naming a plant is a gesture of respect towards its unique individuality, its distinction from the generalised green blur. You wouldn't do anything less for a friend.

And the process of learning that identity brings you closer. I remember the first time I was shown 'keying out' by a professional botanist friend. We were in The Burren in Ireland, surrounded by a dazzling display of sky-blue gentians and vermilion cranesbill. And near our faces (we were lying down) was a stumpy orchid, not pretty but enthralling in its drab compactness. Clapham, Tutin and Warburg took us through its features – the thin lines of spots along the leaves, like trails of rust, the dense, creamy flower-spike, a scent of vanilla. Hello, *Neotinia intacta*! Now I'll remember that Irish May, and Rachel, whenever I see it again.

But plants aren't just 'species', members of an abstract class. They have addresses as well as names, spots where we've found them, befriended them, shared a moment and a place in our lives. John Clare knew 16 orchids from Helpston in the 1820s and logged them according to his personal map of the parish. Early marsh orchids (he called them 'cuckoos') grew 'by a brook side in a close near Brigges's Barn – was very plentiful before the Enclosure on a Spot called Parkers Moor near Peasfield-hedge …'

That was real neighbourliness – knowledge, affection and concern brought together, and I wish I'd felt that when I rashly went off on a plant twitch in spring. I was tetchy from some legal business and the gnawing anxiety I always feel when the summer migrants are late arriving. So I drove north to Wayland Wood, the site of the *Babes in the Wood* legend and the only place in Norfolk where the yellow star of Bethlehem grows and has done 'since records began'. I didn't so much want to see it as to *find* it and to prove that all was right with the world – and right with me, too, that I hadn't lost the knack of finding a plant. But I'd failed to track the shy flowerer down 25 years ago, and I did no better this time. I quartered the wood, peered around every conceivable niche, nudged down stopped-off paths. But I hadn't a clue about either the place or the jizz of the plant. I was a stranger and a trainspotter, and it served me right. When I gave in and just meandered, the wood became enchanting, spangled with wide-open celandines, wood anemones and the first early purple orchids. And just coming into flower all over the wood was something special I did know: the white, warm-flour-and-honey-scented racemes of bird cherry. At once I was in the Yorkshire Dales in June 1985. I was with an exhausted film-crew, and we were saying an emotional goodbye to each other after a long shoot in desperate weather. The bird cherry around us was still in flower, but quite leafless from the predation of ermine moth caterpillars, and decorated instead with their silken canopies. The bird cherry may be indifferent to our relationship, but for me it already spans moods and miles and decades.

2003

THE NORFOLK BROADS

Anyone who thinks that the 'problems' of the Norfolk Broads are new should read G Christopher Davies' *Handbook,* which almost single-handedly opened the place up as a leisure resort in the 1880s. Thanks to him the place was fast becoming a rowdy, refuse-strewn, gun-happy frontier-land, and in his 18th edition he tried to introduce a code of etiquette for the 'bottle shooters, coot potters, and noisy revellers'. He suggests that 'Young men who lounge in a nude state on boats while ladies are passing may be saluted with dust shot or the end of a quant.' And that was long before the arrival of motor cruisers and nitrate pollution.

So when Polly and I decided to have a Swallows and Amazons weekend ourselves, a few eyebrows were raised, as if we were planning a short-break in a caravan outside Norwich City football ground. We had the last laugh, as we knew we would. In the last decade the Broads have been transformed. The sewage outfalls have been cleaned up, speed-limits imposed on the boats and the whole place designated as a national park. It's now a model for the multiple-use of wild places.

It began as it was to continue. Going downstream from Wroxham, with low clouds scudding in the June gales, we saw our first hobby inside ten minutes, breasting and stalling into the wind like a pigeon. The next was a quarter of an hour later, over reed-scrub on the edges of Wroxham Broad. It was doing something I've never seen in a hobby before, hovering like a kestrel, but with its wings vibrating as fast as a hummingbird's.

Hobbies were almost constant companions over the next few days, and spotting them became part of our shipboard routine. One of us steered, the other kept look out from the bridge: hobby (or harrier, or heron) at 11 o'clock! We cruised into various Broads, chugged more slowly past private pools with their unbreached rafts of water-lilies, and gazed out over the vast landscape of tossing reeds and alder-swamps. In the evenings we became more intimately tangled with the vegetation, as we tried to find places to moor. Hemp-agrimony proved a doughty anchor tussock. Wild blackcurrants went into the muesli. The carr, so often dismissed as some inferior habitat to reed and sedge, was hectic with what we came to call edge-warblers: a convivial mix of first-brood Cetti's, reed and willow warblers, and tits of all sorts.

The intimacy of the birds was extraordinary. They weren't exactly tame, but were quite unfazed by the boats. Terns and swallows skimmed the water continuously. We watched kingfishers feeding while we were having breakfast, and great crested grebes all day. This may be the densest population of these birds in the country. On the rivers we saw a pair every 200 yards. They would swim close to the boat, often with their zebra-striped chicks tucked under their wings, or float by – head tilted to one side, almost flat against the surface of the water, spying for fish. But often they would swim straight at the nose of the boat and dive into the bow-wave, surfing past in what I think was the pure pleasure of messing about with boats. The butterflies and dragonflies were just as confiding. The one swallowtail we saw seemed enraptured with the unfurling sail of our little dinghy, and weaved flirtatiously among its folds.

It's frustrating, but probably fortunate, that you can't get off a boat and plunge straight into some of the great marshland wildernesses, like Catfield Fen. A green and impenetrable wall of alder, willow, sweet-grass, bristling with ferns and guelder-rose thickets, stands in between. We knew we'd have to go the long way round to get into the wild heart of the Broads, round Hickling. It wasn't easy. We missed the low tide, and couldn't get under the medieval bridge at Potter Heigham. Rather desperate (it was our last day), we hired an electric day-boat, and as the cloud and rain came down yet again, purred up Candle Dyke among marsh harriers patrolling the reed-swamp and lagoons. We moored and hiked to the Norfolk Wildlife Trust's reserve, and made it to the celebrated bittern hide just before the storm broke. A few weeks before one of the local pairs of cranes had raised two young in a nest just outside the hide. Now the family were hiding out in the reeds, and hard to see. But as we walked back, the rain passed, and we saw a bittern, a barn owl and two hobbies, very close, hunting for dragonflies from a thorn tree, like flycatchers.

Back on our boat, we cruised through the wonderful jumble of riverside dwellings at Potter Heigham, a frontier village of anglers' shacks, thatched retirement bungalows, mock windmills and self-build cabins customised with sculptures of Andy Capp and voluptuous Greek goddesses. Broadland is no place for snobs. Both birds and people are adaptable and opportunist here. Swallows nest in the prefab boathouses, and real geese feed next to the topiaried ones on the riverside lawns.

That evening the sky cleared and an almost luminous mist, 6 feet thick, came down over the entire marshland landscape. We moored up smartly on a long anglers' pitch and, at about 10 o'clock, the bats arrived. My bat detector went off like a football rattle. Accusing fishermen's torches were trained on our boat. The bats – Daubenton's and pipistrelles – were materialising out of the mist, crackling like furious black sparks, flickering over our deck. It was about 7°C, but party time for all of us.

2004

PLAY TIMES

By the eighth week of the most extraordinary of summers (2003), everybody was at it. In our market town, Diss, the entire population went into hot-weather moult and partied by the Mere. And so did the local swifts, whose flight games over the water were nothing short of pyrotechnic self-indulgence. In the hottest weeks, I watched them quite deliberately slaloming through telephone wires.

The normally serious business of gardening also turned positively playful. Down our lane, a neighbour put out a cardboard box and a single cabbage, price: 40p. The whole countryside was riotous with these festive and uneconomic mixtures of social display and enterprise – 'oven-ready rabbits, RARE HOSTAS', three bunches of sweet Williams, 'Honey, Goshawks!' (the latter for watching, not eating). Even the meadow and wayside flowers were blooming in the kind of billowing profusion we hadn't seen for two generations, making hay while the sun shone. The whole landscape was *en fête*.

I'm intrigued by play, and for that matter by all gratuitous, extravagant and *unnecessary* business. It often seems to me that we are closer to nature when we're playing than at any other juncture of our lives. Of course, our needs for food, sex and territory are absolutely animal-based. And because play is so intricately linked with art, it can somehow seem unearthly, as abstract as higher maths. Yet I've a hunch that it, and a philosophy based around it, may be our 'way back'.

I doubt that even the most ardent behaviourists can believe any longer that animal play is simply a utilitarian rehearsal for more functional business. Sometimes it looks more like the point of life. In the spring, I went back to the Chilterns hoping for a nostalgic glimpse of the red kites. The hills were looking their best – gaunt, reckless, poised for action – but it was cool and blowy, and I doubted the birds would show themselves. As soon as I turned up towards the scarp, though, there they were, hanging like crossbows against the leafless ridge-woods. They weren't sheltering in the lee of the beeches – they were out riding the wind, bold as brass. The further south I went, the more kites appeared. They were sporting over the villages, lifting on gusts that took them sailing clean over cottages, then down to the level of the birdtables. Then, suddenly, the sky was full of kites, a shifting mesh of flight-lines that stretched as far as I could see in all directions. There was no way of counting the birds, but there were at least 60 in the air at once.

It was the most extraordinary spectacle. The birds were deliberately using the gale to try out their flying skills. They were using their tails like rudders, sometimes spiralling round with them so fanned-out that their distinctive forks became invisible. One stooped, falling out of the air like a peregrine. Another allowed itself to be slewed sideways for about 100 metres without moving a feather. Then they'd turn into the wind, raise their wings – as relaxed as a dancer's arms or a half-full jibsail – and gather the air in, fold it into themselves. It was so perfectly beautiful, so naturally muscular, that I couldn't help flexing my own shoulders, in sympathy. I didn't want to fly, or be a bird, but they transported me, back to being six years old again, rushing down a hill with my arms held out.

Occasionally, the birds' mewing calls blew my way, but this was no mass courtship display. Red kites aren't communal birds as their black cousins are, and there was no pairing visible, except for a few brief chases. The birds, I am sure, were simply playing, responding to the rhythms of the air, just as we might to music. For some reason, it reminded me of an enthralling description by an anthropologist of the antics of bowls players, cobbled together out of sensuous instincts and bits of sympathetic magic: 'A bowler aims and plays his ball, wishing it to run true and hit the jack. He watches eagerly as it rolls, nodding his head, his body bent sideways, stands balancing on one leg, jerks over violently to the other side as the critical point is reached, makes as though to push the ball on with hand or foot, gives a last jerk ...' Play can be an approach to life as well as a pastime. Back in the early 1970s, Joseph Meeker, one of the founding sages of Deep Ecology, wrote his inspiring *The Comedy of Survival: Literary ecology and a play ethic* about the pragmatism and playfulness of nature. He outlined a common ground for humans and nature, which he called 'the Comic Way'. It is the polar opposite of Management by Objectives. It's against gloom and ideology, and for improvisation, optimism and freedom. The principles he draws up for this 'Playbill of Rights' (for all species) include: 'All players are equal, or can be made so ... Boundaries are well-observed by crossing them ... Novelty is more fun than repetition ... The best play is beautiful and elegant... the purpose of playing is to play, nothing else.'

2003

* * *

I imagine everyone has their own vivid recollections of the August heatwave: hosepipe bans and wasp plagues; a giant Caribbean turtle gulping jellyfish in the English Channel; beechmast so heavy that it made the leaves look as if they were brown in July; and that rare experience in Britain of heat intense enough to come close to the pain threshold.

But how long will they last? Our climatic folk memory is notoriously short and erratic, and full of a gloomy mythology whose only silver lining is a vague belief in ancient Golden Summers. It is as if, living in a part of the world where the weather will always be capricious, we daren't allow ourselves the luxury of remembering particular weather instances for fear of developing foolhardy expectations.

Who now recalls the summer of 1983, which had the hottest July for 300 years? Or 1975, which started on 6 June after snowfalls on the

2nd and stretched to the end of August? (And hands up all those who are thinking 'surely he means the 1976 heatwave?' universally remembered, with typical British masochism, because it led to a drought.) I hope I'm not being smug. I doubt if I would remember them myself if I hadn't kept a weather diary for 20 years. I certainly can't imagine what my most abiding image of 1990's heatwave would turn into if I hadn't written it down.

It was a Sunday night at the beginning of August, and too hot for sleep. I was lying on the bed gazing idly out of the window, when the sky suddenly became full of careering balls of light. They were round and hazy and darting about in a way that made them look indisputably alive. I was mesmerised at first, then alarmed, but by the time I had summoned another member of the household as a witness they had vanished. For the next few days what I thought was a firmly rooted natural scepticism had a very rough ride indeed. I thought up every possible rationalisation. I wondered if I had witnessed a bizarre electric storm or a giant corn circle being formed, or in fact was suffering from heatstroke and had witnessed nothing at all. I even toyed desperately with the possibility that they might have been bats which had picked up phosphorescence in their roosts, as barn owls sometimes did. Four days later the local paper saved me from panic, if not embarrassment. The lights had been seen all over the area, and had come not from UFOs or luminous bats but from a Tina Turner rock concert at a park more than 15 miles away.

1991

HOUSE AND GARDEN

I've moved house again. Not far, just a mile north over the River Waveney. But this time it's our own place, and as it stands on a fair-sized patch of land, it's going to make me think about that philosophical divide between the wild and the tame in more practical terms than I ever have before.

Both sides seem to have already staked their claims. The house was built in the early 1600s, from timbers that in places still carry fragments of impacted bark. The walls were cobbled together from clay and flint, and above them some of the roof-laths are still lashed down with woven willow. The whole place seems barely to have disentangled itself from the landscape outside.

Our patch is surrounded on two and a half sides by dead-flat Norfolk prairie. But more ancient systems of farming have left their echoes. We have a pond that was probably first dug to provide the clay for the walls, and then used as a 'retting' pond, for soaking hemp fibres clear of their husks. Hemp, for cloth and rope, was the great smallholders' and commoners' crop in the Waveney Valley (and would be again if it wasn't for the Home Office's paranoia). On the 1839 Tithe Map the 10 acres then attached to our farmhouse were all labelled as 'Hempland'.

This pond, 18 feet deep and fed by a cold spring, is the epi-centre of the garden, the hinterland between nature and culture. Goldfinches and woodpeckers drink under cover of the tangled tree-roots that drape its sides. Six species of dragonfly hawked over it in the summer. But its artificially steep banks maintain it resolutely as a garden pond. Should we free it up a bit, scallop in some shallows, give nature more of an edge, trade off some old culture for some new?

On the domestic side of the pond, so to speak, the decisions are easier. Polly will grow vegetables in the walled garden we're build-ing. I'll indulge my Mediterranean longings with a patch of garrigue, with lavenders and cistus and asphodels. (It has what I hope are honourably recycled foundations: a load of limestone rubble from a Lincolnshire quarry that serendipitously found its way to Norfolk as ballast for an empty lorry.) And I'm working on a bird-feeding station made out of agricultural junk. It's a feeble ecological joke – turning ploughshares into swards – but I rather like the idea of all that ambitious ironware rusting into oblivion among the flowers.

But beyond the pond, nature will have a louder say. We've about half an acre of grass, which will slowly be teased into meadowland.

We had it cut in August. A farmer friend from Thrandeston came over with a haymaker so gigantic that I blanched when I saw it lumber through the gates. But he cut the whole lot in four or five sweeps without knocking a single apple off the Bramley.

Now we've got a cropped sward speckled with invitingly bare skid-marks and molehills. I can't be doing with the conventional technique of spraying the whole area with heavy-duty herbicide and reseeding from scratch. Instead, in what I hope is a simulacrum of the way that grasslands evolve naturally, these little opportunist patches will become the growth points. We're helping them on their way, scattering seeds gathered on the local greens – sorrel, wild carrot, knapweed, fleabane, vetches – like spices into an already seething pot.

Only a tiny fraction will be accepted, but with luck the grassland may come to resemble the lost common that once adjoined our house. Or then again, become whatever it chooses. Our insects have already decided. They are ancient occupants. All last summer, they swarmed through the house and garden. First were the black ants, a ceaseless tide flowing from every crack between plaster and floor. There were more, plus weevils and spiders, in the thatch. Sometimes we would watch green woodpeckers and wrens clinging upside down to the netting and feeding from the straw-ends. When the heatwave began, hummingbird hawkmoths spent breakfasts darting between the honeysuckle and the muesli bowls. But most touching of all were the crickets.

Green oak bush-crickets came into the house soon after the ethereal green tortix moths and stalked everywhere (beds included) on their prodigiously cranked-up legs. A dark bush-cricket turned up in the sewing-box, exploring a chunk of magnet. That evening we found him squatting on a dimmer switch – a hippy cricket, fond of good vibes. My field-guide says his night-time song is a 'staccato psst-psst'.

This unexpected intimacy with insects has had a deep effect on me. The whole property is coming to seem not so much an invaded (or invading) colony, as a kind of joint carapace, a complex living shell generated by all its occupants. Gardening is not necessarily about fussy meddling and regimentation. It can also be romantic, playful, intimate, wild, an equal dialogue with nature, and maybe the best model of all for the relationship we should aspire to.

2004

* * *

The hornet burst into the kitchen late one night after one of those interminably wet and cold August days. I had no idea hornets were in any way nocturnal and do not know what drew it towards our open window. But for a quarter of an hour its intense presence dominated the room. It thrashed frantically against the walls. It flew so heavily, its segmented body trailing almost vertically downwards, that it looked like two insects clasped together. Close-to, I could see its thorax pulsating like a bellows. It was hyperventilating. This wasn't the furious hornet of popular myth, but one, I think, in the grip of a panic attack. I caught it eventually, with the help of a plastic beer mug and a large birthday card, and put the whole lot out into the drizzle, hoping that at least that might be preferable to the cosy prison of our house.

Back in the spring I wrote about how moving to an old house has meant a new intimacy with the mysterious lives of insects. This is partly the result of what an estate agent might call its 'characterful' fabric. It is, forgive the pun, an accommodation with the wild. Beetles sidle in under the ill-fitting doors. Crickets hang out in the lamp-lit corners of the living room. Goodness knows what's going on in the thatch.

But I also have the sense of the house being a kind of squatters' encampment on anciently occupied territory. The emergence of the black ants this year again seemed a ritual of frustration and bewilderment, an awakening into a world turned upside-down. It is supposed to be a brilliant, ephemeral marriage rite, a brief glitter of sequined wings on one special day each year. The winged males and females fly up and mate. The females descend to Earth, pull off their wings and begin searching for nesting sites. But our house ants poured out of their winter quarters for two months without cease, spilling from alarming new holes in the floor and marching along the tops of my treasured botany books. They shuffled this way and that, across the carpets and up the windows, but seemed desultory and lost, uninterested in getting outside for their nuptial flights. In the evenings they retreated back into their crevices. I helped as best I could, taking ant-covered rugs into the garden and leaving doors and windows open, until the house was overrun by opportunist blackbirds and robins. It was not until mid-August that they finally vanished from the house, or back into it, with, it seemed to me, the next generation unassured.

As I watch our insects as closely as I can, such mysteries proliferate. In June I was mesmerised by the courtship flights of ghost swift moths, in which the males danced and swooped over a patch of reed with wings vibrating so fast they looked like tiny balls of mist. And just before the farcical hoverfly 'invasion' of the Essex coast in July, when these most benign of pollinators were being vilified as 'pests', I watched hundreds of thin, Latinesque hoverflies feeding on our knotweed. They were the only species on it, and were nowhere else in the garden. What extraordinary refinements of scent and sight must have brought those two organisms together. Later, I tried to capitalise on moths' sense of smell by painting a few trees and posts with that traditional entomologists' mix of beer, brown sugar and black treacle – a potion which seemed, during the brewing, to be rather too tasty to devote to the moths. It was. During the endlessly cool dusks they remained untempted and invisible, hiding out in the herbage. A few – oak rollers, blood-veins, indistinguishable noctuids – hung still and heraldic on the walls, their lives, I felt, only half-lived.

How does one write about creatures whose states of consciousness are so remote from ours, whose lives are so brief and mercurial and full of what we see as the horrors of cannibalism and slavery and living parasitism? Not, certainly, by trying to interpret insects' behaviour in terms of human institutions, as in so much writing about social bees and ants. The great Jean-Henri Fabre perhaps came close in his intensely observed, empathetic and non-judgemental essays.

But perhaps a truly sympathetic approach would need a non-Western mind-set and a willingness to embrace an idea of consciousness not rigidly welded to the individual organism – to see insects as subjects not objects.

And yet, when I think of our ants and hornets, I know there are experiences we share, too. The Greek political prisoner George Mangakis befriended three mosquitoes during his long solitary confinement. 'They were struggling hard to resist the cold that was just beginning,' he wrote in *Letter to Europeans*. 'In the daytime they slept on the wall. At night they would come buzzing over me. What were they asking from me? Something unimportant. A drop of blood – it would save them. I couldn't refuse. At nightfall, I would bare my arm and wait for them. They would come to me quite naturally, openly. This trust is something I owe them ... It shows the solidarity that can be forged between unhappy creatures.'

A few weeks later the hornet returned – upstairs this time. We switched off the light opened the window, shut the door and left it to its own secret devices.

2004

* * *

From my study I can just see the tideline of cowslips that's edging into our scrap of meadow, a ripple of yellow between the trees and the sandy grassland. Actually tideline's an exaggeration: close-to it's more a ragged scatter of plants advancing from one self-sown clump. But they thrill me more than the chunkier flowers struggling through the rank grass nearer the house – so obviously the result of my half-hearted attempts at deliberate seeding. Why on Earth, you may well ask, do I feel differently about them? A cowslip is a cowslip. But I confess that in striving to keep as much of our garden as wild as possible, I'm attracted by the idea of wildness as a *style,* not just a collection of species. I love the surprise and serendipity of natural succession, of watching, in my own patch, the ancient processes of decay and colonisation.

There's no problem achieving this with mobile creatures. We have as many hornets round the lamps as moths. Great tits are nesting in a chimenea we failed to seal properly over winter. And I think we may be one of the very few homes to have green woodpecker on the 'inside-the-house' list. But vegetation sometimes needs a kick-start to become half-way natural – which raises the interesting philosophical question of how much human intervention you can have before a garden ceases to be 'wild'.

There's nothing new about an interest in what I might call a wild aesthetic. It was the guiding principle of the Picturesque school of landscape designers in the 18th century. Uvedale Price was the main scourge of the formal landscapes championed by Kent, Repton and Capability Brown. He was scathing about their lack of 'enrichment, variety, intricacy ... above all connection' (though stopped short of his friend Richard Payne Knight, who wanted their creations blown up). He called his contrasting approach 'picturesque', but reading his account of it two centuries later it seems more ecological. He praises the rugged quality of pollards, and how the 'mosses on the bark, the rich yellow of the touchwood, with the blackness of the more decayed substance' give them enormous visual appeal – precisely the qualities that would be praised by an ancient-tree conservationist today. He talks about the attractiveness of 'playful wildness' in landscapes. He urges us to note how 'Time ... converts a beautiful object into a picturesque one' – the prelude to a tremendous essay on the diversifying and naturalising effects of weather and epiphytes. His blueprints for tree planting could have come straight out of a textbook on primary forest: 'Natural groups are full of openings and hollows; of trees advancing before, or retiring behind each other – all productive of intricacy, of variety, of deep shadows, and brilliant lights.'

A century later William Robinson extended these ideas from the estate down to the smaller garden. He challenged the Victorian obsession for formal borders and bedding plants, and the way they carried 'the dead lines of the building into the garden'. In *The Wild Garden* (1870) he celebrated the rightness of plants allowed their natural settings: lemon globe-flowers in a dark, damp hollow; the unprompted hedginess of a wild rose scrambling over a fence. Wild gardening, being a way of fostering the natural groupings of plants, also encouraged a way of looking at their convivial growth in the wild. Robinson loved what he called 'indefinitenesses' – drifts of naturalised bulbs in grassy drives, a clematis sprawling over a pear tree. He also believed that, in gardens at least, exotic temperate plants could be naturalised alongside natives, and it's partly his inspiration we have to thank for the wonderful drifts of escaped American golden-rod and Michaelmas daisy on railway embankments.

Does wild-style gardening make any contribution to conservation? Perhaps less than it contributes to our intimate perception of natural processes. But I'm convinced it opens up opportunities for natural 'events'. I'm heartened by what's happening in our garden. I planted field maples and hornbeams because I didn't think they'd get here unaided. But they've been swamped by the self-sown oaks and cherries. Primroses, left to their own devices, have reached weed proportions. They've colonised the gravel, the lawn, the vegetable garden edges and the odd tree stump. Next stop the thatch. It's the pond that's the problem. Dug four centuries ago it's very steep-sided. It's hard to get water plants to colonise the edges. But I've heard of a fascinating phenomenon on the Norfolk Broads – small islands of matted marsh-grasses which float about on the water, and become anchorages for other species. That's my next project, to bodge some together out of sedges and bits of cork, and see how long it takes the seeds of our local glory, the marsh orchids, to blow in from the common …

2006

* * *

With wildlife gardening's profile high, I felt it was time to have another critical squint at my own patch. It's chastening to do this retrospectively, and see how the usual mode of wild-garden writing

– the chirpy advice to make a log pile, plant pyracantha, avoid baking hedgehogs in the bonfire – measures up against what actually goes on. I suspect a Crime Scene Investigation unit would catch the flavour better than a team of motivational pundits.

I last wrote about our 2 acres in Norfolk nearly three years ago, and a lot has happened since then. There have been plenty of serendipitous visitors. Two winters ago a drake harlequin spent the morning on the pond, and then shot off across the meadow like an Exocet. Last May a newly hatched four-spotted chaser dragonfly hung itself out to dry on a cistus bush. An exquisite Cretan endemic campanula somehow found its way into my Mediterranean bed. But a tick list doesn't come close to describing the dramas and dilemmas of wild gardening. What did was a remark I heard recently from a reserve warden on the north Norfolk coast. 'We're not bothered about climate change or the sea breaking in,' he said, 'our main business is *predator control.*' I was mildly shocked, but there's no doubt he pinpointed the major dynamic force in wild places, feral gardens included. I don't go in for predator control myself, but predators – or rather that unspeakable habit wild species have of eating each other – certainly control the garden.

Our bit of meadow came good last year. From being largely swamped by aggressive grasses, it exploded with patches of ox-eye daisy and musk mallow and bird's-foot trefoil. Some of these came from seed I'd scattered in little patches of bare soil opened up by moles and ants. But most – like the six bee orchids that sprung up under the washing line – arrived of their own accord. But in May, it started to go tatty. A marauding herd of herbivores – pheasants, rabbits, hares, muntjac deer – crept out of the cover of our bit of woodland and began nibbling the flower buds as if they were cocktail snacks. They had a malicious preference for cowslips and meadow buttercups. Then the hay rattle turned nasty. I'd introduced it as a way of sapping the vigour of the coarse grasses (it's a partial parasite), but it was now turning all my clover and vetches into dwarves. When I looked it up I found that it was parasitic on at least 14 plant families as well as the grasses. They don't tell you that in wildlife gardening columns. For a while I went into a sulk that my meadow wasn't going to challenge the Prince of Wales's, and considered fencing off the whole patch. But by midsummer the browsing had calmed down, and most of the beheaded plants (cowslips excepted) had put out new flower buds. And once the hay rattle had seeded and died off, its hosts regained something of their normal proportions. Chastened, I remembered that a wildlife garden is not just there to satisfy its keeper's aesthetic sense. The more it's chewed and frayed by other creatures, the better it's doing.

The wood itself seems immune to the fact that deer nibble the bark off some of the younger saplings, though it's mounting its own defences. Many of the trees are now big enough to be visited regularly by tawny owls and two species of woodpecker, and old enough to be producing plenty of seed. And sure enough, close by, their offspring are regenerating exactly as they are supposed to: ash, hazel and oaklings, shooting up through the protective cover of bramble patches.

The problem habitat is the pond. It's deep, steep-sided and partially shaded by two huge ash trees. I've managed to get some edge vegetation going – purple loosestrife, sedges, yellow flags – and there are great crested newts, water measurers and pond snails. But these water animals thrive or decline according to the state of the aquatic vegetation, and this does vanishing tricks of its own. The reason is those pesky herbivores again. Most of the summer the pond is full of mallards, of dubious origins. They munch the pondweed into oblivion. And that's not all. Sometimes they munch each other. Ducks bring their broods to the pond from a wide area, and Duck Wars invariably follow. A couple of years ago I was horrified when dead ducklings started appearing on the surface the same week that bird flu had been discovered at a farm nearby. But the next day I watched one of the mothers systematically catching and drowning the chicks of a rival brood. Wildlife gardening? It's a jungle out there.

2009

* * *

We put it up among the fading cow parsley in the middle of June, a bird feeder so outlandish I worry that the council may pounce on us for breaching planning law. It stands 2 metres tall, its twin trunks bristling with rusting spikes and stalks like some prehistoric radio mast.

I'd long dreamed of a feeder that was personal, an offering from me, not just something off a production line. A couple of years back I did an experiment with some pieces of derelict farm machinery, hoping to enjoy the poetic irony of birds gorging themselves on the remains of outdated agrobusinesses. But I hadn't the skill to make anything either striking or even functional out of it. Then I realised I had a string to pull – and now, as they say, an interest to declare. My partner Polly's daughter is Kate Munro, the sculptor who created some of the great wood and metal installations at the Eden Project. I put my plan to her, and in a matter of weeks she'd come up with the brilliant notion of modelling the feeder on giant hogweed, turning upside down the bad image of this demonised alien.

Kate and her kids came and stayed for a week to make the sculpture on site. She debarked two hunks of a windblown garden sycamore to make the twin stems, and sat among the moon-daisies welding the blooms from an extraordinary collection of recyled junk: spiral fence-posts, coil springs, steel washers. When it was finished and in place by the pond, it was so beautiful, so absolutely right amid the skeletal cow parsley, that I could hardly bear to drape it with titbits. But I did, and the birds began to trickle in within an hour. Nothing special so far, but it seems to fascinate families of fledglings. They come en masse and leap about the umbels as if they were climbing frames. They seem intrigued (or puzzled) by the odd spatial arrangement of their perches, and their explorations seem to echo the opportunist, playful way Kate made them. Yesterday I watched a young robin meet an equally youthful but considerably more authoritative great tit on an iron stalk, and go into that little shivering motion robins do when begging for food. For once, I can't wait for winter, when the Hogtable should be as lively as a carnival. But another part of me worries that it's just a folly, a piece of self-indulgent tomfoolery. Or worse, that it's a kind of circus, making a spectacle of the wild.

'Wild' is the new 'natural', a quality whose moment has come at last. Jay Griffiths' *Wild*, Robert Macfarlane's *The Wild Places*, and Roger Deakin's *Wildwood* – incandescent, austerely beautiful and comic by turns – were all published this summer. The Wildlife Trusts have at last remembered that the word is part of their name, and in a historic policy document last year committed themselves to landscape-scale rewilding. There is wild garlic on pub menus and 'wild apple' in perfumes.

But what does this word mean when it's used not just as an adjective but as a description of some kind of quality in nature? It isn't the same as 'natural' and isn't about 'kinds' of organisms. Falconers' peregrines and foresters' nursery-grown oaks may be 'wildlife', but they are not 'wild'. I share the growing belief that there are special qualities in free, self-willed organisms and ecosystems that are to do with sensuousness and inventiveness, and which can vanish under the heavy hand of management. Most importantly (and this is the argument of all three books I mentioned above), these are qualities in the human mind, too: right-brain – bird-brain – creativities that spring from our common evolution. And there seems to be a wonderful reciprocity – glimpse the wild in nature and you glimpse the wild in yourself. Discover your own deep-seated wildness and you intuit new things in nature. You are gazing in a mirror that is 3,000 million years old.

Which is why I don't think the Hogtable is any kind of peep-show. I see it as a kind of gateway, a portal between two wild imaginations, the inquisitive bird's and the playful sculptor's. If we need devoted, loving observation to understand nature intellectually, we also need our wild imaginations to re-enter it emotionally. So here's to David Rothenberg, jamming on his clarinet with Albert's lyrebirds in the Australian bush; to the thousands of Swedes who dance with the returning cranes in April; to every child who has ever drawn an imaginary animal; to Kate and her robins' play-station. I suspect some of the creatures enjoy these contacts as much as we do. But it's the opening of *our* minds that also matters, the realisation that though it may be a jungle out there, it's also a ball, and we're all invited.

2007

POOTLING

Does anyone go walking for its own sake any more? Everyone I come across on my own meanderings is always *up* to something: exercising the dog, jogging (a practice more in need of planning control than afforestation, I reckon), swarming about in sponsored migrations, brandishing tokens of activity – easels, picnics, more dogs – as if moving without obvious purpose was a sign of mental instability. I am beginning to be looked at as if I had just jumped out of a bush – or was just about to jump into one.

We seem to have come full circle, for it isn't much more than 200 years since the sheer fun and physicality of strolling about first began to be realised. When even the roads were morasses for much of the year and walking the only means of transport available to the vast bulk of the population, anyone seen just roaming aimlessly was regarded with the deepest suspicion. Many of the pioneering mid-18th-century naturalists were harried and attacked while out on their rambles.

Joseph Banks was seized on suspicion of being a highwayman in 1760 while poking about in some hedges near Hounslow and hauled up before the Bow Street magistrates. Edward Lhwyd, one of the most adventurous of all early field botanists, was repeatedly taken for a Jacobite spy or tax collector, and hounded out of parishes all over western Britain.

It would be hard to disentangle the progress of footborne exploration from the increasing fascination with the *detail* of the world that characterised the intellectual and artistic awakening of the 18th century. Up on top of a coach, or struggling to work through the mud, you missed so much: the sounds of limestone clattering under your feet, a dim flower in a hedge bottom. Inquisitive walking may even have played a part in undermining the formal and generalised views of nature of the pastoral tradition, and in ushering in the Romantic era.

Think of the poet Thomas Gray, whose *Elegy Written in a Country Churchyard* has had its political message quite obscured by that static, lulling opening verse, 'The Curfew tolls the knell of parting day'. When Gray stirred his stumps and followed the tourist trail to Malham, picking his way tremulously up the limestone crags below Goredale Scar, he was transfixed enough to write one of the first great accounts of a face-to-face encounter with a wild landscape:

> *The hills opened again into no large space, and then all farther*
> *away is barred by a stream, that at a height of fifty feet gushes*
> *from a hole in the rock, and spreading in large sheets over its*
> *black front, dashes from steep to steep, and then rattles away in*
> *a torrent down the valley ... the drops which perpetually distil*
> *its brow, fell on my head ... there are loose stones which hang*
> *in the air, and threaten visibly ... I stayed there (not without*
> *shuddering) a full quarter of an hour ... the impression will*
> *last for life.*

But I don't think it was just the new intimacy with the natural world achieved by walking that helped make it so popular. It also gives you an exhilarating sense of *possession*. When you physically set foot on a piece of land, in one symbolic sense you stake a claim to it. A walk becomes a beating of your own bounds.

I find that I am lured back, quite compulsively, to routes I've walked before. And not just to the bare bones of the route either, but virtually to my own previous footsteps: along the *top* of the bank where the woodruff grows, keeping to the left of the lane round the next bend, a short detour to the bridge with the overhanging hawthorn ...

A walk, of course, provides a ready-made framework for a writer to hang a narrative account on, just as 'the tour' did in a previous era. Yet what is fascinating is the way that different styles of exploration on foot appear to have found their way directly into the style of the written account. One critic has suggested, for instance, that W. H. Hudson's rambling prose 'perfectly echoed the long, slow, unhurried tramping of his feet as he roamed through the gentle southern counties each summer' – though, for me, Hudson's peerings through the window of country life in books such as *Afoot in England* (1909) summon up the echoing, misanthropic tread of the census officer.

Far better is middle-period Richard Jefferies, when he was producing a prodigious quantity of effervescent journalism for the new urban audience. The essays in collections like *Round About a Great Estate* (1880) are addressed directly at this audience. 'If you should happen to be walking ...' so many of them begin. It is quite infectious. The reader is taken by the hand and *led*.

John Clare, on the other hand, seems barely to consider his readers at all. He is caught up in the immediacy of the moment, or perhaps the remembered immediacy of his childhood, and his many poems which are based on walks conjure up an image of a man darting in barely controllable excitement from one side of the path to the other:

> *When jumping time away on old cross berry way*
> *And eating awes like sugar plumbs ere they had lost the may*
> *And skipping like a leveret before the peep of day*
> *On the rolly poly up and down of pleasant Swordy well*

The end of this kind of writing lies really with the modern books of walks, which are instructions about where to go rather than descriptions of real voyages of discovery. There is nothing wrong in beating another person's bounds; I have followed in some of Edward Thomas's melancholic tracks round Hampshire, and had the thrill of finding a few of the same fragments of willow-pattern china in a woodman's garden that he likened to out-of-season periwinkles. But if there is no person behind the route-map, no voice, then I think one might as well gather up the dog, put on a tracksuit and let the whole scene go past in a blur.

1984

* * *

Having been an obsessional map-browser for most of my adult life, I feel rather smug about their recent rise to colour-supplement fashionability – not as mundane charts or guides but as spurs to our imaginative sense of history and locality. Perhaps it's a sign of our growing anxiety about losing our place.

I think it was the feeling that there were stories between the contour lines that first turned me into a map-worm. I still love reading them like coded scrolls, imagining the layers of landscape that lie under the surface structure. Will there be bird's-eye primroses in that fuzzy junction between the limestone hill and the beck-rinsed moor? Will a jumble of Suffolk green lanes, moats and coppices seem as anciently rich on the ground as it does on the plan, or just itself be a ghostly reminder of something long vanished? And what lies, unrecorded, in all the white spaces between?

Modern geographers now separate true maps, which are to do with 'performance' (interpretation, physical contact, and so on), from 'tracings', which are hyper-realistic ground-plans. Yet I have found evocative charts in both styles. One of my favourites is the record which Joseph Johns made in 1847 of the standing and fallen trees in a marked plot of Boubinsky Prales, a virgin forest in southern Czechoslovakia. What is uncanny about the map is its sense of time: the trees are mapped (from above) with such precision that you can see where and how the fallen ones are entangled; how they are split, broken, weathering at the tips; which have kept their root plates; where new trees are growing and what their girth is. It is like a snapshot, a frozen moment, yet conveys the most powerful sense of the ceaseless slow decay and regeneration of the wildwood.

At the other extreme is an exquisite topographical map of Great Yarmouth in the town's museum. It was painted in 1570, from an imagined high point on one side of the town. The town began as a shanty settlement built by migratory fishermen on a bank of silt that was forming across the river – the Yare-mouth – 1,000 years ago, as this bit of East Anglia began to tilt upwards. Five hundred years later, the map vividly shows the ridges of housing development following the contours of the receding high-water mark – and east Norfolk's great grazing marshes forming around it.

Yet perhaps even the most minimally objective maps can be constraints on us, encouraging us to see the world in too set, too routine, too human-centred ways. The other day I read a short essay by Paul Evans about, basically, wandering off; and I felt shamefaced at what a creature of habit I had become in my own meanderings and map-followings. Like William Hazlitt, 'I can saunter for hours, bending my eye forward, stopping and turning to look back, thinking to strike off into some less trodden paths, yet hesitant to quit the one I am on, afraid to snap the brittle threads of memory.' A rut is a good thing to follow, but not to be stuck in – map-bound, as it were. Paul Evans describes how he did 'strike off' in a Shropshire wood, and the moment of revelation that followed, when he discovered multitudes of cryptic footprints, and imagined the myriads of creatures 'from beetle to badger' whose paths had crossed here before making off again, and who had created on their way a route-map for a whole ecosystem. I suspect we understand and contribute to these charts more than we realise. Perhaps they are our equivalent of aboriginal songlines. I know that when I do go free-form walking like Paul Evans, I am tugged this way and that by gaps in hedges, whiffs of fox, shapes glimpsed in trunks, barely understood prompts from rocks and bushes. As signals, they are no more rationally mappable than birdsongs are transcribable, but they are part of that sense of territory that is one of our closest links with other creatures.

1995

* * *

Much as I think we can learn from hunter-gatherers, I've no ambitions to be one. I'm too sentimental to be a hunter, too dilettante ever to become a serious gatherer. But I do aspire to be a rummager, a general browser after stuff, to indulge in an honourable 'treading lightly' version of living off the land. Except that, given the trade I practise, this is also likely to involve foraging for stories, gossip, finds.

Pootling about like a part-time nomad is how I tend to spend my afternoons, and at least once a month this involves doing a circuit of my home-range, checking out the lie of the land. Back in the Chilterns, my cats used to do this every morning, reading the smells and traces of the night as assiduously as a breakfast newspaper. 'What's about?' they'd sniff, in that splendid interrogation that the cat world shares with birders and ancient East Anglians.

I'm nosy, too, and some of this browsing is just neighbourly curiosity. Over in Thelnetham, a house among the trees has an elaborately printed board outside: 'What was Willow Cottage is now Jumanji'. In Redgrave, an old cottage with the most desirable view over the fen, a place where you might watch marsh harriers without leaving your bed, has got planning permission to replace its thatch with pantiles. Whatever next!

I always do a circuit of the local fen and greens. They still have their late autumn colours, and those that were cut or grazed early now have a second flowering of the classic local mix: knapweed, fleabane, wild carrot and tufted vetch. There's a late speciality, too, the little drab yellow umbellifer pepper saxifrage (no relation to either of those families). It's a marker of damp and ancient land. William Turner made the first written record in 1586, in 'ranke medowes'. On the greens, the travellers' horses – part currency, part status symbols – are looking splendid, all blond fringes and highly rated spots. There is a first-year foal exactly like the tarpans that graze Redgrave fen, and I entertain the wicked thought that the travellers may have 'borrowed' the wildlife trust's roving stallion for a spot of freelance stud-work.

Feeling a bit of a gipsy myself, I slip into the grounds of one of the local big houses. Yesterday I'd seen a little egret here, wafting across the ornamental lake. It was an astonishing sight, an icy, virginal presence among the rowdy natives. And they didn't like it, finding its alabaster oddness too threateningly alien. Everything from moorhens to greylags went for it, a screaming, pecking mob of vigilantes that harried it across the water and into a tree. But today they've calmed down. I spot the egret beating towards me, in a group of about 500 lapwings on one of their loose, take-it-or-leave-it fly-rounds. It follows their every move, matching their wingbeats, even aping their jinking 'falls' just before coming in to land.

It's gleaning time as well. The wild harvest has been extraordinary. Hazelnuts, damsons, hops, wild seed for our meadow. Today, I fancy getting one up on Delia, and finding some authentic *Norfolk* cranberries. There's a patch of ancient swamp here called Cranberry Rough, which had enough of the fruit once to be named after it. I plunge in, full of derring-do, into what looks safe enough alder carr, and get the fright of my life. There are patches of real mire here, and I keep going in up to my knees, even after the drought. It's too over-grown for cranberries, I reckon, but it's a strange and atmospheric place, draped with marsh fern and mosses I can't identify. And on the way home I find the biggest feral pear tree I have ever seen, in a hedge. It's 40 feet tall and three feet across, and covered with a Norfolk speciality, little Robin pears, crisp and bright and blushing. I pick 10lb off the verge – a completely unexpected crop. On the radio I hear that English Nature has accidentally set fire to Scolt Head Island on the Norfolk coast. They were trying to incinerate some fox earths and 'lost control.' I love it when the wild cards come into play.

Back home the rummaging continues, as I go free-range reading. My treasured *Flora Diatetica* (1783) doesn't list Robins in a catalogue of pears whose names read like the Song of Solomon: Chaumontelle Wilding, The Green Sugar, The Golden End of Winter. But it taunts me over the one-time abundance of Norfolk cranberries: 'They are collected by the country people, who carry them to market towns for sale.' I long to ferret for more about them in an unpublished manuscript Ted Ellis once told me about, the 18th-century Norfolk shoemaker Lilly Wigg's *Esculent Plants*. But it's deep in the British Museum. So I console myself with Virginia Woolf's account of her holiday in our fens, a hundred years ago. She described a landscape humming with dragonflies and the marzipan scent of meadowsweet – and then fell into the Little Ouse. 'Although a walk in the fen has a singular charm,' she wrote, 'it is not to be undertaken as a way of getting to places.' But whoever wants to get to places when you can be getting about.

2003

... AND FORAGING

Twenty years ago this autumn I finished work on my first full-length book, a guide to edible wild plants called *Food for Free*. It was a modest success in its own way, enabling me to risk becoming a full-time freelance, and I shall always be grateful for that.

But it also had the kind of oddball subject matter that gets one typecast. A few years after publication, I was introduced to a well-known photographer at a party. 'Ah yes,' he mused, peering closely at me, 'you're the man that eats weeds. What an interestingly *earthy* face.' This, I felt, shrinking with embarrassment, was taking the idea that you *are* what you eat a sight too literally, and ever since I have distanced myself slightly from that early guide to greens.

I still enjoy feasts of seasonal crops: samphire from the north Norfolk marshes in summer, wild raspberries from my own wood, local hazelnuts for Christmas. But for the most part I have become a rather precious wayside nibbler, indulging in what the 1930s writer and fruit gourmet Edward Bunyard christened 'ambulant consumption' – single wild gooseberries (squeezed to test for ripeness first); sweet cicely seeds on walks before dinner, a kind of herbal aperitif; squidgy dewberries eaten on the stalk, like cocktail cherries.

But this year, with an anniversary to celebrate and an odd pattern of weather whose effects on normal fruiting patterns I was curious to explore, I felt inclined to go for a proper, inquisitive foray, a working lunch, so to speak. So I map out a route over familiar country near home which takes in some old hedges and one-time mushroom pastures, hoist a gathering bag over my shoulder – and then curse the fact that the mid-October day that I have carefully planned for this expedition turns out to be the most dismal of the autumn so far. But half a mile on, I find I am quite enjoying the mist and fine drizzle. The berries on the trees, dust washed off at last, have an inviting dewy sheen. On the grassland, now thoroughly moistened, patches and rings of darker green grass that may be signs of underground fungal growth are materialising like watermarks.

I start browsing out of a sense of duty to begin with, and drench myself with showers of settled rainwater every time I reach into a bush. Things are already remarkably ripe, even though there have been no air frosts yet. I nibble a few agreeably soft haws, whose flesh reminds me of slightly overripe avocado pear, then start on the blackberries, which are still swelling in good numbers, despite all those saws about not picking them after Michaelmas. Even berries from adjacent bushes can taste quite different, with hints of grape, cherry, plum, and with subtly varied textures, reminding you that there are 400 micro-species of bramble in Britain.

But I draw a blank with hazelnuts. It was not a good year for them to start with, and this year's explosion in grey squirrel numbers seems to have put paid to the few that did form. I try a few tricks, such as getting inside the bushes and looking out, hoping that any clusters will be more visible against the sky. But all I find are a few rather stale cobs already fallen to the ground. I munch some elderberries for consolation, but overdo it, and that slight cloying sensation, of having sucked fruit-flavoured frogspawn, won't go away. But there are clusters of miniature wood puffballs on the tree-stumps, and I find that chewing some of the white flesh takes the elder aftertang away.

My route takes me up into the Chiltern foothills, and a labyrinth of green lanes. Long-tailed tits are dithering through the hedges, and the first chaffinch flocks gathering – though there is no beechmast either for them or me. I am heading for a wilding apple tree I discovered last year – sniffed out, actually, since its lemon-yellow fruits smelt deliciously of quince and scented the air for dozens of yards around. (They were too hard and acid to eat raw, but were spectacular roasted with meat.)

The tree has fruited quite well again, though it is too early for the fruits to have taken on their heady aroma. But there are plenty of other wilding apples about. I bite into one and it has the bittersweet, almost effervescent zest of sherbet. On another tree in the same hedge the apples are like miniature pippins. A third has long pear-shaped apples that have an extraordinary warm, smoky flavour behind the sharpness, as if they had been baked. I ponder the huge genetic storehouse represented by these wayside wildings, all sprung from discarded cores.

But I'm disappointed at how few fungi there are yet in the hedges and copses, and start hallucinating them. A promising mound under an oak turns out to be a toy bubble-car, and every white flash in the field is in fact an upturned flint. But as I turn for home through the valley meadows, with rooks massing above the woods on either side, I begin to strike lucky. There are freshly sprung field mushrooms, pink-gilled and unsullied by insects. There are fairy rings of eight-inch-diameter horse-mushrooms and of shaggy parasols (no good for eating raw, but I pick a bagful for later).

And in the ridgeway hedges on the last lap before home, the wild damsons are perfectly ripe and beginning to drop from the trees. The bushes line an old orchard and were, I guess, originally planted as a combination windbreak and pollinator for the cultivated plums. But they have spread some way beyond their original site, and suckers and seedlings (including a wonderful cherry-plum with round, thick, orange fruit) crop up for hundreds of yards along the hedge. There is one new taste sensation here. The hedge was cut in the summer with the fruit already formed, and the trimmings lie beneath it, covered with dry, wrinkled damsons that taste exactly like thin-fleshed prunes.

So this was my midday meal, ambulantly consumed but in strictly correct order: young field mushrooms and a few soft chestnuts, finished with wild plums and strips of lemony apple. After three hours of continuous nibbling it seemed, I will confess, rather on the acid and insubstantial side, and I began to yearn for a bowl of pasta. But never believe anyone who says there is no such thing as a free lunch.

1991

2. WINGS

The inspiration of birds.

EARLY BIRDS

Searching for early chiffchaffs is a personal spring ritual which I think I have tracked back to source. When I was about 10 my elder sister pressed on me a book by Vera Barclay, called *Joe, Colette and the Birds* (first published in 1934). It reads like a schooldays yarn in the best Arthur Ransome mould at first: two youngsters (Colette is 'all long brown arms and legs') are diverted during the Easter holidays by a 'rangy' young man who is convalescing at their house. To pass the time he decides to initiate them in the delights of birding. Off they rush, marking up their respective lists. They were confirmed twitchers from the outset, and I was instantly in thrall myself.

I was surprised, reading the book again after an interval of more than 25 years, that it had views on conservation, and advanced and uncompromising views, too. Its young hero and heroine are spared none of the details of Mediterranean bird-catching, or the local killing of rooks and raptors. 'Why are farmers such fools?' one asks.

But at 10 I only had eyes for the tallies. Joe and Colette passed the 50 mark in three days flat, and I was determined to do better. I'm sure that I did, but within a couple of years birds began to seem less important as ticks on a list than as potent personal totems, keepers of secrets and emblems of place and season. A barn owl's evening flight-path marked the edge of our local gang's territory. Moorhens on the lawn meant the winterbournes were rising. A chiffchaff singing and surely the Easter holidays must be about to begin …

I made no more lists until my mid-twenties. Birds seemed a frivolous diversion when I was at university during the Cold War days of the mid-sixties, and it was only afterwards, when I was holidaying in the Camargue and the Spanish sierras, that they swam back into my life. Rollers and bee-eaters flicking above the bars seemed like vivid flashbacks, and back home I picked up the threads with an old friend and travelling companion, first at Tring Reservoirs, then on the north Norfolk coast. I remember that, to our eternal shame, we spent much of our first visit to Cley Marshes watching migrating waders from inside our car, keeping the visibility up with the windscreen wipers.

My inspiration then, more prosaic and serious than Joe and Colette, was the Collins *Pocket Guide* (1952), illustrated by the late and legendary Richard Richardson. We had no idea Richardson lived in the area until we met him a couple of weeks later, holding court on Cley's east bank. He was dressed then as he was just about every time I ever met him later, in woolly hat, denim jacket and motor-cycle boots (he rode a Norton).

I had never met a birdwatcher like him. He had come from the East End, was merciless with posers and pedants, but generous and helpful to a fault with those who cared about birds. He had taught himself painting and, to my knowledge, the only thing he ever wrote was the *Check-List of the Birds of Cley and Neighbouring Norfolk Parishes* (1962). But in a way he was himself the Book of Cley. His knowledge of local birds was so exhaustive and idiosyncratic that it assumed the stature of an alternative parish history. It was not just for the latest bird-chat you went to him, but for news of the human passage migrants, the likely outcome of the weather and the conditions of fish and chips.

I can recall him sitting on the bank, a cross between Mr Punch and a weatherbeaten rocker, rolling minutely thin cigarettes, doing outrageous and often libellous impersonations of other birders, raising his binoculars occasionally (though he barely needed them) to verify a wader half a mile away, whistling a flock of whimbrel in from the sea.

But it was his uncanny ability to see the world from a bird's point of view that was his most remarkable gift. Of all my memories of Richard, it is a trivial, unfinished but premonitory sentence that always comes first to mind. He was gazing at a flock of terns loping in to fish in the pools, and said simply: 'It would be worth a skua's while …' It was.

Richard died tragically, a few years later. But on that first meeting at the end of April, 1968, he showed us a feast of birds such as I have never seen before or since: a purple heron in the reeds, Montagu's harriers harrying godwits, avocets, black terns. We watched the sun set from the very spot where we'd huddled inside the car a fortnight before, and as the harrier hunched on a post over-looking a vast marshland panorama still shimmering with terns, I felt that I was entering a new world, not just watching it from outside.

Next year I read – though that is too feeble a word for a process that involved all the senses – J A Baker's now classic book *The Peregrine* (1969), by common consent one of the most remarkable and passionate explorations ever written of our search for a place in the natural world. It is the imaginative distillation of a 10-year odyssey after the peregrines that winter around the Essex coast, 'a dying world, like Mars, but glowing still', that becomes a voyage of discovery into Baker's own vestigial instincts.

The sustained intensity of the descriptive writing is hard to bear at times. In opening himself to the pain and sheer quickening of a bird's world, he reaches a heightened awareness of place and time, a sense that we all live in the same fragile membrane: 'Learn to fear. To share fear is the greatest bond of all ... What is, is now, must have the quivering intensity of an arrow thudding into a tree. Yesterday is dim and monochrome. A week ago you were not born.' And perhaps it is a yearning for that sense of immediacy and presence that makes the spring's first chiffchaff remain an obstinate Grail for me.

1984

MIGRATION

The March equinox is not like the other great hinges of the year. It doesn't slip by imperceptibly, like midsummer or midwinter, or drag out elegiacally like hallowtide. It's a portal between the seasons, a stargate, a time of momentous rearrangements of the northern hemisphere's air and water. And strange things can happen during it. Down in Cornwall a few years ago, I sat in the hanging oakwoods by the side of the Fal Estuary and watched the spring high tide, stained pure white by kaolin from the old china clay works, rise up through the trees. It was a hallucinatory vision: ferns rippling under water, primroses flowering in a bath of milk. There's less clay in the water now, but a high tide in a springtime wood is still a sight to see, a fantastical incongruity, an emblem of this moment when the shock of the new crashes into the moody inertia of winter.

At last year's equinox, I was on the east Norfolk coast with Mark Cocker, hoping for a few spring migrants to brighten the end of a damp and gloomy month. We glimpsed the first wheatears in Winterton Dunes, heard the ventriloquial courtship clinks of toads. But again it was that great collision between the end of one season and the beginning of another that electrified us. All along the grazing marshes between Hickling and Horsey the lapwing and golden plover flocks were resting in the grass, as tense as watch springs, waiting for their moment. Above us, a male marsh harrier, its breeding plumage as sparkling as if it had been dusted with frost, sky-danced in the high mist. The plovers rose in formation to mob it, and the marsh harrier responded by loosing his irritation on a hen harrier, a hapless passer-by also at the end of its winter sojourn. Mark had a sudden vision of the whole east coast of England pulsing with excited birds like these, all about to leave for their breeding grounds; a revelation that migration is about departures as well as arrivals.

I become a restless migrant myself at this edgy moment of the year, saying my goodbyes and desperate for the new show to begin. I flit from parish to parish peering for barn owls in the riverside meadows, straining my ears for the chiffchaff's sweet and simple 'see-saw', the first new notes of the spring. But always, the geese draw me back into winter. Here in Norfolk, we're the privileged hosts of half the world's population of pink-footed geese, 150,000 birds in a good year. On the north coast, around Holkham, their dusk flights to roost can take away not just your breath but your mind. The endless scrolls of birds, the ebb and flow of that ancient cackle, that celestial static, fill the sky, fill your head. I've more than once involuntarily dropped to my knees under them. And gliding home by boat in the Broads one evening, when it was already dark at ground level, I've seen skeins of pink-feet so high, that their bellies too were pink, still basking in the light of the setting sun.

What do migrating geese say to us? That the Earth is one place, that there are more majestic forms of globalisation than the bickering models of the free traders? Aldo Leopold, in a famous passage in *A Sand County Almanac,* saw them as agents of another kind of trade, messengers who barter food for light in their annual journeys between the Arctic and the temperate zone, and become 'a wild poem dropped from the murky skies upon the muds of March'.

But now they're being looked on askance, as possible carriers of a less poetic burden, avian flu. The meanings of migration have always been complex and fluid. I think about that moment 10,000 years ago when the last of the Paleolithic hunters met the first of the summer birds. Some morning in early May, the wild game dwindling, and in its place these screaming black birds, flint sickles in the sky. What did the hunters, so familiar with mammal migration, make of them? A diabolical replacement perhaps, long before the idea of the devil had been invented?

Now swifts are the very symbols of summer to us, like swallows and cuckoos. But as the climate changes will they always come back and reassure us, in Ted Hughes's words, that 'the globe's still working'? Will the geese no longer need to travel south? Or the swallows ever leave? How will we cope if not just the climate, but the ancient cultural icons through which we've made sense of the seasons are also transformed?

2008

MARTLETS

Sometimes I worry that I am spending too much time in Gilbert White's company. As I write this column in the middle of July I find, wrily, and for the umpteenth time, that we have had the same things on our mind. It is 1774: 'July 12: Martins build nests and forsake them, and now build again. July 13: Martins hover at the mouths of their nests, and feed their young without settling. July 15: No young martins out yet. Creeping white mist. July 24: Some young martins come out.'

Almost every July White's journal crowds with notes on the fortunes of the 'martlets' that nested under his eaves. The entries have an endearing mixture of excitement and anxiety – sometimes bordering on the first real display of empathy for wild creatures in literature – that will bring a rush of recognition to anyone who has had birds living close to them in the breeding season.

House martins returned to nest in our road about 10 years ago – half a dozen pairs scattered over a few hundred square metres – though not to our house at first. They have come back every year since, surviving, with varying degrees of success, the whims of the weather and of their human hosts.

In the blisteringly hot summer of '76, for instance, they were all multiple brooded, and conditions in some of the nests must have been like those in the Black Hole of Calcutta. Next door, one pair came up with an ingenious solution I have not seen recorded in any textbook. They built a kind of mud verandah next to the main nest, on which the first brood spent their siestas while the second was being incubated.

The following year the occupiers of the house had a Public Health Inspector round to poke out the nests, because the martins' parasites were apparently invading their bedroom. The birds were on eggs at the time, and this act of vandalism, dubious in its legality, soured our neighbourly relations for a long time.

Fortunately the martins recognised a soft touch, and a few years later began building on *our* east-facing wall. I don't think I have had a truly restful summer's day since. I swing between moments of ecstatic excitement – the evening in late April when they flash past the window, back to the old nest, the little pile of neatly cracked eggshells on the ground that announces the hatching of the young, that day when the dark crowns of the nestlings begin to bob above the entrance hole, and the parents are able to 'feed their young without settling' – and moments of utter anguish. Whenever there is torrential rain, or the parents take it into their heads to rush off and mob a passing sparrowhawk, I might as well pack up work for the day. Even when things are quiet, I am absurdly solicitous, and have caught myself chattering away to them, oblivious of the amused passers-by in the road.

But it has been worth it. The four months they spend with us each summer have been a lesson in the sheer vitality of nature, what John Fowles once called 'the poetry of survival'. Every week brings its moments of poignancy and drama. One evening last June I heard the male bird sing for a whole 10 minutes from *inside* the nest. Sometimes when I arrive back home late at night, I can see the two parent birds' faces lit up by my headlights, peering down as I park the car. Sometimes it is their two tails, side by side, and that is even more of a throat-catcher.

I remember, too, the day I was lucky enough to be watching the nest when the first young ones flew. They had been very active for a couple of days, flexing wings, peering at birds, butterflies, raindrops and cars passing the nest, and performing contortions to try to follow the route of a bluebottle up the bedroom window. Then that morning, one came to the nest hole, stretched out its neck with a strange exultant, churring note, and popped out like a champagne cork. The second left a few minutes later, and they were soon flying as airily and confidently as adults, dashing back and forth to the nest entrance and trying to chivvy out the two remaining youngsters.

But last year there was a disaster. One afternoon in mid-June I happened to notice through the window a great hubbub round the nest, with the parent birds flying distractedly back and forth. I rushed out and found that a great chunk had been torn out of the nest, close to the entrance, and that the whole brood – four blind nestlings – were scattered dead and bloodstained around our drive. I have no idea how this happened – whether it was an attack by a woodpecker or even by one of the unpaired martins that often try to get into the nest. The adults vanished for a whole day, and I was heartbroken, burying the little birds under a rose bush near the wall. Then late that evening the parents came back, and spent most of the night in deep conversation in the nest. Next day they worked feverishly, repairing the breach, and within seven weeks had raised another brood.

I defy anyone to look into a bird's eye in July, at the urgency and clarity of purpose in it, and not be chastened and uplifted. I hope I'm not crediting the birds with human emotions like hope and joy (though I'm sure they have their own); but that is what they can inspire in us, when we recognise that we are all part of the same web of working, feeling, surviving, interdependent life. And for that we must feel a debt of gratitude to White, who was beginning to explore this idea 50 years before the Romantics.

A couple of years before his death he saw another kind of contiguity: 'Sept 7: Young martins, several hundred, congregate on the tower, church, and yew-tree ... Such an assemblage is very beautiful, and amusing, did it not bring with it an association of ideas tending to make us reflect that winter is approaching; and that these little birds are consulting how they may avoid it.'

1984

The 18th-century parson Gilbert White appears many times in these columns. His Natural History of Selborne *(1789) was the first work of literary ecology. I wrote a biography of him,* Gilbert White *(Century, 1986). [2009]*

NIGHTINGALES

There were nightingales in the next village this summer, the first to nest locally for more than a decade. I heard the male bird in that warm snatch at the end of May, and spent two spellbound evenings listening to him flood a whole scrubby hillside with piercing notes.

Then, as no one will need reminding, came June. The pinching rain reduced even the most fulsome singers to short and tetchy phrases, the barest shorthand that would serve to establish a presence. Even listening to them was a dispiriting business. By the time fine weather did return it was July, and most birds were past their song times. I retreated to the garden, and for consolation tried to draw up my personal selection of Desert Island Birdsongs, the sounds I could least bear to be without and dream of hearing again during the long winters. I also began to muse about why the territorial signals of one order of creation – purely functional, or so we are told – should be so universally appealing to another.

As a groundbase I tried listing those songs that I relished for their musical qualities alone. I got as far as the pure soprano of an early season blackcap and that was it. Everything else was hopelessly enmeshed in tangles of memory and association. There were songs which conjured up favourite places, childhood holidays, heartbreaks, adventures, the comings and goings of whole seasons. Even the blackbird's nonchalant warblings, so familiar and conversational as to be almost hackneyed, can make my throat catch. Whenever I hear the first of the year – wafting from a cramped backyard in central London as often as not, and cutting clean across the traffic – I am 14 again, listening to them reminisce in the garden lilacs, in those first magical days of the Easter holidays when there was, at last, daylight after tea.

It is particular moments of the year that birdsongs seem to evoke most powerfully, and which conversely seem incomplete without them. Early March, and mistle thrushes – stormcocks as they are sometimes known – skirling through the gales; wood-pigeons calling endlessly from midsummer woods, like birds stirring in a dream; and the thin, poignant notes of robins in September, the last song of summer.

But it is the willow warbler's tumbling song that cheers me the most. It is the surest sign that spring is here, and always sounds to me as if the bird were leaning back against the first new shoots and whistling at the sky with sheer relief.

Some songs are so atmospheric that they can conjure up a whole cameo of memories. This for instance, from the trilling of common sandpipers. Late April in Abernethy Forest. A dawn walk through the native pine woods to the osprey hide. Roe deer and red squirrels, and capercaillie blustering in the tracks. And echoing across Loch Garten, whooper swans, sandpipers and the wild, banshee cries of black-throated divers.

Or this, from the other end of the country and another kind of climate. A baking day at the start of July. Lolling on a Chiltern chalk down overlooking a sweep of unsprayed corn. Fragrant orchids, and the scents of crushed thyme and burnet. A family of fox cubs playing among the poppies. Then, quite unexpectedly, the whetstone call of a quail, first one, then another – the only ones I have ever heard in this country, and sounding like an elegy for this almost vanished world.

There are other quintessential summer sounds. The scream of swift packs, which always reminded Gilbert White 'by an agreeable association of ideas' of fine weather. The assorted churrings and gratings of the birds of dry heathlands – yellowhammers, nightjars, whitethroats, turtle doves. It is remarkable how many birdsongs seem to have been scored to fit their surroundings. The lilting of curlews over an empty moor. The shivering song of a wood warbler in a wooded Welsh valley in May. The jangling of corn buntings over sun-baked wheatfields. Is it just familiarity that makes these associations seem so appropriate? Or do birdsongs have a kind of ecological design that we can dimly sense?

The nightingale's song does not quite fit into this pattern. It is not so much a song of a particular place, as of particular moments, of warm, still, moonlit spring evenings; of quiet – which it seems able to impose on other birds. And it is a song whose power lies to a great extent in its own use of silence, of exquisitely timed dramatic pauses.

'It can be curiously seductive and maddening,' wrote H E Bates in 1936 in what is still the finest description of the song, 'beginning very often by a sudden low chucking, a kind of plucking of strings, a sort of tuning up, then flaring out in a moment into a crescendo of fire and honey and then, abruptly, cut off again in the very middle of a phrase. And then comes that long, suspended wait for the phrase to be taken up again, the breathless hushed interval that is so beautiful. And often, when it is taken up again, it is not that same phrase at all, but something utterly different, a high sweet whistling prolonged and prolonged for the sheer joy of it.'

In Francis Willughby's *Ornithology*, first published in 1678, there is a first-hand account by a man so impressed by this oratorical quality in the nightingale's song that he believed he had heard them debating in human voices. He was ill, a long way from home and lodging at an inn where there were three in a cage, and night after night he listened to them swapping local gossip: 'I who could not sleep whole nights together, did greedily and attentively hearken to the birds, greatly admiring their industry and contention.' We shouldn't laugh too loudly at him. I think we all respond not just to birdsong, but *through* it. The bird becomes a kind of medium, another avenue for experiencing those senses of season and territory that mean so much to all living things.

1987

SKYLARKS

Hail to thee, blithe spirit! February is, and has ever been, the skylark's month. It is the one bird which will be reliably in song on that legendary moment for the pairing of the birds, St Valentine's Day. The lark – the laverock, 'heaven's minstrel' – is, by a long measure, the most versified bird in English literature. From anonymous 8th-century Celtic bards to Ted Hughes, writers have poured out their own 'silver chains of sound' in tribute. Only nightingale poetry can match it, and it seems odd that it is these two species – one, a bird of dark and wood, the other, of sun and air – that should be the most celebrated. Yet maybe it is their shared aura of otherness, the near-invisibility given by both darkness and the immense spaciousness of the sky that's allowed us to project on to them our yearnings for freedom. A bird which sings as it mounts towards the sun could hardly fail to inspire the most exultant dreams of all – of flight, escape, transcendence.

Yet we now know some hard truths about the lark. We know that its skirling song is a statement about its place on Earth as well as a symbol of freedom. And we know that, as far as human listeners are concerned, it is a plea which has fallen on deaf ears. Skylarks are still in catastrophic decline, down almost 60 per cent since 1965, to about a million pairs. Since 2000 the decline seems to have been compounded by the fashion for the early sowing of winter wheat, depriving the larks of winter stubbles and nesting habitats. Did the poets, unfamiliar with science and bird psychology, intuit anything of its vulnerability, and the subtle meanings of its song?

In medieval verse, the lark is an angel, a busy morning messenger, a clarion. 'A timid persistent frail creature sings at the top of his voice,' wrote an admiring 9th-century Irish poet. In the mid-17th century an extraordinary anonymous poem gives an almost modernist vision of the bird at the shimmering climax of its ascent:

> *Throned on the welkin's crest, her voice the stair*
> *Stills with her wings, and here becomes a chair:*
> *Where seated, in a calm sweet strain she sings ...*
> *[or] like a silver bell, that stands brim-full*
> *Of its own sound ...*

George Meredith echoes this idea in his 'The Lark Ascending' ('up he wings the spiral stair') and then intuits the *un*symbolic essence of the song: 'By simple singing of delight, / Shrill, irreflective, unrestrained'. Wordsworth penned no less than three tributes to the bird, including his resounding anthem to freedom, 'Liberty':

> *Who can divine what impulses from God,*
> *Reach the caged lark, within a town abode,*
> *From his poor inch or two of daisied sod?*
> *O yield him back his privilege! ...*
> *A wilderness is rich with liberty.*

Thomas Hardy imagined a particular lark, the lark that Shelley heard, now sleeping in a kind of immortality: 'A pinch of unseen, unguarded dust ... Maybe it rests in the loam I view'.

But it was in the First World War that the skylark's emotional charge became most intense. Great war poets and trench-shocked infantrymen, finding verse the only way of making sense of the nightmare around them, turned their eye skywards. The lark stood for home, for escape, for a life beyond mud and death. Larks are there, alongside the Flanders poppies, in the bitter verse of John McCrae that inspired Remembrance Sunday. Sergeant John Streets heard a lark and suddenly 'My soul rushed singing to the ether'. He was killed in the trenches in 1916. Isaac Rosenberg had a brief moment of joy in 1918: 'Heights of night ringing with unseen larks: / Music showering on our upturned listening faces.' It was a joy experienced on the German side, too. Franz Werfel saluted the bird: 'Thou doest thy life, / Thou singest thy song, and / Thou art what thou art.'

This is close to the interpretation of birdsong given by the celebrated ornithologist Charles Hartshorne: 'Since there is not an immediate and single practical meaning for song, it will not have a crude or narrowly emotional character, like sheer hostility as in growls ... but will be such as to fit a more balanced and normally cheerful, though mildly excited state such as is suitable both to interest in a mate and to interest in the privacy of territory' (1958). Most scientists would now accept that birdsong is less a linguistic than an expressive communication, an outpouring of individuality and exuberance. 'I am here. I am what I am.'

Can we find new insights from this 1,000-year-old poetic tradition – and from Hardy's vision of the last of the larks singing over the dust of their ancestors – to fight for it, as the trench soldiers did?

2007

CRANES

I daydream about cranes. Ever since I first glimpsed the colony that haunts the eastern reaches of the Norfolk Broads, they've become a kind of Grail for me, an unfailing lifter of spirits, what Aldo Leopold called 'a symbol of our untameable past'. So it was no real surprise when, a few months back, a film title popped unbidden into my head: *The Cranes are Flying*. I couldn't remember a thing about it except that it had been a cult art-movie when I was a student. I got hold of a copy, and it proved to be a touching if dated love story, set in wartime Moscow. But it is framed by shots of cranes flying over the city, first as the lovers chase each other round the streets, then as Moscow celebrates the end of the war, and the heroine braces herself for a future without her lover, killed in action.

Would cranes raise people's heads – and hearts – if they flew over London? All over the world, wherever one of the fifteen species occurs, they are symbols of hope and healing. They are one of the very few species of bird to figure in prehistoric cave paintings in Spain. In native American mythology cranes were renowned for the oratory of their trumpeting calls and were the 'Speakers for the Clans'. The now universally recognised symbol of the peace movement is based on a Hopi Indian sign for the footprint of a crane.

In Australia, the Brolga crane is part of the Dreamtime mythology. A typical story is of a young girl called Brolga, who was the best dancer in the land. She dances in the shade of a coolibah tree, 'moving with the shadow of the old tree's branches. As the wind swayed the tree, Brolga swayed, dancing out into the sunlight.' But she is spotted by an evil spirit, Waiwera, and is spiralled away in a whirlwind. She changes into a crane and begins to dance again before flying away. So the Aborigines named the bird Brolga, because Waiwera couldn't take away her elegance and love of dancing.

The crane's dance is a graphic sequence in Marjorie Kinnan Rawlings's 19th-century novel, *The Yearling*, set in Florida:

> *Two stood apart, erect and white, making a strange music that was part cry and part singing. The rhythm was irregular, like the dance. The other birds were in a circle. In the heart of the circle, several moved counter-clockwise. The musicians made their noise. The dancers raised their wings and lifted their feet, first one and then the other. They sunk their heads deep in their snowy breasts, lifted them and sunk again. They moved soundlessly, part awkwardness, part grace.*

These were almost certainly whooping cranes, now rare in the United States. However powerful and celebratory the mythology of cranes, it hasn't prevented them and their habitats being trashed across the planet. In traditional Japanese culture, the red-crowned crane was a symbol of eternal life, and it was revered for its longevity. As a real bird it was all but hunted out by the end of the 19th century. Yet folding paper cranes was supposed to bring luck. At the end of the Second World War, a young girl folded 645 before she died of cancer caused by the atomic bomb dropped on Hiroshima.

Is this the danger in mythology, that it can provide a kind of virtual reality, where symbols and even emotions can be experienced regardless of whether the flesh and blood creatures that first generated them still exist? Yet this isn't how it has happened in Vietnam. During the Vietnam War, in which US troops blitzed the Mekong delta marshes with defoliants and napalm, sarus cranes vanished. They began to reappear in the 1980s, and their gradual return has been encouraged by Vietnamese villagers as part of a 'regreening' of the country in which almost the whole population has taken part.

What is it about cranes that has elicited this kind of response, across the globe and throughout history? Does their sociable dancing – a habit they break into whenever they are excited – have something to do with it? Of all bird behaviour, it is the most easy for us to relate to, a bond that cuts across species barriers. At Lake Hornborgasjön in Sweden, where up to 50,000 people gather every April to welcome the cranes back, many join in with the birds' dancing. Yet surely the dance is, in both species, a celebration of something deeper – a homecoming, a renewal, a link with our common past, the completion of an annual journey which these ancient and majestic birds have been making for maybe tens of millions of years.

2005

A BRIEF TWITCH

During those spells of very fine weather in early summer, when the winds were blowing in continuously from the Continent, Britain was invaded by waves of exotic migrants. Bee-eaters flickered about the south coast, and carillons of golden orioles sang on the Isle of Wight. The West Country, on Birdline's recorded daily bulletins, sounded increasingly like the Camargue, with black-winged stilts, woodchat shrikes and purple herons loafing in the Cornish marshes. Scores of red-footed falcons patrolled the skies above eastern England. At Stodmarsh in Kent, there were four at once, hunting with hobbies in a display of aerial power that must have made the local hirundines wish they had never left Africa.

I heard too late about the flock of eight cattle egrets that had arrived improbably on a Hertfordshire gravel pit, just fifteen minutes' drive from my home. They wafted in from their breeding grounds in North Africa and, a few days later, wafted away again. I appeased myself by saying that I wasn't really a twitcher anyway – a piece of blatant self-deception. When I heard that some of the flock had turned up at the Ouse Washes, I was there with my telescope like the rest.

It was worth it. There were five birds in the flock, feeding and striking poses in a rough pasture by the side of the A1101, and they proved to be the most handsome and obliging of creatures, spending much of the time within 40 or 50 yards of the road.

Every so often one would fly a short distance to a new feeding or idling spot, with that deliciously nonchalant flight-style that egrets have – so much billowy white wing that they seem to be being blown along like scraps of stray sheeting. Three of them had the distinctive buff plumes on crown and breast that are part of the species' breeding plumage.

They shared the field with a herd of Friesians and looked thoroughly at home, poking around for food close to the feet of the meandering cattle exactly as they do by the Mediterranean. The cows were less familiar with this symbiotic arrangement though, and every so often would make half-hearted charges. One even tried to butt an egret into a dyke. The birds were unperturbed and continued to give their practical lessons in coexistence.

Despite their promising plumage (and, apparently, a perceptible northerly expansion of the species' breeding range), they didn't stay and try to nest. But for a few warm and congenial days they provided another startling tableau of the surprise and vitality of nature. I do hope they got home safely.

1992

Cattle egrets did eventually breed in the UK in 2008, in the Somerset Levels. [2009]

BARNIES

Some 80 years ago the 'Transactions of the Norfolk Naturalists' Society' carried an extraordinary account of what was almost certainly a pair of luminous barn owls. They were seen on a misty February afternoon floating like will-o'-the-wisps above a patch of marshy ground. One 'emerged from a covert about 200 yards distant, flying backwards and forwards across the field, at times approaching within 50 yards of where I was standing … it literally lighted up the branches of the trees as it flew past.'

The owls – if that is what they were – had probably picked up phosphorescence from roosting in the crumbling 'touchwood' of a tree smitten with honey fungus. Yet they were an eerie enough sight to convince one astonished Norfolk naturalist that the birds had the power to generate their own illumination.

Barn owls have always hovered between the light and the dark. They have been viewed with admiration and superstitious nervousness in about equal measure. Of all our birds of prey they have lived on the closest terms with human beings, and yet are still surrounded by mystery and folk mythology. There are stories of owls being burned for witchcraft in the Middle Ages. Their screeching call is an almost universal omen of bad luck, and dead birds were sometimes nailed on barn doors to frighten off evil intruders – of all sorts and substances.

At the same time they were respected by farmers for their prowess at keeping down rats and mice, and increasingly over the past two centuries, their pale vigil kept over the winter pastures has seemed like a reassurance. They are village familiars; white witches, if witches at all.

Of all the barn owls I have watched – fewer each year, sadly – I cannot recall ever seeing one more than a few hundred yards from a village or human settlement. They haunt the roughest, oldest edges of the parish landscape – the green lanes and stackyards and hedgebanks – and with those open, inquisitive faces that look as if they are mounted directly on to the wings, seem like guardian spirits, patrollers of the bounds.

In the Cornish churchyard of St Filii de Eglosros, one first day of spring, I saw a barn owl cross paths with a tramp, headed east with a full backpack. In Dorset, another peered inscrutably out of a hole in an old lime kiln. In East Anglia, during the sixties and early seventies, they were constant evening companions, dipping along the verges in front of the car. This March, in north Norfolk, I watched one in mid-afternoon, endlessly quartering a patch of rough fenny grassland that bordered a village green.

But no barn owl can ever match the first. Our childhood owls nested in a barn just 30 yards from the A41, and their hunting range corresponded almost exactly with the territory of our local gang: over the old brick piles that were all that remained of a Victorian mansion, up the ivy-clad wall that lined the council estate, across the steep field we used for tobogganing, then down, if we were lucky, through the bosky edges of our back gardens. The memory of them beating past the poplar trees – burnished gold wings flickering against lime-green leaves in the evening light – is one of the few images of childhood I can recall with absolute clarity.

Those home owls vanished just before the barn was demolished and the whole area was given over to a housing estate. Now they are almost extinct right across the Chilterns. In the country as a whole the population is only a third of what it was 50 years ago. The barn owl has been under enormous stress during this period, from pesticides, unscrupulous gamekeepers, loss of nesting trees. As many as 5,000 may be killed every year on the roads. But none of these factors, taken either separately or together, seemed sufficient to explain such a continuing, remorseless decline.

Now a new report seems at last to have solved the riddle. Putting an immense body of field records through sophisticated computer analysis, Colin Shawyer has shown beyond any reasonable doubt that the barn owls' decline in Britain is a result of a deteriorating climate and the loss of hunting (not nesting) habitat. Taken together these factors severely limit the small mammals on which the barn owl depends. Even if the adult birds survive a hard winter, they can find it impossible to raise young in our increasingly cool, wet springs. One of Colin Shawyer's most inspired and convincing programs was to correlate nesting sites with rainfall. It turns out that in the dry east of England, barn owls nest chiefly in trees. In the high rainfall areas of the west and north they nest almost exclusively in buildings, despite an abundance of suitable natural sites. What they are after is a roof over their heads, something to keep the rain off their easily waterlogged fledglings.

But the overriding impression of this report is of barn owls as human familiars, haunting the margins of our own society. They will nest in almost any kind of man-made structure – chapels, mine shafts, even motorway bridges – provided they are not too sanitised and tidied. They hunt along the margins, too, in those leftover patches that are neither wholly cultivated nor wholly wooded: the boundary hedges, the streamside roughs, the muddles and back-lots, all those places that are today so ruthlessly gobbled up.

Ten years ago, I wrote in the conclusion of a book called *The Common Ground,* that we might do worse than reintroduce the ancient idea of a tithe – an offering of a tenth of the land to ensure the continued fertility of the earth. Most of our fellow creatures depend more or less on this marginal fraction, and to the barn owl it is critical. The owl's sad decline is a reflection of our own greed, and its return to our parishes would be the surest indication that we have mended some of our ways.

1987

* * *

All spring the tousled sweeps of Tring Park seemed to be thickening, like a cat's new coat. I'd catch glimpses of it from the bypass, and even from a distance I could see the tide of young ash rising in the storm-blasted beech hangers and new shoots seeping up through the tawny stems of last year's ungrazed grasses. The whole prospect stirred perceptibly in the breeze. Something was going on in there.

It is a spectacular place, but I had stayed clear recently while it weathered one of its periodic crises. Back in the 17th century it was the north-west tip of Tring Common, a tract of woodland, grass and heath that stretched over more than 3,000 acres. But gradually it was eaten away, one slice appropriated for a private park in the mid-18th century, more for plantation woods, the last 300 acres filched and enclosed by Parliamentary enactment in 1853. The parkland area became grazing land and an unofficial public open space after the war, but a few years ago it was bought by Whitbreads, who had ambitions to turn it into a golf course and country club. Fortunately, it lies in the Chilterns Area of Outstanding Natural Beauty, and the brewery's original schemes were summarily turned down by the planning authorities. For the past 18 months it has been a brooding and deliciously unkempt waste, getting its breath back.

I gave in to its seductive new charms in June. I had just been to visit the Buckinghamshire soldier-orchid site, and had been delighted by the spreading colonies, which are no longer barricaded off, as they were in the 1970s. I remembered that Tring Park was one of the orchid's last Hertfordshire sites in the 19th century, when it grew 'abundantly' in sunny places by the edges of chalky woods, and I had a wild fancy that it might just have reappeared in the tangled west-facing slopes. I didn't find any, but the whole place had an invigorating sense of profusion. There were drifts of cowslips in seed, enough salad burnet to stain the steeper slopes claret and, in the half-shade along the wood-edge, a glimmering brocade of bugle and jasmine-scented valerian.

Then I began to hear the stories of the barn owls, which have not bred in this corner of the county for maybe 20 years. There were sightings by the village allotments, and one spotted on a path, munching a vole. They were all centred on Tring Park. I took to going for dusk-time walks among the overgrown paddocks and ragged hedges that lie between my wood and the park. I didn't see the barn owls, but the smell of hay, the feel of rough grass on bare legs, and the low sun striping the beechwoods with shadows, conjured up powerful memories of evening walks as a teenager and school holidays spent running wild. Our playground then was also an abandoned park, once the grounds of a long-demolished mansion. There had been barn owls there, too, nesting in the old stables and patrolling the lines of poplars and crumbling walls that marked our common boundaries.

Then one evening in July, feeling lucky after watching two of the Chilterns' red kites circling a village further south, I stopped off for a quick look at the park. It was about 8.15, and I saw the owls immediately, quartering the bleached knee-high grass that was now dotted with orchids and scabious. They were diving for prey roughly every 30 seconds, and catching something on about one strike in ten. I kept low and edged in the direction they were ferrying the food. They seemed quite unperturbed by my presence, so much so that I began to wonder if barn owls have slight tunnel vision. So when one flew straight towards me, I stood my ground. It sheared off with a screech when it was about 20 yards away, and went and hid in a tree. I retired to the cover of a hedge, too, and followed them more discreetly to the nest tree, which proved to be an ancient beech with half its top blown out. Burying myself in the hogweed nearby, I had the magical experience of the owls wafting past me just feet away, as silent as a breath.

I went back to the park often over the summer, and each time the owls came out to hunt a little later. And each time I glimpsed, for just a few maddening seconds, the silhouette of a third owl. I thought at first that it was an unusually dark-plumaged barn owl, but am now convinced that it was a long-eared, which would be a testament indeed to the teeming mammal life in this Chiltern pampas. My last visit was on a moonless night before the rains began. It was almost too dark to see, but I could just make out the adult owls dancing around among the branches, and I guess the young were on the point of leaving the nest.

The future of Tring Park looks bright at present. Whitbreads has settled for a small housing scheme in one corner of the park, and agreed to sell or lease the remainder to a conservation body. Then, I suppose, it will have to be managed, otherwise it will all turn into woodland within a couple of decades (what it really needs is a hurricane once a century and an occasional, passing herd of bison). But I hope whoever has charge of it will have seen it this summer in its prime, with the wild woods tumbling into the valley, and the owls beating over a mile of waving grass that looked less like tame old England than the Elysian plains of John Muir's California, before the ranchers came.

1993

* * *

I'd been living in the Waveney Valley, a place full of wild grassland and gently decaying barns, for a whole year before I saw the bird that should be one of its signature species. The word came from a friend, who'd been tipped off by her window-cleaner, who regarded it as a matter of course: yes, he saw a white owl most evenings when he was taking the dog for a walk, in that little side-valley, back of Botesdale.

I went there at dusk the next day. I settled down close to where I guessed it would hunt, beside a stretch of streamside rough, scattered with newly-planted saplings. A roe deer grazed nearby. A woodcock slipped into the stream a few metres from me, probing and preening. In the half-light, its two pale back-stripes seemed to sway disembodiedly, like eels. At 40 minutes past sunset the barn owl just materialised, rose up out of the grass in front of me. It took off, soft as thistledown, its head like a quite separate creature riding shotgun out front. It passed through the saplings, wing-beats quickening to negotiate the gaps. It was winnowing the grass, threshing it for food. Through my binoculars I could see the last light from the west shining through its wings, picking out the dense primaries from the almost translucent trailing feathers. It had four wings, two in the day and two in the night, shuttling the evening forward. Then it stalled, hovered on tip-tail and plunged into invisibility again.

Now I'm becoming a creature of the dusk myself. It's when the action is. At the moment when I used to look at my watch, or the sky, and think 'time to go home', I now think 'time to go out'. In the notes I made of evening walks a year ago – maybe still in the closing stages of a long low mood – I saw the dusk as an ascetic experience, a medium for confronting the awful sterility of East Anglia's farming landscapes. The twilight seemed to clarify things, strip away all the frivolous excess of flowers and flitting songbirds, and leave you with the sombre realities: dark bare fields, treeless banks, the silhouettes of remnant copses that might as well be banks of grain-silos. Now that image has flipped over, come out like a positive print. The amorphous field-shapes have retreated into the background, and I notice instead the brilliant fringes of things: tricks of the light through the tracery of twigs, dusking moths, the beginnings of spring swelling in the turf. And, of course, the great dramas of roosting. There are niches in time which cut across the patchwork on the ground.

They begin in late afternoon, in the arable fields north of the house. The golden plovers are feeding in the winter wheat. As the sun goes down, they become more restive, darting about in urgent bands, slicing through the sweeing lapwing flocks like arrow showers. Then, pouring in from the south and east towards a roost I haven't yet discovered, endless trails of rooks and jackdaws. They put down here and there on the way and turn the fields black.

A dozen miles west, at a winter-flooded mere. This is the wild-fowl's moment. Bands of wigeon and shoveler hurtle about the sky, beating the bounds of the water and then shooting off on tangents over the nearby houses and fields. It's an exultant, infectious display. Other birds get caught up in it. I see a single starling flying deep in a wigeon flock, then a dozen teal riding with the mallards, and matching every wing-beat and swerve.

But this amicable suspension of the species' barrier is nothing by the side of the great communal roost in the heart of the Broads, now almost a sacred site. Sit here in the winter gloaming and you can see things you should not see in Britain: 30 marsh harriers (which should be in Africa), floating above the reeds; a handful of cranes (which should be in Spain), skimming low to a hidden lagoon; if you're lucky, hen harriers, short-eared owls, merlins, too; and hundreds of teal darting furiously over the marsh like bats.

What do these vespers rituals mean? Conventional theories explain communal roosting very plausibly, in terms of 'safety in numbers' and the sharing of information about food sources. But as so often in nature, it's too extravagant, too excessive to be so simply utilitarian.

The great assemblies, the prolonged flight displays (I wrote about the red kites' two-hour spectacular last year), the mixing of the species (sometimes of predator and prey), suggest something more fundamental is going on. Would it be too anthropomorphic to think that other creatures also like to see in the night in company, to mount a show of solidarity and mutual confidence-boosting against the dark, much as we see out the old year in a riot of song and dance?

2004

PREDATOR

I got the news purely by chance: a barn owl was roosting at my old lodgings, down in the valley. I found the barn floor covered with pellets, in that strange, dark lacquering. And three vole skulls in each pellet. From some intuition, or too many hours spent in thrall to these birds, I knew where it would be hunting. So at last light, in the rough paddocks by the river, I put up my glasses, and there it was, hunched on a fence post. It was a beautiful bird, so gingery I promptly named it Orlando. It also proved to be a mercilessly successful hunter.

Barn owls haven't wintered in this stretch of Norfolk valley for decades, and I hadn't lived that close to one since I was a child. But back home the day went sour. Our local paper had as its letter of the day news of a new threat to the owls: they'd become, so the writer complained in graphic detail, the latest victim of that avian hooligan, the sparrowhawk. I felt affronted – not because of any imagined danger to the owls, but because (though they're predators themselves) they had been dragged in as hapless stool-pigeons in what is an increasingly insidious campaign of victimisation of birds of prey.

When this began, back in the early nineties, it seemed a rather sad joke. I remember the Duchess of Devonshire famously proclaiming that 'sparrowhawks use my birdtable as if it were the snack bar at the Ritz' (a hint of the kind of possessiveness that has come to mark the campaign). Now it is a fully fledged movement, organised under the banner of SongBird Survival (SBS). Its argument is that sparrowhawks are vicious killers, parasites on people's generous feelings towards small birds and responsible for a critical collapse in their populations. Their proliferating numbers must be 'controlled' to avert that decline becoming irreversible.

I understand the feelings of stewardship that people feel towards birds that grace their gardens. When martins used to nest on my house, I used to jump and scream whenever hobbies came near. But I hope I never felt that the predator was doing something wrong or should in some way be prevented from going about its natural business. Witnessing these ancient and dramatic transactions between our native birds seemed more like a privilege.

The SBS campaign is not only an indirect threat to our birds of prey, but a telling example of the way that dangerous myths develop, especially those that scapegoat the 'Evil Intruder' (a process we need to be increasingly alert for against the background of avian flu). First, like all such myths, it denies history. The fact that sparrowhawks and songbirds lived in a dynamic balance for thousands of years before the invention of birdtables and gamekeepers is ignored. 'Balance' must be created by human intervention. The farming writer Robin Page, for instance, argues that the 'normal' population of hawks was once very low, because hen-keepers routinely shot them. But the authority Leslie Brown (in *British Birds of Prey*, 1976) estimates a historic baseline population of 75,000 pairs. This plummeted to about 5,000 pairs because of pesticide poisoning in the 1950s and 1960s, but has now recovered – though currently declining again – to about 30,000 pairs (British Trust for Ornithology figures).

But mythic victimisation has never been much influenced by evidence. The assumption on which SBS's whole case rests, that there has been a massive, general slump in songbirds, goes against the evidence of BTO's censuses over the past 40 years, the period of sparrowhawk recovery. Of our 20 commonest songbirds, 10 have increased, including chaffinch, robin, and all the garden tits. Eight have declined, including skylark and house sparrow. But of this eight, four, including song thrush and dunnock, have increased over the past ten years. Year-by-year fluctuations reflect weather conditions here and in Africa, changing agricultural (and gardening) practices and, of course, shifting predator pressures. But sparrowhawks couldn't drive their food species into irreversible decline without becoming terminally starved themselves. That is the iron law of supply and demand in nature.

I don't personally think that the distress of SBS members has much to do with the endangerment of species by predation. If so, they would worry about the impact of robins on rare invertebrates, of that omnivorous birdtable favourite, the great spotted woodpecker, on its lesser spotted cousin, of the barn owl on the vole. I think that at its deepest level it is a revulsion against trespass. For centuries we have kept the wilderness at arm's length, allowing it in only on our terms, clasping the prerogatives of life and death like Roman emperors. Then, at our breakfast tables, comes this sudden intruder, the barbarian with the incandescent eyes, to remind us that the whole exquisite intricacy of life – ourselves included – depends on the consumption of one organism by another.

2006

EAGLES

The quarrels surrounding Natural England's dream of reintroducing white-tailed eagles to East Anglia have now entered a surreal phase, and seem to me to have implications for our whole frame of thinking about the future of UK wildlife.

This is the story so far. White-tailed eagles – aka sea eagles – were once widespread across the British Isles. They were our top avian predator, an awesome, 2.5m-wingspanned, all-purpose hunter and scavenger. Predictably, they were driven to extinction by game-keepers by the early 20th century. They were reintroduced to Skye – the site of the last breeding pair – in the 1970s. Three years ago Natural England put out for consultation a plan to restore the eagle to England, and chose the mosaic of coastal marshes and woods near Dunwich in Suffolk, which is pretty representative of the kind of places the bird haunts in Europe. They hoped that it might become a totemic bird for the public, an electrifying symbol of the regeneration of England's wild places. In this they were inspired not just by the restored population in the Hebrides, but by the huge success of red kites in the Chilterns. These reintroduced birds have prospered beyond expectation, and have had a dramatic effect on tourism and the public perception of wildlife in the Thames Valley. There's also the example of Oostvaardersplassen on the Dutch coast. Cattle carcasses left on the reserve attract bands of wandering sea eagles, which are now breeding there, just 150 miles from the East Anglian coast.

But back in East Anglia, the consultation foundered. The RSPB protested that the eagles might take one of the few female bitterns in Suffolk, the Country Landowners Association that they might snatch a few piglets, though both objections were on the further shores of possibility. There was talk of moving the possible site to the Thames Estuary or the Norfolk Broads, but Natural England eventually opted for the immense marshlands of the north Norfolk coast. Again they've been rebuffed. Poultry farmers (who have been promised recompense if any of their birds are taken) have claimed that even an eagle flying overhead would cause their birds 'stress', that they might 'injure themselves fleeing into fences' and 'lay strange-shaped eggs' – protests that in all fairness might also be levelled against hot-air balloons. Even local naturalists have berated the idea, insisting that there's no evidence the eagle was ever native in the region, and that the birds might well decimate colonies of local rarities, such as avocets.

On these last two objections, this is the evidence – though obviously this argument is not really about 'facts'. White-tailed eagle bones have been found in post-glacial sites across England, for instance in the Lake District, Yorkshire, Somerset and Essex. There is circumstantial evidence, too, in place names. The Anglo-Saxon name for the bird was 'erne', and the historian Margaret Gelling has identified 30 place names (in 14 counties) which almost certainly mean 'eagle place'. Earley in the Thames Valley is one, and eagle bones were found during the excavation of a 5th-century site just 20 miles away.

As for the eagle's diet, the research is very extensive. Fish and seabirds are favourites, though it almost never attempts to catch birds in flight. It has a distinct liking for seagulls, which might be a plus in some conservationists' eyes. Dead animals, requiring no energy-expensive chasing, are also favourites: the carcasses of seals, deer, lambs and, yes, piglets, though the taking of live stock is exceptionally unusual. The snatching of small pets has been recorded on a few occasions, and there is just one well-substantiated case, from Skye in 1695, of an erne carrying off a human baby (it was quite unharmed and later rescued). And it would be foolish to ignore the possibility that the eagles might raid tern or wader nesting colonies – though to suggest, as some nervous naturalists seem to be saying, that they have a twitcher's taste for rare species is bizarre. Birds do eat each other. It is a fact of life in the wild. In 2007 a family of cranes, East Anglia's current star bird, ate all the chicks in a colony of avocets, the symbol of the RSPB. At the root of this argument are different visions of the future of our countryside. One is a safe, conservative and deferential model, in which human livelihood and convenience are always put first, and animals with attitude are regarded as suitable for foreign parts but not for heavily populated Britain. The other welcomes top predators as proper ingredients of large landscapes, accepts a degree of danger and inconvenience as integral parts of wild ecosystems, and feels that they might even serve to remind us of our place in the scheme of things.

2009

At the time of writing, the possible introduction site has now switched back to the Suffolk coast. [2009]

* * *

There can't be much doubt about the origins of the recent spate of escaped eagle owls. But four birds in the space of a month is hard to put down to coincidence. One rescued by the Fire Brigade in Harpenden; another from a tree in Burnham Thorpe, Norfolk (I have David Cobham's snap of it in front of me); a third haunting the lanes in Fleet, Hampshire; and finally the Nottingham bird that became famous for strafing Rottweilers. What is going on? Is some enthusiast determined to try to naturalise the species here? Is it an example of Rupert Sheldrake's mysterious 'morphic resonance' at work, making it a doddle for all eagle owls to escape once one has learned the knack? I personally rather hope it is a mass protest by Owls' Lib. The most frightening aspect of these stories is what they reveal about the number of these magnificent birds – 2 feet tall and 5 feet in wingspan – kept in captivity. Their taste of freedom, alas, will probably be short. But they should spark off some local legends every bit as Gothic as the Surrey puma. And if that deters people from keeping owls as pets, and keeps nervous Rottweilers off the street, I for one will be happy.

1991

ON SWIFTS

By the time you read this most of Britain's swifts will have gone, leaving a melancholy space in the summer skies. Yet four months ago it looked, for a few stomach-wrenching days, as if they might not be coming back. Despite seemingly perfect weather, the early birds were a week late. The main body eventually drifted back with tantalising nonchalance to their native parishes, but they seemed – at least throughout May – to be perceptibly fewer.

I find the possibility that our most exhilarating summer bird might be on the slide hard to contemplate. Yet the British Trust for Ornithology's surveys show that breeding pairs declined by 41 per cent between 1994 and 2007. There are now less than 40,000 pairs in the UK. When I first saw that figure I assumed it was a misprint, that one or two noughts had been missed out. Swifts seem to be uncountable in high summer, to fill the skies with their ecstatic races. Yet most of the birds we watch aren't breeders at all, but youngsters, which don't nest till they're 3 years old, during which time – it is one of the swift's great marvels – they will not have come to Earth once.

It is their unearthliness, I think, that is part of their magic. They are creatures utterly of another element. You never see their faces. They play, drink, sleep on the wing. They even mate in the air, and if you are lucky enough to witness their brief moment of coupling, it's like a glimpse of some huge primordial dragonfly. Yet their unfettered, switchback sky-rides touch a deeper chord of sympathy in us than perhaps any other creature. They're our inner bird, yearning to be wild and reckless and yelling at the sun.

It seems to be a modern response. There's little early poetry or even interest in swifts (Gilbert White excepted). They were regarded as distant, unpicturesque, devoid of improving moral lessons. They were widely known as 'devilings'. Now their raciness seems a tonic for the times. When the first birds arrive, two-word emails shoot round between us swift addicts: 'They're back' (a phrase from Ted Hughes's famous poem). No need to say what.

When they're late we also seek communal solace. Two springs ago I tracked down a migration website, a sort of helpline for sufferers from Swift Obsessive Disorder. Andy from Spain was more comfort than he knew when he posted on 1 May: 'For those lacking common swifts in northern Europe, this afternoon was evidence of a huge arrival over Torremolinos.' Two days later they brought the Costa del Sol to our glum shores.

I know my own anxieties are excessive, but the swift has been my talisman since I was a child, and over a lifetime I think I've begun to understand a little about our cultural feelings for it. Aged 12, I used to walk to school on May Day, clutching my blazer collar for luck to try to bring them home for that special spring festival. Later there were evenings toasting the birds at a canalside pub, as they raced between the Victorian terrace houses and the factories like a ragged black comet. The pack races of 20 or 30 birds (or hundreds down in southern Europe) are swifts' most intoxicating display, a delirium of full-pelt aerobatics and the fizz of communal joy-riding. I don't think Ted Hughes was being the least bit anthropomorphic when he compared them to a gang of teenage bikers. Their urban aura may be another reason why swifts chime more with modern consciousness. I've seen them in purely natural territory (they nest in old pines in the Cairngorms), but they look weirdly out of place.

These days – perhaps age is catching up with me – there's a more courtly swift manoeuvre that touches me. I call it The Dip. Two birds, maybe siblings or a pair forming for the following spring, are flying in parallel, then suddenly swoop down together in a deep parabola. It is gracious and perfectly synchronised and reminds me of an ice-dancing move. Certainly it is a beautiful act of bonding.

Anne Stevenson, in another great 20th-century swift poem, warns against pressing these human analogies too far. The birds are 'not parables but / Bolts in the world's need: swift / Swifts, not in punishment, not in ecstasy, simply / Sleepers over oceans in the mill of the world's breathing.' Yet so intimately, so publicly do they penetrate our human landscapes that they can't avoid becoming symbols. In 2007, during the Israeli bombardment of Lebanon, I happened to see a live evening news bulletin from Beirut. Halfway through, the reporter was suddenly surrounded by a flickering ectoplasm of swifts. They, of course, knew nothing of what was going on.

But as their silhouettes passed back and forth against the flashes of exploding shells, their message to us was very clear. 'Choose life,' they screamed, 'choose life.'

2009

One of the reasons for the rapid decline of the swift in the UK has now become clear. Modern building regulations mean that there are very few openings where swifts can enter eaves and lofts to breed. Specialist nesting boxes – and 'swift cities' mounted on poles – are now being developed. [2009]

TOTEMS

We'd been out to watch the pink-footed geese on their dusk flight. It was a miserable afternoon in January, nothing about, a wet, bone-chilling mist clamped like gauze over the saltmarshes. The birds looked like a break in the clouds at first, a single wavering line that seemed to stretch across the whole arc of the horizon. Then they were overhead, the long skein unravelling and re-forming, an immense living calligraphy that, however many times you see it, still spells out 'This is Great Business'. It is as near a sacred message as you will get from the natural world.

Back home by the fire, we fell to talking about the sanctity of wild creatures. My friends had enjoyed a farmed goose for Christmas, and we wondered if any of us, after what we'd just witnessed, could ever eat a wild pink-foot. We felt we shouldn't, but, more importantly, couldn't, though it was hard to think of any reason that didn't smack of hypocrisy. Pink-feet are common in Norfolk, and it's legal to shoot them, though not to sell them. What if we'd been offered one as a Christmas gift?

The only answer, I suspect, is to be honestly emotional, and to accept that, like any indigenous people, we too can have personal totems, creatures whose presence touches the heart, and whose wilful killing seems a kind of blasphemy, an offence against one of the family. In East Anglia, the animal most widely regarded as a totem is the hare, 'the scutter, the fellow in the dew, the looker to the side, the hedge-frisker, the stag of the stubble', as a wonderful Middle English poem describes it. Hares are also common here, but it's a long time since I've seen one hung up outside a butcher's shop, as happened when I was young – a sign, I think, of changed public sensibilities. Instead, what are hanging up are votive images of the hare. Every gallery and gift shop is full of them. Hares are painted on the outside of buildings. There is a Leaping Hare restaurant, decorated with Georgina Warne's wry portraits. And a couple of years ago the Wildlife Art Gallery in Lavenham devoted an entire exhibition to hare art. The hare, as local totem, has become big business.

Across the world, too, the hare is one of the oldest and most wide-spread animals in mythology. It's been a fertility symbol, a moon-creature, a fire-devil and a trickster. Brer Rabbit was a hare. The poet William Cowper's touching account of his pet hare Puss (1786) is a landmark in the mellowing relationship between humankind and animals. Variations on the parable of the tortoise and the hare can be found in almost every language from Bantu to Tibetan. Across parts of North America the Great Hare was the lynchpin of many creation myths. A very moral Chinese folk tale tells of a hare living in the Buddha's sacred grove. One evening the Buddha comes disguised as a starving peasant. The hare bounds to his aid: 'Master, I, who have grown up in the forest nourished by grass and herbs, have nothing to offer thee but my own body. Vouchsafe me the favour of feeding thee with my own flesh.' He then throws himself on a charcoal fire, but not before stopping to gently pick the fleas from his fur, saying: 'My body I may sacrifice to the Holy One, but your lives I have no right to take.' And an Egyptian hieroglyph from 2000 BC of a hare over a ripple of water means simply 'to exist'.

What is it about hares that has touched so many cultures? Spring is their great moment of the year in Britain. In the field at the back of my study there are a dozen or so lolloping about, a motley bunch – 'the way-beater, the one who doesn't go straight home, the light-foot, the sitter-still'. Where have they been all winter? I see them singly at night, but never in the gangs that suddenly appear in spring. No wonder that in folk culture they have so often been seen as shape-shifters, transfixing us with their appearances and disappearances, their prodigious running, their fascination with, and nimbleness in, fires. But there is something else too. Much of the current art of hares portrays them in a kind of conversation with their fellow creatures of the field, gossiping with rooks, running with curlew. This echoes the Chinese story of the hare and the fleas, and an extraordinary moment last spring, when I watched a barn owl fly down to sit among a group of hares. This is how we know them best, as twitch-nosed watchers, weavers of the fields. They are a presiding presence, like roost-bound geese.

Of course, our special affection for creatures like hares and geese is a kind of sentimentality. But it's also a sign that we still have a sense of wonder about the great mysteries of communication between our fellow beings.

2009

3. LEAVES

My adult interest in nature was rekindled by plants – and by buying an ancient wood in the Chilterns in the 1980s.

WOODING

'Back to the woods': what a catch-all phrase! We use it for fleshly frol-ics and for 'going bush' and for trying to find some simpler, more natural way of life. Yet sometimes it hints at a search for something far from simple: for the tangle of feral energy and myth that the idea of the forest has formed in our imaginations.

I felt a bit of that yearning myself this spring, and a craving to go back to my old wood in the Chilterns. Two years in the Waveney Valley has opened my eyes to whole new worlds, especially to the buzzing luxuriance of the fen in high summer, and the watery magnificence of the Broads in winter. But in April and May there is really only one place to be, and that's in the thick of a burgeoning wood, rippling with tides of flowers and dappled twiggery.

We don't have much in the way of woods left in agricultural south Norfolk: clumps of alder and willow on the edge of the swamps and along the riverbanks; new farm plantations and roadside thickets that may, one day, become woods of a kind; and a handful of tiny ancient woods – though they are chiefly drab ex-coppices, dog's mercury monocultures saved for the sake of the pheasant.

When I made it back to Hardings Wood this spring, I realised that the element that was really missing was my own involvement in the local woods. In Norfolk, I'd been neither intimate witness nor active woodland creature. In the Chilterns, I'd held the deeds of Hardings for more than 20 years and had got to know every square foot. I could never get my head round the idea of being a land 'owner' (how on Earth can anyone presume to possess a whole wild community?), but the sense of having some kind of responsibility for the place had bred an intense attention to its evolution. I knew when individual ash seedlings had grown a single inch, where windfall branches had dropped from, exactly how big our colonies of wood-vetch were, where flash-floods would travel, where badgers had walked the night before.

And on that wet, early May afternoon, I found those two decades of on-going memory suddenly visible again, as if I had drawn out a layered peat-core from my mind. The glades we'd cut out by clearing the last owner's plantation poplars were now soaring, naturally regenerated woodlets. Three years ago they weren't much taller than me. We'd not planted a thing, but close on ten species of tree had come in of their own accord: ash chiefly, with hazel, hornbeam, maple, beech, cherry, holly, blackthorn and hawthorn. And underneath there were already tufts of colonising spurge laurel and shield ferns. Up on the acid plateau at the top of the wood the bluebells were even thicker than I remembered, but still blooming at the same moment as the unfurling of the beech leaves – that wonderful, luminous conjunction of colours that always reminded me of swimming under water. I'd often worked up here by myself, ring-barking the planted poplars so that, in their fallow years, they could at least be useful to tits and woodpeckers. Now I could see how far the trees had collapsed, and the way the young oaks beneath were insinuating themselves between the dead branches. It was, over maybe half an acre, just like a real forest.

But there were more playful touches, too. The ash seedling that we'd naively put a tree shelter round was a quarter of the size of its unprotected neighbours. The oakling lawns that had sprouted after the great acorn autumn of 1994 had all vanished. A thin trickle of garden columbines and meadow-rues up the edges of the main track. Woods have ancient rhythms of their own.

All this will go on, as the wood is now in the care of a village trust. So this was a journey back to the woods in the richest possible sense, a rediscovery of their mystery and resilient independence, and of the possibility that we can be part of their continuing evolution.

2004

I owned Hardings Wood in Wigginton near Tring between 1981 and 2002, and ran it as a 'community wood'. Since I moved to Norfolk it has been in the ownership and care of a village trust. Aspects of its story are in my books Nature Cure *(Chatto and Windus, 2005) and* Beech-combings *(Chatto and Windus, 2007). [2009]*

THE GREAT STORM

One hurricane, to misquote Lady Bracknell, may be regarded as a misfortune. Two in the space of little more than two years looks suspiciously like carelessness. If the greenhouse effect (ie, 'us') is to blame, then we can be reasonably sure that there will be more of the same in the years to come. This will mean a drastic rethink not only of such matters as weather-forecasting and house-building, but of the whole way we regard and care about trees.

The January 1990 storm was different from the one in 1987 in coming when the trees were not in leaf, but it affected a much greater area of Britain. The Midlands, Wales and the West Country were all badly affected. We got our come-uppance in the Chilterns too. Thirty trees were down in my own wood – six times the number in '87. In Frithsden Beeches, one of the best surviving examples of an ancient wood-pasture, more than a third of the vast beech pollards were blown out of the ground.

But the lessons of 1987 still apply, perhaps even more urgently. It is now accepted, for instance, that in many places more damage was done by overhasty and insensitive 'clearing up' than by the gale itself. Trees which had lost a branch or two but were otherwise perfectly safe and healthy were assumed to be dead, and were felled. Young self-sown trees and shrubs were crushed in the manic effort to clear fallen wood away. Down in Sussex I saw bulldozers clearing the ground for replanting by scraping away the topsoil plus its carpet of young seedling trees.

In places where there has been less interference the process of natural healing has been spectacular. Many of the trees that fell into damp ground weren't killed and simply resumed their lives in a horizontal mode. I've seen oak hedges sprouting from reclining trunks, and willows sprouting almost under water. In the Chilterns we also have a nice addition to the landscape in the form of wild cherries flowering at knee height. Down in the Hampshire Weald, where the beech hangers were especially badly hit, a more natural tree community of ash, maple and hazel has pushed up clean through the wreck-age, growing six feet in two years in many places. The National Trust's wood at Toys Hill, perhaps the most comprehensively devastated in the country, was already carpeted with birch, whitebeam and beech seedlings only a year after the storm. Many of the stumps which had been relieved of their trunks and pushed back in the root hole were sprouting, too. (All of which was rather more optimistic than the Trust leaflet which declaimed in apocalyptic terms that 'the Great Storm desecrated the past and betrayed the future'.)

Enough evidence is now available to suggest some tentative rules for speeding up the recovery of storm-struck woods. One: remember that fallen or tilted trees aren't necessarily doomed. Oak and ash with deep roots often survive and reroot themselves along the trunk. Two: remember that even 'dead' wood isn't useless. It is a normal and essential component of woodland ecosystems, an irreplaceable habitat for fungi, mosses, insects and birds. In natural woodland 'fallow' wood makes up more than 50 per cent of the total timber mass. Three: natural regeneration (in woods at least) is a quicker, cheaper, more natural and more resilient way of restocking woods than planting. Four: where planting is felt to be necessary it should be of small saplings, and done without staking, so that the trees can acclimatise to the wind.

In the longer term, we need more whole woods, and less concentration on wind-funnelling belts and clumps at the edges of the fields. We may also have to regard beech trees as something of a luxury. Their top-heavy, shallow-rooted habit has made them far and away the most vulnerable species in the two storms so far. It seems extraordinary now that landscape gardeners and early ecologists could ever have regarded beech as *the* climax forest tree in southern Britain.

1990

TREE-PLANTING

It is, as I write, the season for tree-planting. All over the country, on roadsides, village greens, school playgrounds and abandoned fields, saplings are being reverently set in rows. Children are gathering basketfuls of acorns, hazelnuts and haws, and are sowing them in little pots on classroom windowsills. It is our great annual ritual of reparation, a token of our desire to make amends.

Yet do we ever pause to think rationally about this curious rite, about what it does to the land and to the attitudes of the planters? Trees, after all, grow quite naturally in our climate and succeeded in foresting Britain long before Plant a Tree Week was invented. Turn your back on a piece of land, and it is, in a few years, a wood. Much of the activity of farmers, developers and nature conservation managers is, precisely, the killing of trees, for their impertinent insistence on growing where they like. Agriculture – and civilisation itself – are founded on a constant battle against incipient forest regeneration. Yet with our green hats on, we seem to doubt trees' biological ability to reproduce themselves.

Perhaps the best that can be said about planting is that it's more important symbolically than ecologically, that the planted trees become visible monuments to the dedication of a piece of ground to woodland. At its most damaging, it is pure PR, a clichéd gesture of correct intentions by politicians and corporate bodies. The Woodland Trust, one of the biggest planters in the country, privately admits it would like to see more natural tree growth, but does not think its members would tolerate years of scrubby young seedlings on its holdings. They want instant woods, woods as responsive to human intervention as a herbaceous border.

What must humouring this attitude do to people's view of nature's independence, especially children's? Doesn't it simply reinforce the ancient heresy – one of the root causes of our environmental problems – that nature is subservient, incapable of surviving without our assistance? And, more practically, what does it do to the planted land, stuffed full of often random assortments of saplings in ordered rows? Are these really trees, or a kind of living signpost, put there for our self-gratification?

Every time we're tempted to plant a tree anywhere that isn't a garden, we should go and meditate on one that has grown of its own accord. Go and look at a so-called 'derelict' hedge, at the mazy growth of the upward shoots from the knotty horizontals, at the give and take of the trees. Then look at it after it's been dug out by one of the countryside agencies and replanted with nursery saplings. Go to a wood hit by the 1987 hurricane, and compare the neat rows of planted beeches with the teeming sheaves of naturally sprung maples and ashes, all in places and patterns they have chosen themselves. Go to the New Forest, and see how the new generation of self-sprung forest trees – oak and beech principally – grow through and are protected by thickets of holly and gorse, known locally as 'holms' or 'hats'. Look, too, at an old tree untouched by tree surgeons and branch-pruners. Look at its body language, the natural balancing of the branches, the scars where limbs have been shed, the generous, conciliatory shapes of the healing tissue: what we describe, anthropomorphically, as damage or degeneration may be nothing of the kind. But most of all, just go to any patch of 'waste' land (a set-aside field will do) – the kind of land usually chosen for tree-planting – and count the tree seedlings already there. Why are we so contemptuous, so untrusting of them? Why do we prefer *our* trees, rather than wild trees which have sprung naturally in positions which suit them, and whose survival potential is a good sight better, despite a few years of entirely natural accompaniment by brambles and weeds? The honest answer, I fear, might not be very complimentary to us.

The conservation of wildness is the blind spot in the 'wild'-life conservation business in this country. Except in a few token 'non-intervention zones', it simply isn't considered. We're eager to conserve species, carefully defined habitats, that mysterious collective known as 'biodiversity', and all our human designs and ambitions for the biosphere. But not that untamed, inventive energy that makes nature different from a suburban park. The wisest, most reliable and most respectful way of establishing trees (in places where they are wanted) is simply to allow those that spring up naturally to continue.

2005

ARBOREAL HYPOCHONDRIA

Britain's trees, the press has been trumpeting, are in a state of terminal crisis. Racked by hurricanes and drought, poisoned by acid rain, millions are shedding their leaves months before time and giving up the ghost. A United Nations report has just rated our tree population the sixth worst afflicted in Europe. It is like the spectre of Dutch elm disease writ large, an ominous and premature new Fall.

Readers may remember an outbreak of similarly bleak prophecies during the drought summer of '76 (when many defoliated beech and birch trees were felled in the mistaken belief that they were dead), and again during 1989. I wrote about the scare that October, and wondered if the state of a tree's foliage was really a very reliable guide to its health. The shedding of leaves (or the development of unusually small ones) is a perfectly natural response by shallow-rooting species to drought conditions, a way of reducing water loss by transpiration. It is equally normal to find tree foliage in a state of disarray by midsummer because of weather damage and predation. Indeed it would be a sign of sinister ecological goings-on if this were *not* so, as it would mean some catastrophe had befallen the leaf-feeding insects, with consequences that would reverberate right up the food-chain.

No one would dispute that the last few seasons have been very stressful for many tree species. An unprecedented orgy of bark-stripping by grey squirrels this spring has been the last straw for young beech trees already weakened by three years of drought, and has pointed up the folly of imposing such huge monocultures of this tree across southern England. London's planes (another virtual monoculture) are widely stricken by a fungus disorder, though this may not be terminal. And along the edges of motorways and trunk roads all kinds of species are showing the cumulative results of root damage, over-use of salt last winter and exhaust pollution.

But lumping all these incidents together as some kind of gener-alised 'tree crisis' runs the risk of obscuring the complicated factors at work in each case. In a big city like London, for instance, trees are at risk from a whole range of barely connected factors, not least of which is (still) the hostility of some ratepayers. The reasons given to council Tree Officers by householders wishing to cut trees down paint a depressing, tragi-comic picture of our supposed new mood of green enlightenment: 'Trees cause rats.' 'I hear the roots under the property.' 'Pine cones and branches may fall on my chihuahua.' 'Trees produce carbon dioxide and can poison you when you are asleep.'

No sooner have we begun to grasp that trees are the air-condi-tioners of the planet, that in cities they filter out soot, dampen noise and calm the natives, than the old miserly superstitions return: trees are too dangerous, too dirty, too long-lived to be allowed a free rein in the civilised metropolis. Or, you may hear, they are just too fragile. A whole mythology about their imagined frailty has meant that the trees which are officially encouraged in London are a dour and monotonous bunch. The plane Janes especially have become as ubi-quitous and predictable as sugar beet in East Anglia.

Plane trees look absolutely right among the white buildings and fierce light of southern Europe. But in London, with uncertain skies and looming grey backcloths, their dense leafage can be almost fu-nereal. Yet they continue to be planted in the belief that their toler-ance of pollution (thanks to leathery, drip-dry leaves) makes them uniquely suitable as city trees. No-one seems to have reckoned on the impact of root-borne salt, or the boon which street after street of a single species provides for the spread of disease.

There are plenty of better models for city trees – the locust tree *Robinia pseudoacacia*, whose airy, acacia-like leaves give a real touch of the Mediterranean to some streets in the Greek quarter of Blooms-bury. Or the floppy, lime-green leaves of the big catalpa in St James's,

Piccadilly, which really shows up the moroseness of plane shade. This is arguably the best tree in London, especially when its flowers are out and smelling like concentrated sweet-peas. It is neither a victim nor a producer of 'poison', and to my knowledge has never dropped so much as a twig on a passing chihuahua.

There are trees, native and exotic, sprouting of their own accord in every waste patch, too: birch and willow in pavement cracks and National Car Park borders, figs and fruit trees on old walls. And during the last prolonged dustmen's strike a seedling tree of heaven was seen rising defiantly out of a lidless bin. Sadly we rarely permit these embryo, wild trees to survive, and maybe one thing that does link the various threats to trees in London and the country as a whole is the assumption that trees are a kind of pet or domestic retainer, to be chivvied, fussed over, disciplined, given almost anything but freedom and respect.

1991

THE OLDEST YEW

If you travel through Glen Lyon in Perthshire you soon become aware that, in this already heritage-drenched landscape, ancient trees have become tourist business. Signs to what the local Tourist Board call 'Big Tree Country' line the roads. The 250-year-old so-called 'Mother Tree', the ancestor of the 27 million larches which the Duke of Atholl plastered across the local hills, is at Dunkeld, 10 miles to the east. So is the Birnam Oak, the last remaining tree in Macbeth's infamous mobile wood. But the Great Yew at Fortingall trumps them all, being reckoned by believers to have clocked up 5000 years and to be the oldest living thing in Europe. It was here before the making of Stonehenge and the Neolithic burial chamber at Maes Howe in the Orkneys.

This is my first time in Fortingall. It's winter, and the entire landscape is still in brown tweed. I know old yews well enough not to expect a skyscraper, but I'm looking forward to seeing the tree arching over the road in a froth of evergreen shoots. I'm not at all prepared for the diminutive tuft, no taller than a teenage hawthorn, that's tucked under the lee of the Victorian church. Nor for the fact that it's in a cage. This is to keep us, the itchy-fingered public, out, not the tree in; at least that's the story on the noticeboard. When the yew was first 'discovered' in the mid-18th century, it had a bad time from souvenir hunters, who hacked pieces from the already collapsing trunk until it effectively turned into two separate trees. By the end of the century, the gap between them was wide enough to carry a coffin through.

Squinting through the bars and reading the captions becomes, alas, the 'yew experience'. You feel voyeuristic, as if you're peering through a prison door hole at an inmate slumped in the corner. The yew seems hunched as much by the enclosure as by its own ageing timber frame. The northern half – a sheaf of thick knotted stems, each as thick as a sheep – has a few thinner branches which lope across the pen, and then stop dead at the fence. The southern trunks are propped up by crutches, and here and there by the wall itself. The interior is too dark to make out any of the exquisite texture you sometimes find in the interiors of ancient yews, and the trunks seem to be regressing to the quality of rock, not wood. But I can make out the circle of posts that have been hammered into the ground to trace out the original circumference. It was 56 feet. Twenty people could have joined hands around it.

What bothers me, looking back, is how disappointed I was by the Great Yew. The cage didn't help, but I was expecting something more intricately beautiful, more awesome, as if the tree had some kind of duty to impress me. Alas, this is the way we all too often regard ancient trees, judging them not in their own terms but by how they reflect and echo human history. Old yews have been especially vulnerable, because of a still-unexplained mystery: almost all of them grow in churchyards, and almost all of them are vastly older than the church itself. How could this be? Were Christian churches built on the sites of earlier, yew-centred pagan sites? Did the Celts plant yews or congregate round wild ones? The Fortingall Yew, the oldest of the tribe, is revered by Druid revivalists, nostalgic wood-folk, patriotic Celts, even Christians with a strong sense of their church's roots. A florid New Age folklore has blossomed around it. Jesus visited it during his 'lost years'. A starburst of ley lines – from the Holy Isle of Iona to Montrose (Mount of the Rose), from Tober-mory's Well of Mary to Marywell on the coast, from Eilean Isa (island of Jesus) to Lindisfarne – converge at Fortingall, the *axis mundi* of alternative Scotland. Churchyard yews everywhere have been anatomised, blessed, danced round. And it is not much differ-ent with all our ancient trees. We give them human names, invent historical narratives about the long chain of human events they might have 'witnessed'. In all this their own stories, their lives simply as trees, not landmarks or symbols or trophies, are forgotten.

Later that afternoon in Fortingall, I went back to the yew. Its new shoots were foxy with pollen-heavy male flowers. It looked as if it could easily live another few thousand years, but only by becoming a kind of low hedge, or a rockery plant, and abandoning the energy-expensive business of keeping a trunk alive. Could we cope with this? We expect trees to conform to our ideal images. We manage them into acceptable shapes, perform surgery to prolong their lives, over-ride their own attempts to keep their genes alive. The Fortingall Yew would root along its drooping branches if it could, but there is a cage around it in our minds as well as on the ground.

2008

THE END OF THE ELMS?

Do you remember the English countryside before the elms vanished, those towers of brooding foliage which seemed to echo the piling masses of summer cumulus? It's now 30 years since Dutch elm disease virtually wiped out our second most important hardwood tree. Since then the disease has waxed and waned, as the fungus responsible develops diseases of its own and then bounces back in new resistant strains. But the popular view is that the elm, as a presence in the landscape, is finished. The English elm *Ulmus procera* has gone the way of the dodo. Only a handful of wych elms *U. glabra* cling on in isolated woods, and the small-leaved elm *U. minor* of the south and east survives as no more than an elm bush, forever doomed to catch the infection as soon as its suckers enter their teenage years. Can the picture really be as bad as this? Could a natural disease ever wipe out three whole species?

But if the field elms are passing out of personal memory, they are still part of our cultural memory, 'whelming' – John Betjeman's perfect epithet – in generations of landscape painting and poetry. No wonder that, every so often, nostalgic elm fans try to find a substitute, to discover some elm facsimile which might fill the gaps in our denuded hedgerows. The last attempt wasn't the best of ideas. A few conservation organisations attempted to promote the Japanese elm cultivar 'Sapporo Autumn Gold' as the 'elm for England's future'. True, it's a disease-resistant variety, but it bears no resemblance to any European elm, and is no more appropriate for the English countryside than a fancy Japanese maple. So when a West Country nurseryman contacted me recently and told me about his scheme to propagate an American cultivar, the Princeton elm, I was sceptical, and asked if he'd ruled out working from some of the resistant native elm stock instead. I think he thought I was in denial, or a believer in unicorns. But such fabulous plants do exist – or at least did, when I last looked closely at elms 15 years ago. The most promising were in the village of Boxworth, near Cambridge, and I told my correspondent I'd pop over and see how they were faring.

I need to fill in some background here. The small-leaved elm is an ancient native of woods in East Anglia and the south. In the warm, post-glacial climate it reproduced both by seeds and suckers, and built up highly individual, genetically discrete clones in different parts of the countryside. When the great Cambridge geneticist R H Richens surveyed the elms of more than 500 parishes in eastern England in the

1950s, he found such differences in leaf-shape, bark texture and the shapes of whole trees that he was able to name types of elm distinctive to small groups of settlements and sometimes to individual villages. The explanation for this is probably that early farmers, who used elm foliage as fodder, planted out suckers from their local woods around their settlements and cattle enclosures. These 'village elms' spread throughout the locality and survived 4,000 years on. And an additional genetic legacy was that some of them seemed to be immune to Dutch elm disease – notably in Boxworth and Dengie (Essex).

I went back to Boxworth last autumn. There were skeletons of dead elms all the way up to the parish boundary. Then stretches of hedge lit up by the most beautiful tangerine-tinted elm foliage. Inside the village there were large trees by the side of the road, and whole woods full of thriving elms, of every age from one year to a couple of hundred. I could not find a single tree with a hint of disease.

The Boxworth clone can be easily propagated by suckers and has the classic elm form. It would make a prime candidate for 're-elming' England. But would it be proper to spread it about, to dilute its meaning in this way? It is native to the UK, but, strictly, only to these few square miles of Cambridgeshire. The argument is similar to the one which currently smoulders about the spread of the beech to woods in the uplands of Britain. Beech is native to the UK, but historically only to southern and central England, and its opponents say it is 'polluting' native oakwoods in Dartmoor and the Lake District – even though these are the high-rainfall regions to which beech would naturally spread in the face of climate change.

My own opinion is that such purist views about 'indigenousness' are all very well in stable conditions. In times of tumultuous environmental change, of disease, climate instability and increasing landscape fragmentation, indigenousness itself becomes fuzzy, and wild organisms may need a little human help to move to the sites they'd reach by themselves in a state of nature. This is why, so to speak, biodiversity evolved, to fill the gaps in a changing world.

2009

THE COLOUR OF AUTUMN

'If men could disintegrate like autumn leaves,' wrote anthropologist and naturalist Loren Eiseley in one of his notebooks, 'fret away, dropping their substance like chlorophyll, would not our attitude towards death be different? Suppose we saw ourselves burning like maples in a golden autumn.' We all find auguries in the blaze of the Fall, prophecies of the rigours of winter, reminders of our own mortality, or like Keats, some comfort in the 'mellow fruitfulness' – a more warming season, he felt, than the 'chilly green of spring'. Mixed feelings, usually, of poignancy, elation, uncertainty.

But what does it really mean, this great metamorphosis? Why do trees bother to change the colour of their leaves only to dump them almost immediately? Theories have abounded over the years. The coloured chemicals, some thought, helped to keep the leaves warm or to recycle nutrients. The late Bill Hamilton, widely regarded as 'the Darwin of the 20th century', was convinced that the tints were a deterrent to insect predators. As an evolutionary biologist he believed that such expenditure of energy in the synthesis of pigments must be to the tree's advantage, and thought that the degree of autumn colour on any tree correlated with the number of aphid species that might attack it next spring. Alas, Hamilton was more familiar with computer models than nature in the field, and he made a classic blunder that was common more than a century before. 'The assumed attractiveness of bright colours to insects would appear to involve the supposition that the colour vision of insects is approximately the same as our own,' wrote Lord Rayleigh in 1874, 'surely this is a good deal to take for granted.' In fact, all herbivorous insects, aphids included, are only really sensitive to the ultra-violet and blue end of the spectrum. Not one has yet been found with a red receptor in its eye. Yellows are responded to, but only because they are a component of green – which of course *attracts* leaf-eating insects, the very opposite of what Hamilton suggested.

George Orwell, of all people, got a lot closer to the probable truth. In his rumbustious novel *Keep the Aspidistra Flying*, the chief characters, Gordon Comstock and his ever-optimistic sweetheart Rosemary, decide to have an autumn day out at Burnham Beeches in Buckinghamshire. They plunge into the woods, Gordon, at least, smouldering with unrequited lust. The leaves have just fallen, and Rosemary wades around in them up to her knees. 'Oh Gordon,' she cries, 'look at them with the sun on them. They're like gold.' 'Fairy gold,' mutters Gordon. 'As a matter of fact, if you want an exact simile they're just the colour of tomato soup.' Cynical maybe, but Gordon's comparison was smarter than Hamilton's theory and Rosemary's sentimentality. The ripening of tomatoes – fruits of the sun, legendary source of life-protecting antioxidants – may be analogous to what happens to leaves in autumn.

Just why temperate trees shed their leaves in the first place still isn't understood. It may be partly because tree roots don't easily absorb cold winter water and need to reduce the moisture lost through the leaves, and partly to help rid the tree of toxins that have built up over the summer. But what happens before the great shedding is a transfer of sugars and nutrients (up to three-quarters of the dry weight of the leaves) back into the woody parts of the tree for safe keeping over the winter. What remains after the chlorophyll has gone are the natural antioxidants – yellow and orange carotenoids – that help protect the now-vulnerable leaves, and the flurry of chemical activity going on inside them, from the rays of the sun. And there is another protective chemical, the bright tomato-red anthocyanin, that is specially manufactured for the autumn. The season's high colour isn't a sign of deterioration and decline, but of detox vitality. Keats wrote 'To Autumn' in September 1819, already aware that he was mortally ill with tuberculosis, yet still found something uplifting in the season. Do we all share part of his feelings, and intuit the truth about the Fall show, that it is not about decay at all, but about ripening, battening down the hatches, preparing for the next new beginning?

This year the autumn tints began a whole month earlier than in 2007, and in a different order. By the beginning of September the beeches and hazels were already yellowing, and the sycamores were decked out in purple and orange. Last year the oaks and field maples led the show. These premature changes are usually the result of a heatwave summer and of drought-stressed trees cutting down on their water budgets. This year it may be that the tree roots were stressed by too much water. Whatever the reason, I find it cheering that the ancient habit of leaf-fall, which may have begun 100 million years ago, can still duck and dive along with our rapidly changing weather, and continue to surprise and thrill us.

2008

HERBALS

An original edition of the most famous, the most frequently quoted and without doubt the least read book on herbs ever published, John Gerard's *The Herball, or Generall Historie of Plantes,* 1597, will set you back more than £700. But a few years ago Dover brought out a facsimile of the 1633 edition for a modest £25 (not bad for 1,600 pages). More importantly, this edition is 'very much enlarged and amended' by Thomas Johnson, which means that you get the best of both writers.

The amendments, it has to be said, come as something of a relief. Gerard was as shameless a plagiarist as most of his modern-day counterparts. The groundwork and a good deal of the contents of his herbal were lifted, unacknowledged, from an English translation of Dodoens' *A Niewe Herball,* published originally in Latin in 1578. He made bad mistakes. He faked records and, I've no doubt, anecdotes. And for all this he has been severely reprimanded by the botanical establishment (most notably by Agnes Arber and Canon John Raven).

Johnson himself was rather more gentle, and the sternest comment he allows himself concerns Gerard's notorious record for wild peonies on a rabbit warren in Southfleet: 'I have been told that our Author himselfe planted that Peionie there, and afterwards seemed to find it there by accident: and I do believe it was so, because none before or since have ever seen or heard of it growing wild since in any part of this Kingdome.'

A heinous piece of early Piltdownism that, today, would have more likely got 'our Author' drummed out of the Society of Apothecaries than given such a gentle tap on the wrist. But, of course, Johnson understood that the important thing about Gerard was not his scientific expertise but his sheer delight in plants, and a gift for idiosyncratic, inquisitive prose that could turn even a taxonomic description into an adventure story.

Listen to his unquestionably first-hand account of rose-bay willowherb (a rare species then, which he had obtained for his garden from Yorkshire): 'The branches come out of the ground in great numbers, growing to a height of six foot, garnished with brave floures of great beauty, consisting of foure leaves a piece, of an orient purple colour, having some threds in the middle of a yellow colour. The cod is long … and full of downy matter which flieth away with the winde when the cod is opened.'

Despite being customarily referred to as 'Old Gerard,' he was only 42 when the *Herball* was published, and his lack – by modern standards – of integrity was, I'm sure, a kind of playfulness based on a conviction that plants were *fun*. There is an intriguing passage in his chapter on sowbreads (cyclamens) where he warns of the danger of this herb to pregnant women, even those who do no more than 'stride over the same … for the naturall attractive vertue therein contained is such, that without controversie they that attempt it in the manner abovesaid, shall be delivered before their time'. It is hard to believe that such a normally level-headed writer is being serious, certainly not when you read on and find that he has barricaded his own cyclamen with a lattice-work of stick, 'lest any woman should by lamentable experiment finde my words to be true'.

Yet the affection he felt for plants could also be moving, anticipating the sentiments that began to be expressed about them a couple of centuries later. My favourite piece of Gerard is his wise tribute to the healing powers of sweet violets, which is light-years away from the herbal mumbo-jumbo conventional at the time:

> [they] have a great prerogative above others, not onely because the minde conceiveth a certain pleasure and recreation by smelling and handling of those most odoriferous flours, but also for that very many by these Violets receive ornament and comely grace ... yea Gardens themselves receive by these the greatest ornament of all, chiefest beautie and most gallant grace; and the recreation of the minde which is taken thereby cannot be but very good and honest: for they admonish and stir up a man to that which is comely and honest.

As for Gerard's respectful editor, Thomas Johnson, he seems to have been every bit as hedonistic as his mentor. One of the reasons Johnson was able to add to and correct so much of Gerard's text was his experience in the field. He had a talent for leading rumbustious but productive botanical jaunts about southern England. His own accounts of some of these survive, and provide an entertaining insight into 17th-century fieldwork.

His most adventurous trips were made in the summers of 1629 and 1633 to north Kent and were so disrupted by weather, drink and general disarray that it is a wonder his parties saw any plants at all. Ten set out from St Paul's on the first expedition and within a few hours a violent storm had diverted four of them to Greenwich, where they 'went ashore and sought refreshment'.

The rest crossed the Medway to Rochester, and the next day ticked off danewort in a Gillingham cemetery. Along the highway to Sheppey, they recorded lesser calamint, butchers' broom, polypody and broomrape, and looked set for another good day when the Mayor of Queenborough – no doubt slightly surprised at the vision of this band of strangers meandering unsteadily about his parish – demanded to know their business.

They satisfied the mayor of their serious purpose, and after chatting about medical and naval affairs, set about drinking each other's health again. Then, a barge across to the Isle of Grain (noting sea-kale and saltwort on the shore first), and a six-mile tramp 'without seeing a single thing that could give us any pleasure ... In the heat of the day we were tormented like Tantalus with a misery of thirst in the midst of waters – they were brackish!'

What a relief for the bulk of the party to find a brewer's dray bound for Rochester that night. Johnson and Jonas Styles left them 'lolling among the barrels' and went on to find cannabis at Cliffe and an extraordinary collection of chalk-loving plants (including fly orchid, juniper and white mullein) in a quarry at Dartford that is almost certainly still there.

None of this endearing detail comes from outside sources or biographical notes. It is worked into the notes of the trip. Down went the beer and up went the score. What a way to do a survey!

1984

FLORAS

The publication of a new *Flora of Hampshire*, the first for nearly a century, is another landmark in the evolution of that tangy and thoroughly British institution – the county flora. And with more than 1,300 contributors and an open-minded fascination with both indigenous history and botanical immigrants, this must be the most democratic example in the whole tradition. Almost every page throws up some tantalising social detail. Marsh thistle (first recorded 1959) may have reached the county on the clothing of troops preparing for the D-Day embarkation. In Selborne, Gilbert White's mistletoe-laden maples survive two-and-a-half centuries on. There are even revelations about an extraordinary relationship between lizard orchids and Hampshire schoolgirls, who are responsible for almost every record between 1925 and 1943: '1926: Winchester, foot of

St Catherine's Hill, found by a pupil of the County Girls' School ...
1928: Ropley Railway Cutting, schoolgirl Peggy Bampton', and so on.
Doubtless the interwar tradition of awarding prizes for the best
collections of wildflowers has something to do with it. But the smell
of lizard orchids has been likened to rampant billy goat, and anyone
who has read *Cider with Rosie* may begin to wonder if special sensi-
tivities weren't also involved ...

Idle speculation, no doubt, and nothing to do with the proper
purpose of local floras in recording the intimate distribution of
species. Yet, being made largely by amateurs and based on geographical divisions which have nothing to do with science, they cannot fail
to be fascinating social documents as well. They are about the cultural
landscape as well as the ecological, about parochial custom and
feelings for the home place. Ronald Blythe, writing of his Suffolk
boyhood, remembers this link persisting until the Second World War:
'Village people of all ages saw them [wild plant colonies] as a form of
permanent geography, by which the distance of Sunday walks could
be measured, or where tea or love could be made.' We might be cynical about the permanence of their geography now; but one of the joys
of local floras is the heartening message they give about the fragile
but persistent continuity of nature. Many of the species in the first
full county flora (John Ray's *Catalogus Plantorum* of Cambridgeshire,
1660) are exactly where the author found them three centuries ago.

There is continuity – and diversity – in the human voices behind
the records, too. Read Thomas Johnson's account of botanical expeditions to north Kent in the 1630s to catch the flavour of early fieldwork. Or try the polymathic George Claridge Druce, who between
1886 and 1930 personally wrote no less than four county floras, for
Oxon, Berks, Bucks and Northants. In one edition, he describes a train
journey in the company of some Oxford ragwort seeds, which wafted
into his carriage at Oxford and out at Tilehurst. Even more of a hands-
on recorder is Francis Simpson, whose idiosyncratic volume is still
the only one to be named after the author. *Simpson's Flora of Suffolk*
(1982) notes a colony of a very pale-flowered deadly nightshade at

Old Felixstowe and describes the author's own contribution to conserving this strain: 'There is a danger that one day these plants and their berries may be found by some overzealous person and destroyed ... When it is possible I visit the site and remove the berries in order to protect the plant.' Then there is the gentle tone of Rev. Keble Martin's *Flora of Devon* (1939), which includes a catalogue of some 40 species, colour oddities, eccentric shapes and local varieties of violet, including one delectable type found only in the villages of 'Marldon, Berry Pomeroy and Dartington'.

All of these speak volumes about their period and the character and enthusiasms of the people who made them. They are also the best possible answer to those (myself once) who feel that diligent recording might in some way diminish their simple delight in plants. Our contributions, coloured by our lives, will be the next generation's delight.

1996

ORCHIDS

It's orchid time again. Up here in south Norfolk, we're spoilt for them. At least 10 species flower within walking distance of our house, a fifth of the entire British list. Already the green-veined orchids are in full bloom, drifting in their thousands among the cowslips on Shelfanger meadows. Lying down with them, you can see the veins in the flower's hood picked out against the sun, the same lustrous green you sometimes see in mother of pearl. Then come the marsh orchids, four species and as many putative hybrids, including the beefy leopard marsh orchid, whose leaves ripple with tawny stripes. And by the end of June the bee orchids will be out just an amble away from our door. Seeing those fabulous, chimerical blooms, with their velvet bodies and sculpted pink wings, takes me back half a lifetime to when I found my first, on a Midsummer's Eve picnic in the Chilterns. There were quails calling in the fields below, and we felt so enchanted that we fell to pagan fertility ritual, and tipped our red wine into the turf. 'Wet-my-lips', the quails continued to call.

What is it about the orchid tribe that casts such spells over us? At their annual orchid festival this spring, Kew Gardens explored the magical hold they have had over artists. They are one of the four 'Gracious Plants' used in traditional Korean painting, where they're exquisitely picked out by just a few bold strokes of the brush. In Victorian painting it was more like a few thousand bold strokes. 'Miss [Sarah] Drake' was one of the most accomplished flower painters of the time, and lived just down the road from Kew at Turnham Green. She contributed elaborate illustrations to what was described as 'the most splendid botanical work of the present age', James Bateman's gigantic *Orchidaceae of Mexico and Guatemala* (1837-41). This phantasmagorical tome gives clues about the source of orchids' appeal. Bateman's text, a bizarre mixture of cultivation tips, travellers' tales and running orchid jokes, perfectly captures that uniquely Victorian fascination with scientific oddity and imperial conquest. He referred to orchids as 'the chosen ornaments of royalty', and his flights of fancy about the resemblance between orchid flowers and birds, monkeys and monks were illustrated with surreal cartoons by J Landells. Here he is considering the similarity between *Cycnoches* species and swans: '*Cycnoches loddigesii*, perhaps, bears, on the whole, the closest resemblance to the feathered prototype; for the column (answering to the neck of the bird) is long and pleasingly curved, whereas that of *C. ventricosum* is lamentably short,' though it was closest to 'the swelling bosom' of a true swan.

Certainly orchids' uncanny and sometimes suggestive resemblances are part of their glamour. Meditating on why the lure of orchids surpasses that of all other plants, Eric Hansen is tempted towards a Freudian explanation. In *Orchid Fever* (2000) he writes: 'I took a closer look at the flower [of a *Paphiopedilum* hybrid]. The shiny, candy-apple-red staminode that covered the reproductive organs was shaped like an extended tongue identical to the Rolling Stones logo. This shocking red protrusion nestled in the cleavage of two blushing petals then dropped down to lick the tip of an inverted pouch ...'

Yet reading accounts of the orchid frenzy of the 19th and early 20th centuries, I get the sense that it was not simply the beauty and outlandishness of the flowers that mesmerised their devotees and rapacious collectors, but their origins. These were the fabled air-plants, growing without visible nourishment in the most remote and beautiful regions on Earth. To capture them was to regain a little piece of paradise. The romantic novelist Charlotte M Yonge was reminded by the hothouses in which they were kept of 'a picture in a dream. One could imagine it a fairy land, where no care, or grief, or weariness could come.'

Even our earthbound British orchids carry something of this magical power. Searching for our native species takes you into the last remnants of our wild habitats, into bog and fen and ancient wood. But they're a recently evolved, hugely promiscuous and contrary family, and searching for bee orchids especially is just as likely to take you on to a derelict airfield. With windblown seeds like talcum powder they crop up in gravel pits and roundabouts and once, famously, in the telephone exchange car park in Milton Keynes. Our locals grow on a patch of wasteground next to an electricity substation. The flowers are supposed to fool bees into trying to mate with them, but they are in fact self-pollinating. Their purposeless extravagance annoyed Darwin, seeming to fly against his theory and his personal work ethic, and he prophesied they would soon become extinct. Not yet, thank goodness.

2006

WEEDS

One of the unexpected by-products of last summer's monsoons was that roadside verges didn't get cut till quite late. I don't know whether this was down to rain-shy contractors, hunkering down until the grass was less clotted, or to local authorities' ballooning cash crises. But while the warm rain fell and the mowers played truant, the roadside flora had a field day. Willowherbs grew to prodigious heights. Wild carrot, for once, was allowed to come into flower. And ragwort – abominated, sprayed, yanked out ritually on Pony Club weekends – turned the countryside into gold.

I love ragwort. I relish its reckless, rumpled habit, as if a rather tattered yellow bedspread had been casually thrown across a field. So did the poet John Clare, who as a fieldworker himself, ought to be listened to on such matters:

> ... *everywhere I walk*
> *Thy waste of shining blossoms richly shields*
> *The sun tanned sward in splendid hues that burn*
> *So bright & glaring that the very light*
> *Of the rich sunshine doth to paleness turn ...*

But, as every farmer and country dweller knows, ragwort is a killer. It accounts for as many as half of all poisoning cases among livestock. A group of alkaloids, known as pyrrolizidines, cause insidious and irreversible liver damage to animals which eat large quantities, and they usually die with distressing symptoms, including the chaotic muscle activity know as 'the staggers'. No wonder that the plant was included in the Weeds Act of 1959, which requires landowners to take action to prevent it from spreading.

But looked at closely the situation is more complex. Neither wild nor domestic animals will normally touch ragwort if there is other forage available. The vast majority of poisoning cases are from dried plants which have found their way into hay, and from wilted and shrunk specimens which have been sprayed with herbicide – a fatuously counter-productive process, as the plant is just as toxic when it's dead, but less easily recognised by animals.

And why has the plant seemingly become more troublesome over the past hundred years? I've not been able to find any worried references to it in early farming or botany books beyond its early popular name of 'Staggerwort'. John Gerard (1597) describes it as 'growing everywhere' but mentions no problems, and adds that it is sanctified as St James's Herb by flowering on 25 July – the saint's day. Sixteenth-century farming writers such as Thomas Tusser and Fitzherbert don't include it in their black lists of weeds.

Was ragwort more sensibly managed then, or just less common? Might its apparent increase over the past century be, indirectly, our fault? Ragwort's rise has been accompanied by the conspicuous decline of its greatest natural predator, the beautiful cinnabar moth, which in its flighted stage may be suffering the same complex stresses as so many other moth species. Has the flower's naturally ragged look – and the billows of seeds taking to the wing on every summer breeze – made it an obvious scapegoat for our culture of tidiness? And even allowing for the problems it causes on pasture land, are these an excuse for the widespread demonisation of such a striking native flower, to the extent that it was blanket-sprayed on at least two East Anglian nature reserves last year, with resultant 'collateral damage' to other species?

Our social attitudes towards weeds are as fascinating – and often as contradictory – as our attitudes towards animal 'pests'. The definition is, of course, everything. Weeds are often described as 'plants in the wrong place'. English bluebells are widely regarded as weeds when they spread inside gardens, Spanish bluebells when they escape from them. Ashes are called 'weed trees' by foresters growing oak.

But more often it seems as if a 'weed' has slipped out of a whole cultural context, not just its 'proper' place. The litany changes with time and fashion and the perspective of the beholder. At various times 'weed' has meant lowly things, aggressive things, dull things, useless things, alien invaders. Their metaphorical shape is as dominating and tangled as their tendrils. Giant hogweed, introduced here in the 19th century as a temperate rival to spectacular hothouse plants, is now an officially feared weed inside the garden as well as outside. But oil-seed rape, escaped from arable fields and increasingly invading road verges, is not perceived as a weed at all. It's a crop plant, and therefore human-serving, wherever it is.

As for the 18th-century farmer's hit list, it has come full circle, with many old arable species such as corncockle and shepherd's needle – which also began their life here as expansive aliens 6,000 years ago – elevated to the status of treasured and protected rarities. A historical perspective won't solve the ragwort dilemma, but it might help us see it with more discrimination. A weed is a plant in the wrong side of the brain.

2007

DEVIL'S MEAT

Thirty years ago this month the great drought of 1975–76 broke. Denis Howell had been appointed as an emergency minister, a kind of rain shaman, and in a matter of days the heavens opened. The growth of the underground network of fungal 'roots', starved and stressed by years without adequate moisture, was so astonishing that I was sure I could smell it in the air after every downpour – a rich, evocative, deep-wood smell. When the fruiting began a few weeks later, it was hard to ignore. In the Chiltern beechwoods people were picking 50lb of ceps in a single afternoon. Pastures were white with field and horse mushrooms. Forgetting all our traditional qualms we turned into a nation of foragers. The BBC ran information bulletins about the crop and warned not against poisoning but against trespassing. What a hope! By the end of October the mushroom mountain was so huge that they were being given away in pubs, and two 9-year-olds came down our road hawking them door to door at 10 pence a pound.

I think it was that fungal *annus mirabilis* that changed our cultural attitudes towards fungi for good. It was the event that made it possible for UK supermarkets to begin stocking wild mushroom species, for television chefs to feature them without raising revulsion in their audiences. But it had been a long haul. In contrast to almost every other European country, Britain had a deep suspicion of the entire tribe. Until 1976, our opinion of them had scarcely changed since Francis Bacon called them 'venereous meats' in the early 17th century. The poet Robert Graves used to argue that our hostility was a hangover from the time when hallucinogenic species like liberty caps ('magic mushrooms') and fly agarics were the prerogative of a priestly elite, and were surrounded by taboos. Yet this wariness doesn't occur in other nations with similar prehistories to our own, and I suspect the reason lies in our cultural estrangement from woodland as the planet's earliest and most comprehensive deforesters.

What propped up the myths was ignorance about what fungi were and where they came from. Before spores had been glimpsed, toadstools (the name says it all) were believed to be spontaneously generated from mud and dank. In 1751, Otto von Munchausen – a real scientist but with the imagination of his literary namesake – did see spores, but swore that he had witnessed them hatching into small insects in water, and concluded that toadstools should not be regarded as plants at all, but as the dwelling places of small animals. Even the pioneering micrographer Robert Hooke, who mysteriously never spotted spores, believed fungi to be created from 'putrifying bodies ... by the concurrent heat of the Air'.

It was not until the early 19th century that the true mechanisms of fungal growth were understood. Meanwhile, more open-minded naturalists continued their own explorations of the wilder shores of fungal lore. The popular writer 'Sir' John Hill gave a graphic description of what sounds like a pure fantasy – the 'pietra fungaja' or fungus stone – but is in fact a real 'organism', 'which, on being watered produces excellent mushrooms ... The upper part is mixed yellow and olive colour; and the surface is broken in a wild but beautiful manner, into a resemblance of scales or feathers. The under part is white; and in the pores lie the seeds. The substance of the mushroom within is of a delicate and high flavour and perfectly wholesome.' The stone is actually a conglomeration of tufa held together by the mycelium of a bracket fungus.

At the beginning of the 19th century, the botanist James Sowerby described a bizarre fungus (a *Clavaria*) he'd found in a London wine cellar: 'It is remarkable for being luminous in the dark, when fresh, at the end of the shoots. Mr Forster doubted whether this phosphoric appearance may not be owing to some vinous moisture imbibed …' And giant puffballs (though Victorian fungophiles adored them and harvested them in the vegetable garden on a cut-and-come-again basis) continued to bewilder. In 1928, several specimens were found in a drawing room at Kew, and looked sufficiently like human skulls for the police to be called. One found in Kent during the Second World War was believed to be a German secret weapon.

Now, aficionados all, we buy farmed oyster mushrooms, go on local authority fungus forays and take essence of fungus whenever we need an antibiotic. Yet there is one last bridge to cross. The image of fungal decay is still a black one. We need, culturally, to grasp that without the help of these organisms, the Earth would be piled high with undecomposed vegetation. Roll on the rain.

2006

BIOMIMETICS

Back in the seventies, when I first became interested in economic botany, a book appeared with a rather original agenda. Felix Paturi's *Nature, Mother of Invention* was not principally about the usefulness of plants to humans, but about what brilliant architects and engineers they were in meeting their own needs. He talked about the photoelectric cells in the growing shoots of sweet-peas, about the complex management of hydraulic pressure in the 'ponds' of pitcher plants, about the minutely precise, built-in clocks that regulate the reproduction of algae. And he made the suggestion that perhaps these processes in the plant worlds might be as valuable to us, as models, as the plants themselves.

It wasn't an entirely novel idea, of course. Plants have often acted as incidental inspiration for human engineers. In the 1850s Joseph Paxton famously modelled the framework of the Crystal Palace, the biggest glasshouse in the world, on the ribbing of the Amazonian water lily. Ten years later the inventor of reinforced concrete was mimicking an idea found in 250-million-year-old cactus species. Velcro fasteners were inspired by the seedheads of burdock, whose hooked bristles clamp them to any surface they come in contact with, including each other. (A brilliant example, incidentally, of the inexact 'fuzzy logic' of biological problem-solving.)

But the notion of quite deliberately using biological processes as the foundations for technological innovation had to wait for the full flowering of molecular biology and the development of microscopes that could witness just how the world worked at its most fundamental level: 'You just look at the thing!' the legendary physicist Richard Feynman pronounced in his historic paper 'There's Plenty of Room at the Bottom'(1959). In this nano-world it's possible to glimpse – and therefore possibly reproduce – the actual molecular processes by which mussels generate the glue which sticks them to rocks and see the structure of spiders' filaments. The prospect for 'green' engineers is as dizzying as it is daunting. These are engineering solutions which are beautiful, incredibly efficient in their uses of energy and raw materials, making products which are entirely biodegradable. But they do this using principles and techniques almost the polar opposite of conventional human technology. The biological factory is soft and wet, operates at room temperature, uses complex substances, and generates adaptable rather than 'fixed' end-products. But it has become possible to dream of creating colours using the same gentle chemistry as flowers. Of 'growing' ceramics in the way that shellfish do. Of dealing with dirt not with synthetic detergents but by developing surfaces that are self-cleaning, as in the water-lily family. Of copying the 'cold light' of bioluminescence, and – the Holy Grail – of finding a way of fixing sunlight as efficient as photosynthesis. The science – or is it art? – of biomimetics has been born.

Yet, inevitably, there are problems as well as huge possibilities, demonstrated by biomimetics' most dazzling success story yet. The morpho butterflies of the South American rainforest are breathtaking creatures, 15cm across, with shimmering wings which seem to change from dusty silver to brilliant lagoon blue. The colour isn't a pigment, but an iridescence, produced by what has proved to be astonishing tissue architecture in the wings – platforms of scales, covered with ridges, ringed with reflective 'aerials' tuned to the wavelength of light, the whole structure acting like a sophisticated hall of mirrors and prisms. The Japanese company Teijin has succeeded in replicating this structure in its Morphotex fabric, which is being used in the front seats of Nissan Silvia convertibles. But Morphotex needs 61 alternating layers of nylon and polyester of different refractive indices to create its effect – very energy-consumptive to manufacture and far from biodegradable. This may be 'bio-inspiration' but the goal of biomimetics is to grow such substances in the way that nature does.

Yet the technical problems seem small beside the philosophical ones, which the scientists, in their excitement, haven't even raised yet. If biomimetic technology is successful and we become increasingly able to ape natural processes for producing our raw materials and energy, what then becomes the status of nature itself, the model for all this innovation? Increasingly removed from the need to exploit it directly, might we develop a new respect for it in its own right, begin to truly value whole living organisms, not the disconnected fragments we currently use? Or, with less and less need for 'the real thing', might nature become redundant, a once-useful template which a hyper-biotechnological culture could afford to forget and discard? When we have grown butterfly wings for ourselves, will we have left the realm of nature altogether?

2006

4. TRACKS

'Getting about', as we say in Norfolk.

DOCKLAND

It was not the kind of anniversary to hit the feature pages, but 1987 marked the centenary of the death of Richard Jefferies. Jefferies was the outstanding nature writer of the 19th century, and succeeded in combining powerful (agonising, sometimes) spiritual insights into the relationships between humankind and nature with acute first-hand observations. He is best known for his essays and novels based in Wiltshire, but after a year in which the environment of the inner city was rarely out of the news, it is worth recalling that he was also one of the pioneering champions of urban wildlife. He celebrated railway flora and town starlings, and made a passionate defence of the River Thames as an amenity which should be cherished for all London's citizens.

He loved London for the vitality and colour of its street-life, and his dreams of an ideal world were a long way from rustic sentimentality. 'My sympathies and hopes', he wrote in 1880, 'are with the light of the future, only I should like it to come from nature. The clock should be read by the sunshine, not the sun timed by the clock.' He wanted, in Edward Thomas's paraphrase, 'the light railway to call at the farm gate'.

By an odd quirk of coincidence, this vision very nearly came to pass in London last summer. Just a few days after Jefferies' anniversary in August, the first small trains began running quietly along the Dockland Light Railway. This was 'the light of the future' all right, a clean, user-friendly alternative transport system that is regarded as one of the jewels in East London's gigantic urban renewal programme.

But one question keeps nagging me as I tramp about the new Docklands: here is the light railway but where is the farm gate? Dockland is being publicised as some kind of Utopia-on-Thames, a hi-tech symbol of the enterprise culture and a model for urban development throughout the land. Yet it seems to have ignored what is now regarded as a prerequisite of tolerable urban life everywhere else in the developed world: parks and green open spaces and a touch of natural life to give its inhabitants a change from the texture of concrete. I picked up the habit of going walkabout in London when I was a teenager and became besotted with the idea of being foot-loose in the city. Later I used to go winter duck-watching through the palings of the old dock basins, and in summer on botanical safaris after the alien plants that flourished on the rubbish tips. These were, I am well aware, partial, tourist's views of London, as are my current feelings about Dockland, which swing from schoolboyish excitement at the Dan Dare architecture to melancholy at the demise of that earlier, tangier, working East End.

Yet some kind of provision for green space could have been a meeting place between old and new East Enders, between residents and visitors. It is not long before you begin to miss it. The water that has been channelled, mock-Venetian style, between the new design studios and finance complexes is as stark and straight-edged as an industrial canal. A few fish, poisoned by effluent and lack of oxygen, limp round in obscene looping parodies of normal swimming. The vast piazzas that fill in the spaces between the luxury flats and gabled urban cottages are made of exquisitely hand-moulded bricks – but not a single blade of grass is permitted to deface them. Even the trees – and they are a rarity, shamefully – have been planted in austere rows and geometric formations. Your eyes begin to long for anything which would break up the antiseptic tidiness of it all. A mass invasion by hemlock and japweed would be just the thing, but I fear they might get the worst of it.

There are patches of green wasteland, thin strips of bramble and buddleia, but they are mostly barricaded by high security fences. The one or two official public parks that have been marooned amid the development are dismal, run-down places, which make their own comment on how finance is distributed here.

But then, in the summer of 1986, I discovered the house martins. They were nesting in a small colony under the balconies of a block of 1930s flats. It was literally the last building before the immense development site by the Shadwell basin, and I spent an enchanted hour watching the birds hawking over the weed-strewn spoil tips, past the Indian corner shop and over the wretched patch of grass and staked trees that passes for the local park. I have watched them for two seasons now, and seen them gathering mud for nest-building out of the ruts cut up by bulldozers, and one cold September afternoon slaloming after flies among the parked cars, skimming just inches above the road surface. For the most part they feed where they can, over the so-far-undeveloped buddleia patches and the few derelict churchyards (which also happen to be the only untamed sites where children can play).

I am not suggesting that these wastelands ought to be conserved, untouched, as Dockland's open space. But the sense of freedom and liveliness and accessibility that runs through them – and through the martins that depend on them – is something without which a city, however prosperous, will find it hard to stay sane. Yet the London Docklands Development Corporation (LDDC), which is master-minding the whole project, has no plans or provision for open space. Nor does it have any for providing views of, or access to, the Thames, which is locked up behind barricades like all the other natural prospects. The river is the heart and the *raison d'être* of Dockland; Richard Jefferies described it as 'morally the property of the greatest city in the world'. One would have thought that the LDDC, with the immense technical resource at its disposal, could at least have commissioned some kind of walkway along the north bank, to give the East-Enders a sniff of salt-water.

There has been much talk this year about the 'greening' of the inner city. But Dockland, by comparison with the brimming tree-scapes of Warrington, Peterborough – even Milton Keynes – is not only un-green but positively wintry. It may of course be hard to raise the finance for such frippery in a community so devoted to the market. But I hope that industry and business, now apparently so keen on becoming patrons of conservation, take up the challenge of doing just that on their own backyards. Otherwise all of us who live, work or just ramble in the Dockland – and all the other city developments that will be based on it – will end up gazing into the canals at nothing more than exquisitely framed reflections of our own faces.

1988

SOME CORNER OF A LONDON FIELD...

It feels as eerie as walking over my own grave, every time I go there. Marooned among the ragged breakers' yards and derelict rubbish tips north-west of Heathrow is a patch of tussocky grassland with my name on it. Mabey's Meadow, the London Wildlife Trust (LWT) noticeboard announces, as if I'd been slaughtered there in some crucial ecological battle. I first came across it a decade ago, and it took me some while to find out what this flattering dedication meant. Apparently, when the Trust took over the care of the meadow and were casting about for a name, they remembered that I'd helped their ecologists survey this site back in the 1980s. Before that, I'd stalked the whole surrounding territory when I was working on a book on urban wastelands called *The Unofficial Countryside* (published 1974).

The landscape had been a revelation, a testament to the tenacity of living things. I'd hike along derelict canals, watch sandpipers bobbing on floating car tyres, find scraps of medieval hedge caught between the mobile-home parks and totters' paddocks. I'd join the bottle-hunters on the refuse dumps among a witches' brew of thorn-apple and cannabis and deadly nightshade. In late summer I'd go down to the sludge-beds of the now-vanished sewage works at Perry Oaks, a seething artificial swamp at the end of Heathrow's main runway. It was another time of terrorist paranoia, and I'd watch delicate wading birds – little stints, dusky redshanks – flying off to their African wintering grounds under machine-gun cover.

I went back to this old stamping ground in late July, and it seemed much as I remembered it. In the 1980s, the LWT surveyors had found the scarce fern adder's tongue on 'my' meadow, an indicator species of ancient grassland. But this summer what shone out were the flowering plants, a riotous mixture of exotic perennials and relict natives in full bloom, which looked simply gorgeous. Somehow a garden variety of veronica had become the dominant plant, and the whole meadow was lit up by its brilliant blue spikes. It kept company with two species of golden rod from America, Jacob's ladder and the gaudy pink of everlasting pea, both from the Mediter-ranean, and a host of native plants, including castellations of teasels. The whole display was like a carnival float, dancing with grasshop-pers and gatekeeper butterflies.

This stretch of the urban fringe is an unofficial wetland. Deep, compacted beds of London rubbish and tumuli of old bottles are riddled by a labyrinth of flooded gravel pits and flashes. Abandoned mill-leats and Victorian canals burrow through a dense scrub of buddleia, Japanese knotweed and thorn. I took off through a gap in a fence, past lagoons where terns were fishing and gravel-waste islands capped with the moon-flowers of wild carrot. In the River Colne great green wands of club-rush waved above dumped fridges. Emperor dragonflies rested on rafts of floating polystyrene. Carpets of water lilies were sucking at the lager cans. There was no doubt who was getting the upper hand. The whole area had a fantastic, gaudy luxuriance, as if a hundred years of blissful purposelessness has made anything possible.

But the tidying has begun. Much of the land is now in the Colne Regional Park. Wooden seats are replacing the dumped armchairs. The towpaths are being gravelled over. I guess it would be selfish to regret this. The kind of ecological slumming I personally revel in is hardly a viable large-scale land-use. But finding ways of preserving the wildness and tanginess of this unofficial countryside – what you might call, metaphorically, its urban 'accent' – at the same time as making it amenable to ratepayers is a so-far-unresolved problem. Modern urban development precisely targets these so-called 'brown-field' sites. The shameful new runway proposed for Heathrow would go slap through the old West London wetlands. And goodness knows what is happening inside the Olympic building site along the Lee Basin, once the ecologically richest area of East London. Public scrutiny is forbidden. No journalists are allowed through the barri-cades. Even the consultant ecologists have to be accompanied by teams of spooks and security men.

Yet again, maybe the language we use about these places does us no favours. 'Brownfield' suggests deadness and sterility, the precise opposite of the riotous growth that characterises them. The distinguished Sheffield ecologist Oliver Gilbert popularised a much more constructive term – 'the urban commons' – which catches their flavour of kids' playspace and informal park. But he championed their scientific as well as their social importance, as areas where spontaneous natural succession is played out and an authentically urban flora develops. A meadow of adder's tongue and voluptuous garden escapes would be a countryside conservationist's nightmare, but on already compromised urban ground it's a brighter prospect than shaved lawns and municipal shrubs.

2009

GREENING SPIRES

There is no more agreeably green city than Oxford, especially in the spring. Where else can you wander among 40 mazy and entirely individual parks and gardens in less than a square mile, pick medlars in the street, see a herd of fallow deer and a meadow purple with snakeshead fritillaries only a couple of hundred yards from the main through-road? Oxford is so thoroughly infused with greenery that half the time it is impossible to say what is wild and what is cultivated. Relics of old monastic gardens and donnish collections spring up through any unguarded seam (Oxford ragwort went one better and escaped to become one of the nation's most successful weeds). Sparrowhawks jink along the punt routes and over the college walls, which themselves are adorned with extraordinary mixtures of escaped herbs, seedling trees and prize roses.

That all of this has survived is more extraordinary when you remember that, as well as being a university town, Oxford is the birthplace of the mass-produced motor-car. At one time it looked as if the city might be suffocated by its local Frankenstein's monster, and in 1948 Thomas Sharp published his historic blueprint *Oxford Replanned*. It was a landmark in the understanding of 'the spirit of place' and the contribution that nature makes to this in a city. Yet its attitude towards the car – again becoming a national environmental threat – makes you wonder if we have made any progress since.

Sharp, though no friend of the car, would not challenge it, and he proposed to ease the terrible traffic congestion in the High with a relief road driven smack through Merton and Christ Church meadows, the green heart of Oxford and one of the most glorious views in England. Fortunately (especially since the ancient trees that were to ennoble the edges of 'Merton Mall' all died of Dutch elm disease 20 years later), the scheme was rejected. Instead, Oxford decided simply to make things difficult for motor vehicles, with a battery of pedestrian precincts, parking restrictions, bypasses and a superlative public transport system. There is still heavy traffic at rush-hours, but it never threatens to asphyxiate the city as it did a decade or two ago.

Alas, the Department of Transport shows no sign of learning from Oxford's lesson. Official policy is to take the car as a fixed, sacrosanct entity, and to design the rest of the environment around it. Just a few days after the approval of the new Winchester bypass, which will cut a 400-foot-wide gash through the ancient turf of Twyford Down, the Prime Minister made her notorious attack on 'airy-fairy' environmentalists in which she defined modern Britain as 'the great car economy'. What a vision! Britain as a nation of garage-keepers, the Venice of the trunk-roads.

I enjoy the freedom a car gives you as much as anybody, but the conventional assumption that most car-owners would be horrified by any legal restriction on the size, design and use of vehicles is insulting. We might make a start by rethinking the image of the car and making it less brutally individualistic and inimical to other life forms. Why not a fully organic car? I once read a learned paper which discussed the epiphytes of half-timbered Morrises; and one NCC field officer of my acquaintance has a semi-natural grassland under his accelerator pedal that is close to SSSI status. The possibilities in this direction are limitless, and with cars adorned with hanging plant-baskets, birdtables and parasols, traffic jams would become a delight, like gently moving outdoor cafés.

1990

IN PRAISE OF LIMESTONE

I first fell in love with limestone in the Yorkshire Dales, decades ago. I liked its tactility, its warmth and glowing colours, its raggedness, the fact that it was always falling apart, weathering, evolving. It seemed more truly alive than any other rock – which in a way, it is. Limestone was built up like a snowdrift, from the fallen remains of countless small sea creatures. Paradoxically, it is created in water, and then dissolved by it. W H Auden, in his poem 'In Praise of Limestone', suggests that it is this continuing relationship with water that gives the rock its character. He called it the 'stone that responds', the rock 'of short distances and definite places'.

I understand what he means about 'definite places'. Limestone's slow dissolution means that every inch of the landscape is unique, a labyrinth of individually sculptured slabs and fissures and crags, which are bevelled, honeycombed, engraved. Sometimes you can witness the actual process of habitat creation: a pebble caught in a shallow riverbed, whirled about by the current, grinding out the beginnings of a crater; a breeze ruffling a thin puddle on top of a slab – a 'tadpole runnel' which is etching its way into the rock, until it becomes a groove where soil begins to gather.

The geological nooks create vegetational niches. In The Burren in Ireland, miniature hazel woods grow in the hollows, so dwarfed by the minimalist soils that, like some botanical Gulliver, you can have the bizarre experience of walking through a forest that comes up no higher than your chest, and of gazing down at alpine flowers – gentians and mountain avens – growing beneath the trees. In the gorges of Crete it is just the opposite. You walk at the bottom of sheer cliffs, nearly 1,000 metres tall, gazing up at the hermit flora clinging to the crags – endemic flaxes, wild lettuces and nettle trees that have eked out their existences in these exact, 'definite', spots for tens of thousands of years.

But the Dales have my heart. I can still recall precise places and moments, even on just one area of limestone pavement. A 'bowl' of ferns, growing in a depression that had been naturally worn into the shape of a huge vase. A deep, dark fissure where the wild garlic flowers had been drawn up a metre tall in their search for light. An entirely horizontal ash tree, winding its way along a grike, and maybe hundreds of years old. A ribbon of bird's-eye primroses along a peaty fault-line. A bed of lilies-of-the-valley, spilling over the lip of the pavement, their exposed leaves clattering in the wind, and their scent drifting over the whole scene.

Back in the 1980s, I made a film for the BBC's *Natural World* series here. The experience wasn't exactly material for a home-grown 'Tales from the bush' column, but it did provide confirmation of the definiteness of the place. We were working at one point in no more than an acre of pavement, but it was so wonderfully chaotic and labyrinthine that we had to put up a trail of flags to find our way from one marvel to another. And almost anywhere we could put our ears to the ground and hear what was responsible for it all: the sound of water rushing beneath the earth, wearing away the stone.

2008

HOLLAND'S COAST

Fleeing to Holland's northern wetlands from a Britain buffeted by spring monsoons and a string of environmental crises from Sizewell to Sutherland was like journeying to one of those parallel universes beloved of science fiction. The shrivelling weather was as bad (worse, actually), the political climate just as unsettled. But in place of the mood of glum confrontation we'd left behind, there was wit and inventiveness in the air.

The Dutch are masters of the sidestep, the social pun, and faced with a problem seem able not just to think their way laterally out of it but make some kind of parable in the process. Is there another small country where the flower-markets make up for the shortage of garden space by selling full-sized sprouting coconuts as house plants? Or one which edges country park lay-bys with stones painted up like miniature sleeping sheep?

We had gone chiefly to watch birds on the polders, those extraordinary new marshlands won out of what was once the Zuider Zee. Yet the Dutch knack of finding user-friendly solutions to environmental problems was apparent even in the heart of Amsterdam. We inadvertently fell foul of the parking laws on our last day and were wheel-clamped by something resembling an outsize bulldog clip. This isn't the kind of penalty you can buy your way out of with a standing order from petty cash; and not at all like the Byzantine theatre of London clamping. In the city that gave the world the communal White Bicycle, all you do is walk down one of the canalsides to a post office, pay a nominal fine, and walk back. The clamp is freed within the hour, and you feel curiously relieved to have been given such an effective lesson about unsociable street behaviour.

Would this flair for creative compromise be apparent out on the polders? I had heard that the birds were spectacular, but driving out over the arable prairies inland, I found myself wondering whether a programme that had already absorbed most of Holland's natural estuaries could possibly be less damaging than coastal development back home.

Estuaries, of course, are very tempting prospects for a developer. They can provide free water, cheap energy, easy overseas communication, and a workforce eager for the good life on the coast. So the applications queue up – for nuclear power stations, tidal barrages, bunded reservoirs, container ports, marinas.

The RSPB reckons that more than 30 British estuaries are already under threat. The fear is, that with the meeting between land and water made into something much more abrupt, the teeming life of the tidal mudflats would vanish. The millions of birds which winter on our coastal marshes – one quarter of all Western Europe's waders among them – would have to find somewhere else, or perish.

What makes the problem doubly agonising is that some of the proposed developments are for benign technologies that would otherwise be high on any list of green priorities. The redevelopment of the Cardiff Docks, which will turn the Taff Estuary into a freshwater lake, is, in all other respects, an imaginative scheme for reviving one of the most blighted urban areas in Wales. The Severn Barrage could be a real alternative to the proposed PWR at Hinkley Point. So if any way could be found of conserving vital intertidal marshes while permitting urgent (or inevitable) development it would be a great blessing.

The Dutch response to this conundrum is simple: if the original mudflats have to go, make new ones. Flevoland, some 10 miles east of Amsterdam, is the most recent area to have been materialised out of the Ijsselmeer. Of its 100,000 hectares, half is farmland and a quarter residential. The remainder is given over to nature reserves, wild areas and deciduous woods.

Driving on to it we were able to hold on to our scepticism – just – at the hordes of black-tailed godwits, greylag geese and roe deer grazing on the fully drained land; but not when we came to the edge of the saltwater lakes that are next in line for drainage. The gales made it difficult to venture outside the car, but they had also blown in huge numbers of sea-duck for shelter. Rafts of smew, goldeneye, scaup and merganser bobbed in the lee of the breakwaters. Little gulls wafted over male goosanders – an extraordinary contrast of fugitive dark underwing and swaggering peach bulk when a shaft of sunlight caught them together.

On the landward side of Flevoland's coast road there is an immense tract of reed-marsh and brackish lagoons. Marsh harriers were hunting over the willow scrub and reeds, and flocks of avocets and godwits scurried about the mud. The variety of habitats is partly due to the way the Dutch drain these areas. They are first banked, pumped partially dry, then sown with reed seeds (by plane!) to dry them out further, and finally dyked and drained. But in the nature reserve areas, much of the land is left in the reed-marsh stage, though there are large stretches of mud which look as if they are managed for a slightly tidal regime, and which that day were dotted with dunlin and knot.

None of this, of course, is an exact replacement for natural estuaries. There isn't the intricate tracery of creeks, or the magic of a landscape made anew twice daily. Yet in one way, that is precisely the point. Estuaries aren't fixed, irreplaceable habitats like ancient woods. They are intrinsically unstable and mobile, and always have the potential of recreating themselves on the seaward side of any development.

The whole of the north Norfolk coastal marshlands, fed by just four small rivers, and yet of international importance, were, like Flevoland, half a mile out to sea 500 years ago, and have emerged entirely naturally. Every year they change a little as creeks silt up or a sea wall breaches. It's a lesson in natural flexibility which has not been lost on the Dutch either ecologically or politically. The last time their engineers came to Britain they began the process which was to destroy most of our wetlands. I hope we soon ask them back to help find ways of extending what remains.

1987

THE CÉVENNES

It was a good summer for butterflies in southern France. Down in the limestone hills west of the Cévennes, a sharp-eyed acquaintance logged more than 70 species in a fortnight. I was camping there in August with some old friends and their children and as the array of butterfly species – Cleopatra, Satyr, Dryad – began to resemble the cast of a Greek drama, so, doped silly by the afternoon heat, we fantasised our own lists of theatrical sun-flies: the True Blue, the Bent Copper, the Grey-rinsed Skipper (or Old Heath) and the Large White Supremacist *(Eugenia terreblanchea)*.

This was alternative humour showing its middle age, but it did underline for me what a great source of shared metaphors and memories the natural world is. My friends earn part of their keep by running guided walks for other campers. But these familiar rambles are important rituals for us too, a way of beating our tribal bounds and saluting old friends: the dippers, lizards and lilies along the wooded river walk to Nant; the red-backed shrikes and feathery limestone grass, *Stipa pennata,* like the trail left by a sparkler at night, up on top of the radio-mast cliff. One evening we always go to hear nightjars on a high *causse* to the west. This year we were almost past their breeding season, but in one magical moment a pair skimmed down – silent, weightless spectres in the half-light – to hover and drink in a dew pond. There are new experiences, too. The heat, for one, which in early August is stunning. Feeling more at ease than I have for years, I sleep outside, gazing at the shooting stars and listening to the poignant creaks of the children swinging in their hammocks. (They have been making an un-nature trail, hanging strings of garlic in trees, and moulding bird-of-paradise droppings out of striped toothpaste.) One afternoon we go swimming in the Dourbie, my first river-dip for decades. Moving slowly and half-covered by water we seem to be accepted by other creatures. Silver-washed fritillary and banded grayling butterflies as big as warblers fly in procession above us. Crag martins swoop for water a few feet from our heads. Young viperine snakes wriggle past and, to a great cheer, one catches a delta-wing striped horsefly known to us only as 'the thing that bites John'.

And there are daily rituals too. The camp serin, that at 8.30 each morning begins the extraordinary subsong which Rachel christens its *chanson de la toilette*. And in the afternoon heat, lolling in the shade of a tree with our field guides and trying to work out the plants found that day. It can be a delicious but fruitless task, wallowing among the profusion of the French flora. But no matter, for this is a human debate also, a gentle, unspoken exchange of personal whims and ways of thinking as much as an identification parade. We all sometimes use nature like a language. Making private jokes and symbols of it is partly a way of saying we all speak it, of cementing our bonds with each other. But I like to think that being, so to speak, so *familiar* with it, is a way of touching many basic feelings – of continuity, affection, delight – that, for all our word games, are deeper than words, and may be common to living things.

1992

ANDALUSIA

I was last in southern Spain one baking August in the early 1960s, and had an impression burned into me of a region so poor and exotically strange that it might just that moment have floated free of Africa. I remember the scorched red earth, bee-eaters and rollers hawking from the telegraph wires above the pocked dust roads, and my first painful experiments in eating prickly pears. I remember, less happily, the limbless Civil War veterans selling lottery tickets on street corners, and the *gardia civil* officer we befriended who, under General Franco's rule, was obliged to change out of his uniform before he could play subversive flamenco to us.

Well, Franco went 10 years later, and from Norman Lewis's and Jan Morris's lyrical essays about Andalusia, I built up an achingly romantic image of what they still described as the wildest region of Western Europe, where the skies were full of vultures and azure-winged magpies, and the landscape was seared into a crucible of wildflowers.

I went back at long last this March, and found a freer and more sophisticated country. The beggars have largely disappeared, and the roads are as good as anywhere in Europe. But the place also seemed perceptibly less Spanish. Andalusia, once the most cryptic and distinctive part of Spain, is now part of the greater Europe, and the only music you are likely to hear on the street is techno-rock blasting out of car stereos. Maybe it is impertinent of a visitor to lament the kind of changes that are helping Andalusia to emerge from poverty. But I confess I was sad to see that even the landscape was now being updated and converted, courtesy of the Common Agricultural Policy, to standard, flowerless, Euro-arable prairies.

I had thought it was just my bad timing at first. I had scheduled our jaunt for the tail-end of March, which in a normal year is reputedly the time when 30-odd species of orchid and a good number of Spain's 6,000 plant species begin to bloom. But as we meandered through the white-stoned villages between Ronda and Granada there was, by Mediterranean standards, an eerie barrenness along the roadsides. The garigue herbs – thyme, rosemary, cistus – were stunted and a long way from blooming. Asphodel and orchid shoots were only just poking through. Later we found out that there had been an unusually cool and protracted winter that had held everything up.

But it was plainly not that alone. In much of the country below the high sierras, there simply weren't any roadsides – or much wild land of any kind. Most of the fields (and even the olive groves) had been ploughed to the edge of the tarmac. The air was scented, not with orange blossom and Spanish broom, but the stench of insecticide. Livid green, reseeded grassland was spreading like a stain in the valleys, and if you were pitched down here without any idea of where you were, you could easily have mistaken it for Wiltshire or Dumfries – or mid-America, for that matter. Of course there were patches of excitement: the small blue convolvulus on roadwork spoil and chunky winter-flowering buttercups, *Ranunculus bullatus,* on many rocky banks. In Ronda there were lesser kestrels circling in the Tajo, the great chasm that divides the town in two, and from the bridge above the gorge, the males' plain chestnut backs were very clear.

But it was the city of Granada that provided, paradoxically, the most novel insight into Andalusian nature. There is a huge contrast between the detail and ornamentation of the great 14th-century Moorish palace, the Alhambra, and the simple elegance of the Moorish gardens which surround it. The Generalife gardens are not that strong on wildlife (though we missed their famous nightingales by just a few days), but they do invite you to look at vegetation in a new way. They consist of tiers of cool and shaded terraces, each one containing just a few simple elements – orange trees ranged alongside a narrow canal and watered by rows of fountains; single magnolias and judas trees in their own walled alcoves; steps lined with ivy and broom, and carrying aqueducts just a few inches wide along their edges. It sounds as unwild and formal as you could imagine, but the whole stone framework also includes a multitude of arches, peepholes, viewpoints over the lower layers, so that you are forever seeing things from different perspectives:

cameos of plants in separate beds, a close-up of a small square of cypress bark, irises framed by juniper, the movement of water from terrace to terrace.

I imagine this is an expression of the Islamic view of nature, and of finding beauty and pattern in simplicity. But it was also an ecological lesson about hidden intricacy and unexpected relationships, and thereafter we took a more benign view of the landscape as it struggled out of winter. Up in the high Serrania de Ronda, there were still no orchids to speak of, but we took a new pleasure in sheets of storksbill that gave a lilac sheen to acres of limestone plateau, and in a black wheatear flitting about the white rocks.

The car windows began to seem like Generalife spy-holes. Near Antequera, an early party of bee-eaters huddled on a wire above the sun-roof like iridescent stuccowork. A flash of egg-yolk yellow from one of the few patches of unploughed roadside grass was a colony, at last, of *Ophrys lutea,* which had among them a couple of spikes of the scarce and local Atlas orchid *O. atlantica,* with flowers like black velvet. And then, on our last day, we saw, shimmering on the edges of arable fields, a plant which seemed to sum up our glimpse of the new Andalusia: it was the Barbary nut, a dainty and diminutive blue iris with fleeting flowers that appear in the late afternoon and last only a few hours.

1993

THE OLDEST BOTANICAL GARDEN IN THE WORLD

Travelling west from Venice to the oldest botanical garden in the world is like being on a cultural roller-coaster. You leave the most beautiful city on Earth and plunge into a desert of industrial sprawl that is slowly covering the entire flood-plain of the River Po and threatening to sink Venice into the bargain. You reach Padua, heavily bombed during the Second World War, and find the best bits of the old city are clustered around the awesome and outlandish Basilica di Sant'Antonio. Anthony is the people's saint in this part of Italy, a worker of miracles, the patron saint of lost property – and patron too of the humbler animals (a distinction that springs from a legend that he preached to fishes when he couldn't find a human congregation). Most especially he's revered as a healer. The furiously animated sculptures inside show Anthony reviving a baby scalded to death, raising a drowned woman, restoring the severed foot of a boy. Graphic photographs of horrendous car crashes survived and limbs healed are plastered as votive offerings on Anthony's tomb.

Just a hundred metres from this cauldron of raw faith, there's a monument to another approach to healing. The Orto Botanico was created in 1545, three centuries after the Basilica, as a place where medical students at Padua University could study medicinal plants. It's a tranquil, meditative garden, contained within a perfectly circular brick wall. Inside, the plants are grown in stone-edged beds and marked with handwritten labels, giving their vernacular Italian names, scientific names and uses. The collection has moved on since the 16th century. There are drug plants *(Solanaceae* especially) from tropical forests that somehow survive the winter here out of doors. And, perched inside a tower a little like something from the Basilica, there is a 400-year-old palm tree, which Goethe visited in 1786 and used to illustrate his intuition about evolution in his *The Metamorphosis of Plants*. The garden is a shrine to scientific curiosity and horticultural ingenuity.

Yet its origins weren't entirely different from the Basilica's. The hidden agenda behind the 16th-century botanic garden was nothing less than the re-creation of paradise. For much of the medieval period it was widely believed that the Garden of Eden had survived the Flood and existed somewhere on Earth (or, a few thought, on the Moon). But the discoveries of the early explorers scotched this theory. They found too much which challenged the assumptions about creation presented in scripture and the classics: prodigious plants and animals for which there were no biblical names, Adam-like men who practised cannibalism, and everywhere, an exuberant diversity which fitted none of their expectations. So in the growing mood of confidence that followed the Renaissance, a new idea began to take root. At the Fall, nature had not so much been cursed as scattered across the Earth, to be discovered by humans when they were ready. It was humankind's redemptive challenge to reassemble the jigsaw puzzle, and make coherent sense of it.

The early gardens resounded with ambitions to gather together plants from all over the world. The Oxford Botanic Garden (founded in 1621) had specimens from 'the remote Quarters of the World … comprehended as in an Epitome'. John Evelyn's plan for a huge 'Elysium Britannicum' is quite specific in its invocation of a New Eden and, like many of his contemporaries, he thought scientific gardening might restore the fruitfulness which the Earth lost at the Fall. 'Adam instructed his Posteritie how to handle the Spade so dextrously, that, in processe of tyme, men began, with the indulgence of heaven, to recover by Arte and Industrie, that which was before produced to them spontaneously.' Padua's circular design isn't purely ornamental: it was intended to symbolise the four quarters or continents of the globe, the scattered fragments of Eden. Its contemporary documenter, G Porro, described how the curators were 'collecting the whole world in a chamber' and pointed out that species which came from the East (for example, cedar) were planted in the eastern quarter of the garden.

Botanic Gardens now play a vital role in ecological education and plant conservation. The Orto Botanico itself had a splendid and well-narrated collection of rare wild species from north-east Italy. But it's well to meditate on the hubris that gave rise to the idea of botanic gardens in the first place. Garden collections aren't substitutes for the wild, and the belief that 'Arte and Industrie' can in some way improve nature is what got us into the predicament we're in today. Maybe there's an ecological lesson in the Edenic legend of the Tree of Knowledge, that we should begin to acknowledge our limits as a species.

2006

A GREENHORN IN THE STATES

No one can make a first trip to America without a suitcase full of prejudices and fantasies. Any nation that can produce both Aldo Leopold and George Bush – and sell them successfully – is going to deliver dreams and nightmares in equal proportion.

My own dream was to see a bit of wilderness, but we thought we'd do the trip properly and visit New York first. We stayed in the Algonquin Hotel, a writers' Mecca for almost a century. We spent Sunday in the glorious mêlée of Central Park. Polly, my partner, went skating, and I watched a great horned owl slipping through the trees above the frisbee players. When we left town, travelling south on the train, we saw an extraordinary landscape going feral between the railway and condominiums: acres of reedswamp lit up by the scarlet foliage of sumach scrub. Already I had a sense that the frontier was still alive, eddying back and forth.

We hung out for a while in Maryland, by the Chesapeake Bay. The Delmarva peninsula is the most environmentally aware region you could wish for, busy with community conservation projects and water-purity programmes. In one of the Bay's wildlife refuges, we saw the snow geese flying south, a sublime vision of endurance and elegance against a pure blue sky – and still calling after 3,000 miles. On the water were hundreds of ruddy duck, steaming in V-formation, as popular here in their native country as they are in Britain. (Here the Government's anti-alien campaign is against naturalised mute swans.)

The big crop here is soya, and our host's son was growing it for conversion to petrol on half his land and allowing the other half to evolve into prairie, under a scheme similar to our Countryside Stewardship. But the local farmland is shrinking. All through the eastern states, new-growth forest is reclaiming abandoned agricultural land. Vermont has gone from 35 per cent woodland in 1850 to 80 per cent today. Moose have started playing Russian Roulette along Route 128, America's 'Computer Highway'. So have racoons, and our melancholy body-count was 20 road-kills to one live.

We stayed a few nights at a B&B, a southern mansion restored in a style somewhere between Art Nouveau and Mississippi riverboat. It was no surprise to wake up one morning and see a turkey vulture's wing draped over the window. The birds were everywhere, circling the houses, jostling for burger scraps on lawns, hanging like gothic scare-crows in the ornamental conifers. Our landlady, the restorer, cringed when we told her. 'They give the wrong impression of the place,' she moaned. 'My husband throws tennis balls at them to get them off the roof.' Apparently they eat roof insulation and leave unsavoury odours. I thought they were the wildest bit of America we'd seen.

We knew that, if we wanted real wilderness, we'd have to motor west. So we hired a car and took off along Route 66, singing the song like sixties throwbacks. But we'd underestimated the distances and the extent to which the US road culture won't let go of you. Our plan had been to motor down to the Great Dismal Swamp, between Norfolk and Suffolk (Virginia). Coming from the soggy Norfolk/Suffolk borderlands ourselves, this seemed too good a joke to miss. But it was simply too far, and so we headed for the Appalachians and the Shenandoah National Park.

Short on time and planning, we barely got beyond the organised trails. But we saw chipmunks, migrating monarch butterflies, as big as bats, and the tennis-ball-like fruits of osage orange trees. The remarkable thing is that there was virtually no woodland here when the park was dedicated in 1936, on a depopulated area of dirt-farm-ing. Now two fifths of it is an official US wilderness.

We kept to the back roads where we could. In Pleasant Valley, the householders were building up their winter woodstacks, and Dane, of 'Mountin' Man Taxidermy' had his colour brochure in the stores. 'Deer mounts include banded competition eyes. Add $75 for open mouth.' But we couldn't find a way into their woods.

Increasingly it seemed to me that the road was the frontier, the place you staked your claims, strutted your stuff, anything but let other people across. Along stretches of country road that weren't lined with houses, there were 'Posted Private' hunting notices on every roadside tree. But at least there were the parks and refuges. Just outside Washington, we got politely ejected from a National Wildlife Refuge for being there after dark. (It was where they raised the celebrated cranes that were taught to migrate behind a microlite.)

Back in New York State, in the Great Swamp National Wildlife Reserve, Sunday parties were going ecstatic over white-tailed deer. It was, though, as hard to get away from the boardwalks as from the roads. But on the train to JFK, we glimpsed snowy egrets hunched up in the Newark shipyards. We failed to get to the wilderness, but the wild was there, edging back along the frontier.

2004

5. IMAGES

Nature in art – and the art of nature.

ART AND NATURE

Art? Who needs it, when the climate's getting wobblier by the day and the early flowering hawthorns have to be censused and the planning inquiry wants facts not fancies … Art clouds reality and isn't what a natural world in crisis needs at this moment, thank you very much.

On the day that he died in 1851, the painter William Turner was found on the floor of his bedroom, trying to get to the window to look out at the River Thames. His doctor reported that, just before 9am, 'the sun broke through the cloudy curtain which so long had obscured its splendour, and filled the chamber of death with a glory of light.' That cloud was the pall of soot and sulphur-saturated fog (later christened 'smog') that blanketed London during its heyday as an industrial city. Nineteenth-century artists were agog at its visual effects, at the way it misted scenes into essays in impressionism, at its magical softening of detail. London pea-soupers lured Claude Monet over from France. He told his dealer 'what I love more than anything is the fog.' James McNeill Whistler thought the evening smog clothed 'the riverside with poetry', transforming factory chimneys into Italian bell-towers, warehouses into palaces, so that 'the whole city hangs in the heavens, and fairy-land is before us'. Out in the real city, of course, people were dying of asphyxiation, and the fish populations of the Thames were being wiped out.

This rose-tinted view of a grossly polluted city is precisely what sceptics have against the intrusion of art and imagination into the world of natural history. And a wonderfully intelligent exhibition at Tate Britain this spring showed the extent to which Whistler's famously 'atmospheric' portraits of London at dusk – and the glowing, streaked, shifting light in Turner's landscapes (Constable called it 'tinted steam') – sanitised, even glamorised, the city's filth.

Yet were these artists turning a deliberate blind eye, or simply reflecting the complicated and ambivalent ways that humans look at the world – in this case our very understandable desire to try to see hope in dereliction? The business of art – and by that word I mean all human imaginative activities, poetry, dance, myth, language itself

– is to explore the relationships between human feeling and the world outside. And there is no more urgent task, I'd argue, than to carry this exploration into the natural world. We are stuffed with facts about nature. We know more about its mechanical workings than most of us do about our cars. Yet a deep and paradoxical gulf, full of confusions and contradictions, still exists between what we feel and hope and dream about it, and what, as a species, we do. Why do we behave with a suicidal disregard of the facts we so worship? Why do we continue to whip into subservience ('manage' is the euphemism) what we still call Mother Nature? Can we be both animals and humans without disservice to both these parts of our make-up?

The arts have no more 'answers' to these conundrums than science, but they can bring imaginative light to bear on them. The great anthropologist Claude Lévi-Strauss once described the function of myths in early society as 'resolving contradictions'. So they can with us, too, but they have to be constructive, connected myths. And just as myths can degenerate into dangerous superstition, so art can mutate into propaganda and glamorisation and pure delusion.

And art, of course, is as full of paradox as the world it explores – the portrayal of animals as humans (and vice versa) for instance. John Downer's film *Pride* (shown last Christmas), in which a real family of lions had their jaw movements computer manipulated to match a heavily romanticised script, was widely regarded as offensive and degrading. But why then is *Wind in the Willows*, with its much more outrageous merging of human and animal worlds, seen as one of the great literary myths of nature and the countryside?

Are we, at the deepest level, more merged with nature than we acknowledge? Is birdsong a kind of music, or music a kind of human-song? Were the first cave paintings more to do with hunting or thinking? At that very first moment in human art, it is hard to spot any difference between our imaginative and biological responses to nature. Perhaps it could be so again.

2005

PICTURES ON THE ROCKS

The cave paintings discovered at Vallon-Pont-d'Arc in the Ardèche last year are the most remarkable examples of rock art yet found. For a start, radiocarbon dating has put their age at 31,000 years, which makes them the oldest in the world by a considerable margin. They show a dozen or so species, several of them not seen in cave art before. And most significantly, they are hauntingly beautiful, with an expressiveness and vitality and detail that only reappear (in European art at least) in the Renaissance. Many of the animals are portrayed in perspective, with contours scraped into the rock for emphasis.

Now, the first tentative scholarly reactions are beginning to appear – though without much agreement, beyond the fact that these paintings question most theories about the origins of human creativity. Are they examples of hunting magic, attempts to 'capture' (a word we still use about 'likenesses') the animals' spirits? A coded map of their haunts? Or even hallucinations, tricked out on the rocks by drugged shamans?

Yet these possibilities don't really explain two important aspects of the Ardèche paintings. They are *not* principally of food animals such as deer, but of rare, spectacular and often dangerous creatures, including rhinoceros, mammoth, bear, panther, hyena and owl. And the creatures are drawn with a delicacy and sensitivity that suggest not just acute observation but an understanding of the complex mixture of raw emotions, habit and physical response that make up an animal's behaviour.

There is a real appreciation of the changes in muscle tone that accompany feeding, fighting, and resting, which is matched in the depiction of facial expressions. Perhaps the pictures represent not prey but totems, animals that were especially respected and feared, and maybe even worshipped as a result. (One curious example is a chimera – half bison, half human.)

But I wonder if they might not also mark an important stage in the development of *empathy* in the human species. This capacity to understand what fellow humans were feeling seemed to emerge at the same time as dramatic changes in culture and social structure about 40,000 years ago. To me what the Vallon paintings suggest above all else is an extension of that empathy to other species. The bison and the bear are no longer objects, enemies or aliens, but living things whose experience of fear, excitement, anger and kinship is no different from the painters'.

1996

* * *

'Virtually the Ice Age', proclaims the brochure for Creswell Crags, a limestone gorge cut into the unspectacular farming country of north Nottinghamshire. Virtually, perhaps. But the illusion is hard to sustain. The river that helped carve out the valley is now an ornamental lake. A busy tourist road runs between the caves where hyena bones and quartzite spearheads have been unearthed. But it was here, in 2003, that archaeologists discovered the first British Palaeolithic rock art, a series of bas-relief animal carvings which are reckoned to be the most remarkable of their kind in Europe. I'd called in on the off-chance, and the caves were locked-up – a safety consideration that is probably merited for once, given the clutter of raw limestone rock inside. But peering through the grille outside Church Hole, I fancied I could see a bird carved on the ceiling, an arching neck ending in a great beak. It looked a lot like an ibis, and the thought that this image of a creature I knew had been shaped by human hands 12,000 years ago gave me goose-flesh.

The story of how these images were discovered – and why it took so long – is remarkable in itself. Paul Bahn, perhaps the greatest authority on European cave painting, and documenter of the 30,000-year-old masterpieces of Chauvet Cave in southern France, had always been troubled by the apparent absence of rock art in Britain. The caves were there, the animal remains were abundant and the landscape had been occupied by hunter-gatherers throughout the heyday of Palaeolithic art. So in the spring of 2003, Dr Bahn organised a small party to have a closer look at some English caves.

Creswell was the first place they visited and within hours they had found an exquisite engraving of a stag, high on the ceiling close to the entrance of Church Hole. Someone had plainly seen the engraving before and had taken it for a goat: underneath the stag's head a whiskery beard had been scratched and dated 1947. Another 90 images have since been found in the cave, scratched out with flint burins, or sculpted from the soft limestone: bears, horses with fantastic bristling manes, birds that I am pretty sure are cranes. Many, with the wit and artistry so evident in cave art, exploit natural fissures and curves in the rock to outline animal shapes. But they have lost any colouring they might once have had from damp and exposure to the sun, and it's easy to see how they were missed.

The fact that many of the figures are close to the well-lit mouth of the cave is a puzzle given that most images in southern European caves are deep in the darkest interiors. This concealment never squared with the early theories about rock art – that it was a kind of field-guide to potential prey or was imbued with simple hunting magic (draw the beast, and so 'capture' it). Nor did the revelation that there was almost no correlation between the species found as food remains in particular caves and the species most popular in the paintings. As the anthropologist Claude Lévi-Strauss has said: 'The animals were not so much good to eat, as good to think.'

Nowadays more complex psychological explanations are looked for. In *The Mind in the Cave* , David Lewis-Williams argues that these first images, these first representations of thoughts outside the head, were a profoundly important step in the development of human consciousness. He believes that they are representations of things seen during trance states – which, remembered as disembodied, two-dimensional images, were recreated as paintings in the dark hearts of caves.

Whatever their origins, there are two striking aspects of Palaeolithic painting. First, its astonishing sensitivity. There appears to be no primitive, childlike cave art. It suddenly appears, mature and fully-fledged. One of Creswell's bisons is engraved with a few simple strokes that give it the bulk and energy of Picasso's sketches of bulls.

Second, at the moment of this amazing development, this first expression of the human imagination, it was not other humans that the artists envisioned, nor gods made in their own image, but their fellow creatures. I find this the most heartening message about the deep roots of our relationship with nature.

2005

THE CORNFIELD

Is John Constable's *The Cornfield* a glimpse of Arcadia, a vision of an ideal rural landscape where nature and civilisation are in harmony? An enthralling exhibition last month at the National Gallery suggested that even if it doesn't rise to quite this height, it is a picture which arouses fiercely affectionate feelings.

Colin Painter, principal of Wimbledon School of Art, advertised in the gallery and elsewhere for anyone who had a version of *The Cornfield* at home to contact him. He received 509 responses and heard of reproductions of the painting on everything from ashtrays to teapots, thimbles and wallpaper. The exhibition was made up of a vast assortment of these reproductions, set beside the original. But what was fascinating was not so much the sheer ubiquitousness of the image in our culture, as the descriptions the owners gave of what the painting means to them. As part of what Painter calls 'the visual furniture of thousands of people', it is a broad-shouldered token, carrying memories, reassurance, lineaments of the good life.

Constable painted *The Cornfield* in 1826, and it was the first of his paintings to be acquired for the nation. Though he finished it off in oils in his London studio, it was based on one of his favourite haunts – Fen Lane, between East Bergholt and Dedham. This had been his daily route to school when he was a child. In a letter, he describes the picture as 'inland – cornfields – a close lane, kind of thing – but it is not neglected in any part. The trees are more than usually studied and the extremities well defined – as well as their species – they are shaken by a pleasant and heathfull breeze ...'

And the trees that form the main arch in the picture's middle-ground are indeed so well defined that it is easy to see they are elms, fronted by a hawthorn and a pollard oak. In the foreground are the famously out-of-scale boy with the red waistcoat, drinking from a stream, and a donkey and foal, nibbling hogweed. In the distance is the cornfield itself, caught like a sash between the trees, and leading the eye away to a village lying among the Stour Valley water-meadows. Linking the two planes of the painting is a path, followed by sheep and a distracted sheepdog, that curves beguilingly through a broken gate and vanishes behind the elms.

For some of the people to whom Colin Painter spoke, the path is the heart of the picture. It invites the viewer in, gives a sense of depth and of unseen dramas: 'I like the picture not so much for what you can see, as for what you can't. I'm always wondering what's going on round the bend.' Others who own the reproduction view it – quite unlike professional art critics – as something commemorative, a tribute to the English countryside, a yardstick: 'I would like to be able to look at this view from my own window.'

'You know it was summertime because the corn is ripe, you know it was probably a good year because the corn is a lovely golden colour and not flattened; people are working it by hand, so you know that no machines were used; you know it's lush here because of the stream.' For one housewife, 'The *Cornfield* copies I have owned have been given to me with love, so the picture reminds me of love and friendship and the circle of life and death and the past and future … My ancestors (along with those of many other people in this country) were agricultural labourers. The boy in the picture reminds me of my sons.' To a nurse born in Sierra Leone, the boy is a reminder of home: 'I thought the boy was asleep because I would only expect to see something like this in a Third World country – somebody actually lying down and drinking straight from a stream.'

Continuity. Childhood. Security. A lost domain. It is a remarkable list of references for a single painting to encompass. Perhaps *The Cornfield*, with its sense of prospect and refuge, of leisure and work, and above all of a passage between the dappled wildwood and the bright world of cultivation, does come close to touching the formula for a pastoral Utopia.

1996

LANDSCAPE PAINTING

It has been quite a year for reflections on landscape painting, culminating in the 'A Picture of Britain' exhibition at the Tate, and its accompanying BBC tv series. They raised two intriguing questions. Why is the painting of natural landscapes almost invariably done from a distance? And why, given its modern pre-eminence, did it emerge at such a late date? In poetry, naturalistic evocations of the countryside go back to the 6th century. But in painting, the land 'beyond' was always formalised or abstract – as, for instance, in the emblematic farming scenes of the medieval Books of Hours, or stylised arrangements of landscape props and Classical figures in the work of painters like Claude and Poussin. Nothing approaching a view of a patch of the real world appears before the 18th century. It was as if such a thing had previously not been properly seen – or seen in a way that made it transferable to a canvas.

Perhaps there needed to be a critical change in our social and psychological relationships with the land before its representation was possible. It's probably no coincidence that landscape painting as we understand it originated in Holland in the 17th century. This was the time of the great draining and redesign of the Dutch landscape, and the emergence of a new agricultural order out of the wild flood-fields. The community developed the idea of a *landschap* as a portrait of their territory, which was imported by Britain in the colloquial concept of a *landskip*.

The painting tradition which began in Britain in the 18th century was of just such scenes, landscapes literally and metaphorically enclosed by human business. In this period of great geographical and economic change, the natural landscape ceased to be merely a space unself-consciously dwelt in, and became – especially for those with leisure and money – an objective prospect, a possession, a medium for planning and survey, for overview.

The change in meaning opened the opportunity for new ways of seeing and portrayal. Psychologists suggest that our landscape needs can be grouped under the headings of 'prospect' and 'refuge'. There is an abundance of prospects in the British tradition – Turner's seascapes, Samuel Palmer's mystical harvest scenes, Paul Nash's beechwoods – yet hard to find more than a handful of refuges or retreats, interior views, views from the grass roots and hedge bottom. There is simply no painterly equivalent of the intimate poems of 19th-century farmworker John Clare, who could write a bitter commentary on Enclosure from the point of view of 'a piece of ground' and describe a fen landscape as if he were one of its indigenous birds, embattled in its 'huge flag forrest'.

The impact of these lordly surveys on our view of nature and the countryside can hardly be overestimated. Just two centuries of these broad, long-focus capturings – the rolling farmlands, the epic glens, the ordered estates, the wild waterfalls – seem to have created archetypes for the countryside which have made us blind to its details, its contradictions and its movement through time. Is it the painted landscape, not the real, that is now our communal model for how the countryside – and by implication nature – should 'be'? Is our quest for 'timelessness', our nagging sense of loss, quite literally 'picturesque', a regret that the reality no longer lives up to the fixed images made during a short moment in art?

Of course, landscape painting is as full of surface beauty as the countryside it records. Constable's portraits of East Anglia, the Pre-Raphaelites' flowers, Joseph Wright's Black Country parables are memorials to geography, to ways of farming, to real moments of visual revelation. But landscape painting's intrinsic beauty and seductiveness may be its chief problem. It encourages a view of the natural world which is distant, complacent, *over*.

A landscape art which reflects our emerging biocentric view of the world and recognises the living intricacy of what has so far been seen exclusively from a distance, may need the same kind of leap of consciousness that enabled prospect painting to emerge in the 18th century. Ecologically-concerned artists are already exploring the landscape from the inside: Julian Cooper's riveting close-ups of rock faces; Kurt Jackson's pictures of the explosions of light and living matter in the very heart of woods, which are celebrations of the energy of creation, not 'scenic views'. Like Andy Goldsworthy and David Nash, they are pioneering the landscape art of the future, which must surely include, as at least part of its agenda, the idea that humans are *in* the landscape, not simply viewers of it.

2005

FLOWER PAINTING AT KEW

In the late 1980s I spent a fortnight buried in the archives of the Royal Botanic Gardens at Kew, looking at their collection of botanical paintings for a piece of writing I was doing. It was an extraordinary experience, not least because most of the pictures were filed, species by species, among the sheets of dried and mounted plants in the Herbarium: works of art they might be, but they were also works of reference. There were more than a million pieces even then: paintings by the early masters, such as George Ehret, meticulous sketches of new discoveries by Kew's intrepid plant collectors, watercolours donated by colonial governors' wives with time on their hands. And, what enthralled me most, the so-called 'Company Art' commissioned by the East India Company, in which local Moghul painters gave their own highly stylised but unmistakable renderings of plants which 'may prove beneficial to the inhabitants of Great Britain'. They were like flowers imagined into ornaments for the heavens.

Kew's collection – now partly on public show in a new gallery entirely devoted to botanical art – paints a portrait not only of the entire plant kingdom, but also of our different ways of perceiving plants. There are blowsy lovers' roses; fastidious anatomisings of economically valuable species, with the useful bits in close-up; and humble English field flowers magnified into glorious luxuriance.

With works covering five centuries, it's possible to track how each era attempted to resolve botanical art's central dilemma: how to reconcile personal vision with scientific accuracy. By the late 19th century, the breakneck speed of scientific discovery and the economic demands being made on botanists meant that purely functional illustrations began to dominate. In 1831, the writer Goethe, no mean botanist himself, mourned the fact 'that a great flower-painter is not now to be expected: we have attained too high a degree of scientific truth; and the botanist counts the stamens after the painter has had no eye for picturesque grouping and lighting.'

This proved to be too pessimistic a prediction, and Kew's new gallery shows that there are as many 'great flower-painters' now as during the genre's heyday in the 18th century. Shirley Sherwood, a great patron of modern botanical art, helped create this gallery, which has been named in her honour, and which contains many pieces from her own collection. I think it is the most perfectly lit gallery of any kind I have seen. Low intensity and diffused spotlights make each individual work seem as if it's hanging in the dappled glow of a woodland glade.

Another feature is that the pictures are arranged by botanical families (just as they were in the Herbarium), so you can see how an individual species was viewed by artists working centuries apart. The Rt Hon Mrs Thomas Hervey's painting of Gallica roses, c. 1800, is hung close to Rory McEwan's 1974 watercolour of the same subject – and holds its own very well. Susan Christopher-Coulson's *Sweet Violet Scattering*, all texture and shadow, is matched by the prodigious Maria Sibylla Merian's collage – made three centuries earlier – of a multitude of primroses and cowslips blazing across a single canvas. It's clear throughout the exhibition that in terms of detail, technique and the arrangment of a plant on the canvas, the early masters were every bit as accomplished as the modern.

But there have been advances. New painting materials can give irises the voluptuousness of velvet. There is more understanding of plant growth as a dynamic process. A better acquaintance with oriental flower painting (well represented here) has encouraged exquisite experiments in minimalism – single twigs or sprays of flowers, for instance, streaming across the paper with every fleck on the bark caught like calligraphs.

Only one thing bothered me, and it's a worry about illustration in general. Botanical art, like 'wildlife' art, has a self-limiting definition. It has, for 500 years, been overwhelmingly about the portrayal of single plants in abstraction, without any kind of context, temporal or environmental. There have been a few giant exceptions – Marianne North, for example, whose florid Victorian oils of plants pictured in their tropical landscape settings crowd the walls of the gallery adjoining the Shirley Sherwood. But most modern artists shy away from placing plants in their habitat – and certainly not in a visibly threatened habitat. Yet these are the contexts in which we now see and feel for plants.

There's no simple answer. How should a botanical artist respond to climate change? How do you portray 'endangerment' in a picture? Perhaps one solution is implicit in the tradition itself. You try to capture every grain and filament of that species' beauty and intricacy. Pandora Sellars' picture of the rainforest glory lily, a fragile lacework of pink blossom and pencil-drawn leaves, suggests something so precious that its destruction would be an obscenity.

2008

THE BARBIZON PAINTERS

I was in the Forest of Fontainebleau, just south of Paris, on the last stages of research for a book, and felt for a moment I'd been translocated into New York's Central Park. There were tribes of orienteers, joggers, cyclists, horse-riders; rock-climbers finger-tipping their way up the massive sandstone rocks; and solitary t'ai-chi practitioners posed by the side of lissom trees. And all this in an immense mosaic – 140 sq km – of hardwood plantations, ancient beeches, tracts of heath.

But there is one extra-special feature of Fontainebleau. Parts of it were the very first nature reserve to be established in western

Europe, not on grounds of its scientific interest or its biodiversity, but because it had touched the hearts of a spirited gang of local painters, the Barbizon School of the mid-19th century.

As was the case across Europe, there was a massive increase in plantation forestry in Fontainebleau in the 18th and 19th centuries. By 1830, more than 7,000 acres had been planted up with pine. But the forest was beginning to become a retreat for the Parisian middle-classes at the same time, and a campaign against this 'industrialisation' began. The celebrated artist Theodore Rousseau rallied his friends and petitioned Napoleon III to protect the *forêt ancienne* from the debilitating canker of commercial forestry.

The Barbizon School was a large and disparate group, from Corot, Gustave Courbet and Millet – whose uncompromising pictures of working peasants outraged the French bourgeoisie – to Monet and Pissarro, whose work in the forest formed a bridge between the Barbizon School and the impressionists. But they were united in an absolute commitment to nature and to catching its energy in the open air, up close. They worked at the woodface. Nicolae Grigorescu's portrait *Andreescu à Barbizon* is an heroic emblem of what they stood for, a kind of credo. The artist is emerging from the forest like a hatching chrysalis. He has his umbrella and stick over his shoulder, but they have the look of tools necessary for a long expedition, not the bric-à-brac of a day out sketching. He is looking directly out of the picture. But there's no third dimension to the painting, no distinction between foreground and background, just a shimmering plane of dappled green and yellow, a few blurred trunks. The artist is materialising from the greenwood, not as a passive witness but an outgrowth of nature.

For the French government, the simultaneous rise of Fontainebleau as a commercial tourist honeypot and a centre of French artistic excellence couldn't have been handier, and Napoleon III agreed to Rousseau's 1851 petition. He authorised the creation of some 400 hectares of *réserves artistiques,* groups of especially beguiling old trees and rocks, which were to remain uncut and unmanaged. By 1904 the *série artistique* covered one tenth of the forest (4,000 hectares).

But during the period of intense forestry modernisation in the 1960s, large numbers of the old trees were cleared away, victims of the familiar forester's superstition that young trees would never regenerate unless humans cleared their parents away. *Dépérissement* – 'decline' – was looked on not as an entirely natural part of the woodland cycle but a kind of sickness or repressive force. In the more ecologically-aware 1900s, the *série artistique* was formally abolished, and replaced with a series of *réserves biologiques* covering more than 4,000 hectares of which nearly 2,000 were to remain entirely unmanaged.

One of these is La Tillaie, an area of the forest named after the lime trees that would have been dominant here in medieval times. I couldn't 'see' it at first, expecting the old trees to look squat and knob-bly, like they do in Britain. But this is a zone which has never been cut. There are no pollards. What swam into shape as I edged into the wood were the forms of authentic natural beeches, immense tower-ing columns often 40 metres tall, as smooth and uncluttered as trees in mature plantations – except that here large numbers of them were in a state of serious *dépérissement* . Some had already lost most of their trunks from about 3 metres up, the result of invasion by – aptly for this painterly place – what is called artist's fungus, and its relative *Fomes fomentarius,* which forms horny brackets like carthorse hooves. They crash to the ground like meteors as the trees decay. The old beeches were an entire ecosystem, riddled with black woodpeckers' nest-holes and insect borings, and orange globes of *Ramaria* fungi.

And regeneration was, contrary to foresters' beliefs, happening exactly as it should. Around the dead trees there were new beeches of all ages. In one clearing they were growing up between the fallen trunks of four adults which had crashed down together. In another they were filling the space created by a fallen lime, one of the very few still growing here, and which was itself sprouting new poles from its prostrate trunk. It was gratifying that the Barbizon artists' precocious vision of the forest as something which renewed itself as well as them was at last being vindicated.

2007

ART IN THE WILD

Sculpture in woodland is becoming quite a fashion. The Forestry
Commission (FC) now has half a dozen sculpture 'trails' on its prop-
erties, the Woodland Trust has extended its 'Seats in Woods' project
to Scotland, and even the County Wildlife Trusts are beginning to
dip their toes into this not obviously ecological territory. Much
more along these lines and people will begin to expect monuments
among the trees, and we may see the beginning of an artistic version
of twitching ('A first-summer Andy Goldsworthy at OS 256865.
Good shape at present, but apt to sag in bad weather.') I hope this
won't happen, because surprise and incongruity are partly what
these works are all about. Most are explorations of the raw stuff of
the surrounding landscape – wood, stone, water – and, set directly
among the greenery rather than in a remote gallery, are wonderfully
conducive to meditations on the differences between natural and
human creativity.

We have a local trail in the Chilterns now, in the FC's Cowleaze
Wood near Lewknor, and over the past few months I've been amazed
by the sheer breadth of associations it conjures up. My favourite piece
is so minimal as to be almost invisible. It lies in a wedge of land
between two converging paths, in which the trees have been thinned
to pole ash and beech, and consists of a long, gently curving wooden
rib supported at about 12 feet above ground level on trestles.

I still don't think I have plumbed all the subtle ways in which it
affects me. At a purely visual level its thin, tentative – I'm tempted
to say pencilled – horizontal line underlines how much woods are
paramountly places of strong verticals. These are the marks of the
constant spring, how the living shoot grows, regardless of its origins.
Then the rib suddenly seems like a walkway, tracing out the aerial
paths of mice and squirrels; then, at a more practical level, I see the
rough trestle poles (cut from the thinnings on site) as reminders of
a piece of social history – the Chiltern bodgers who used to work in
the woods turning young beech poles into chair-legs.

A couple of hundred yards away is a stranger, more challenging piece: the skeleton of a small tree welded out of iron (and already rusting) and carrying, in place of leaves, individually cast metal fish. I once sat under this in May, and watched a hang-glider pass overhead through a mesh of green leaves and iron carp, an extraordinary vision in three elements.

Another short walk to a pine plantation, and you come upon a huge picnic table, eight feet high, with a painted blue and white check tablecloth. It is visible hundreds of yards away, and is the best visual joke in the wood – acting as a shelter for having picnics *under*.

I accept that intrusive works like this are not to everyone's taste, and are sometimes seen as compromising the 'naturalness' of even conifer plantations. But I rather like the role that they suggest for humans in nature, as a kind of inquisitive, wry bowerbird, leaving spoors, clues, puns and trophies to collapse slowly back into the earth. It is, I feel, a more commendable and modest role than that of general manager, especially as some of the best works often challenge our central, utilitarian assumptions about what woods are *for*. I have to confess that my favourite piece of woodland sculpture is a collection of whittled oddities in Foxley Wood, Norfolk, simply entitled 'Useless tools'.

1992

* * *

A few months back, one of our more elegant East Anglian trunk roads suddenly sprouted a stark white tree. It was rather shocking. One moment there'd been an ordinary dead hulk, bleaching nicely of its own accord and home no doubt to diverse beetles and birds. The next there was this porcelain fork, a manifestation, it turned out, of conceptual art. I wondered what conceivable meaning there could be in the Duluxing of a perfectly lively fallow tree, but from the way environmental art is shaping up at present, I could make a rough guess. A portentous comment on the contrast between the dark road and the purity of nature, perhaps. Or some forced textual joke: a White Elephant, a White Flag (nature surrenders!) – or perhaps a

Whited Sepulchre, the rottenness disguised by human artifice. Tough luck on the beetles, whichever way.

The masters of environmental sculpture like Andy Goldsworthy and David Nash have the greatest respect for their natural raw materials. Working often in situ, they incorporate the processes of growth and decay, and the influence of changing seasons and fluctuating light, *into* their work. That's the whole point of it: to make nature a partner in the work, not something subservient to the artist's grand plan; to start a conversation between natural and human creativity. Nash's *Wooden Boulder,* axed out of a fallen oak, then levered into a Welsh stream to find its own way into the Atlantic, remains the epitome of this kind of work.

But there hasn't been much of this kind of sensitivity in the exhibitions I've seen in woods and parks over the past year. Most of the artists seem to have little understanding of or interest in the places they're working in, and the pieces they make might just as well have been in an uptown gallery. They're full of post-modern irony and bad art-school puns. I've seen a work entitled *Copper Beech,* (a tree hung with pennies on strings) and a kind of wooden dais (looking over nowhere in particular) entitled *A Platform for Self-elevation.* This year's exhibits at the Chiltern Sculpture Park in Cowleaze Wood near Watlington seemed dominated by urban angst. There was an elaborate photocell meant to symbolise photosynthesis, which, unlike the leaves around it, wasn't working. A STOP sign on a patch of tarmac was apparently inspired by the audible closeness of the M40 but might just as well have been a Forestry Commission track sign. Glaring posters stuck to trees emphasised the danger of woods and the sensibleness of running away. What were these pieces trying to say? That woods are no different from city centres and therefore that intrusiveness – the spirit of the graffitist – is justified?

The best environmental sculpture always gives a sense of exploring the place in which it's situated and possibilities for growth and evolution which nature hasn't got round to yet. One recent piece by Chris Drury seems very much in this tradition. Looking down on the flooded Railway Land Nature Reserve in his home town of Lewes years ago, Drury saw a pattern of land and water whose rhythmic movement reminded him of the human heart. He put forward a plan to plant out a reedbed, roughly in the shape of a heart, where water would ebb and flow around islands of land. After long consultation with local people, who were concerned about endangering the wild character of the reserve – and, in a sense, with the place itself, which needs space to evolve and breathe – *Heart of Reeds* was opened last summer, a living, free-form but profoundly evocative piece. As Drury says: 'You can walk the pattern and feel it with your body' – something you cannot do with the Whited Sepulchre of the East.

2006

ANDY GOLDSWORTHY

In the US National Gallery in Washington, just a few hundred yards from the office where the destiny of much of the world is decided, there's an Andy Goldsworthy installation with a quite different sort of power. It's based around one of the glass walls in the gallery, the boundary between 'inside' and the world beyond. Outside are a group of Goldsworthy's familiar cairns, low-slung mounds like stone molehills. Except that two of them have broken through the wall, become both insiders and outsiders, dissolved the barrier.

Goldsworthy currently has a major show at the Yorkshire Sculpture Park. The extraordinary publicity given to this suggests that he's now one of the best-loved modern sculptors. Yet most people know him from his more strictly 'natural' works – the snakes of autumn leaves floating on water, the ice arches, the boxes made of leaves – pieces which explore the patterns and processes of nature, and its fleetingness. I remember the impact made by an installation in the City of London a decade ago. Goldsworthy had made a number of large snowballs, stuffed with layers of seasonal cargo – daffodils, leaves, pine cones – and kept them frozen in a refrigerator. In late winter he scattered them about the City pavements, and as the temperature rose, they melted and disgorged their contents – a précis of all the seasons for this season-free, urban labyrinth.

At another extreme, in the same category as his Washington work, is *The Wall that Went for a Walk*, which he installed in Grizedale Forest, in the Lake District, in 1990. This also questions the meaning of enclosures and boundaries. The wall snakes through the forest, winding this way and that round boulders, down slopes, incorporating trees into its stonework, following the lie of the land rather than riding roughshod over it.

These enduring, politically tinged pieces seem a long way from his 1985 dandelion chain pinned in a ring above a lake of bluebells – the latter celebrating the wildness and changeability of nature, the others musing on the way that human works might 'fit' into the natural scheme of things. But it is precisely because he's exploring the borderlands between these two worlds – the natural and the man-made – that Goldsworthy is such an important artist today. 'Movement, change, light, growth and decay', he's written, 'are the lifeblood of nature, the energies I try to tap through my work. I need the shock of touch, the resistance of place, materials and weather, the earth as my surface. I want to get under the surface. When I work with a leaf, rock, stick, it is not just the material itself, it is an opening into the processes of life within and around it.'

The show at the Yorkshire Sculpture Park marks the 20th anniversary of Goldsworthy's residence in the park, and it's possible to see, from photographs of early works, how 'the shock of touch', and all that implies, has become progressively more important than 'the material itself'. During his 1987 residency – a time when it was still a new idea that art could be 'of' nature rather than simply representing it – he made an exquisite horn, pinned together from sweet chestnut leaves. It was a statement about the potentiality of natural materials, about the relationships between evolved forms. In the early 1990s, in south Australia, he built cairns of bleached sheep and kangaroo bones and turned trees into fossils by caking them with red sand. In a sculpture park in Missouri he wrapped wet leaves round a remarkable lizard-shaped river rock and let them be washed off. The next day, he built a thin vertical wall around the same rock ...

Among the most delightful pieces in the current show are the *Sheep Paintings*, which result from Goldsworthy leaving blank canvases in sheep fields with salt licks at their centres. Over time the sheep build up a picture of their daily activites in droppings and muddy footprints, a bustling record of the chaotic sociability of grazing animals. But it's Goldsworthy's work as much as the sheep's. He chose to make it, as a statement sympathetic to farmers about the 'reality of dung'. 'My art is unmistakably the work of a person,' he insists. And about 'persons' too. Nowhere is this more evident, for me, than in the show's most striking piece. *Hidden Trees* is three walled caverns containing huge, dark, oak logs, salvaged from forestry work in the park. They are bound in and by the walls. The piece is installed in a ha-ha, a boundary ditch popular with 18th-century landscapers, which gave the illusion that the park and the wilder countryside beyond were seamlessly joined. Goldsworthy reveals, in the depths of the ditch, the reality that was hidden: reckless forest clearance, hard human labour. Yet the way the logs are caught by the walls suggests something else as well – that they might be breaking through them. Artists aren't required to give answers, but they make us ask questions. Goldsworthy does this, so to speak, in spades.

2007

DAMIEN HIRST

Is there anything left to say about the artist Damien Hirst? The pickled animal corpses that helped him win the Turner prize last winter have been lambasted in the popular press as little more than tasteless self-advertisements. And the argument about whether they are art rumbles on *ad nauseam,* since any half-sharp contemporary artist will say that he or she is, precisely, challenging the definition of 'art'. But maybe Hirst deserves a second viewing from a greenish perspective, as he has defended his notorious bisected cow (*Mother and Child*

Divided) as an allegory of our treatment of the natural world. And if it stirs up discussion and feelings – even of revulsion or rage – doesn't that, by definition, make it art?

I should come clean and say that Hirst leaves me cold, and that my feelings have been more stirred by the Christmas displays in butchers' shops. I have an old-fashioned belief that artists should give 'added value' to their materials (in the way that Andy Goldsworthy – an artist whose work with natural materials has often featured in *BBC Wildlife* – does, for instance). Merely shifting familiar objects into unfamiliar contexts (carcass in gallery, bed on hoarding) may have been 'art' when Marcel Duchamp first hung a urinal in an exhibition in 1917, but it's a soft, anything-goes option for an artist now, hard to tell from a student stunt.

Yet, perhaps I am being too picky, too fixated on the notion of art as a special activity. Changing the context, the settings, of natural organisms does change our viewpoint on them, and often our feelings, too. One of the best places to experience this, and set Hirst's work in perspective, is the Hunterian Museum at the Royal College of Surgeons in London. John Hunter (1728-93) was the father of modern surgery, but also a perennially curious naturalist. During his life, he accumulated a remarkable collection of biological specimens. These found their way to the Royal College, and though many were lost from bombing in 1941, more than 3,500 of his original preparations survive in beautiful, chilling perfection in bottles of alcohol.

This is no place for the squeamish. Almost the first exhibits you see on entering the long galleries display room are mutant human embryos. Yet there is nothing morbid about the collection. Even the tiniest exhibits have an awe-inspiring intricacy. They fill you with conflicting emotions – sadness, wonder, sympathy, anger, wistfulness. There is the embryo of a hyena with clearly visible stitches in its abdomen, as if it had given emergency birth itself. The gill filaments of an angler fish, still with an almost-luminous sheen. The immense optic lobes of a horned owl's brain. A muntjac's head and neck sliced in half, Hirst-wise, to show its enormous tongue (which I've seen in real life used as an organ of smell). And a poignant row of male house sparrows, taken between January and April to show the progressive enlargement of their testes. So many young lives sacrificed, such happenstance beauty ironically revealed. This kind of mass dissection does not lie easily on our modern consciences. Yet it would be unfair to judge Hunter by our standards, and it is hard not to be moved by his dedication and skills which matched those of any sculptor. He was also a deep and precocious thinker, fascinated by reproduction and adaptation. If he hadn't been dyslexic, modest to a fault, and had lived in a more liberal political climate, there is an even chance he would have come up with the theory of evolution by natural selection almost a century before Darwin. As it is, one of the museum's curators calls the collection 'John Hunter's unwritten book'. I think it is more than that. Collectively it is a stunning work of art, a panoramic meditation on mortality, survival and natural ingenuity, all the more so because it focuses our attention on the *subject*, not the 'cleverness' of the artist.

And changing contexts can work the other way, too. A few weeks ago I heard from a friend who had visited a walk-through undersea aquarium on the East Coast. She had been astonished and uplifted to see, swimming above her, plaice and sole – the dead fish of marble slabs transformed into shimmering movement and colour. Now that *is* art, and I hope all such free-range aquaria will rapidly enter themselves for this year's Turner Prize.

1996

DEREK JARMAN'S GARDEN

I stumbled on Derek Jarman's garden quite by accident while trudging across the Dungeness shingle back in the 1980s. I had no idea it was his at the time; but there was something special about the miniature henges of shells and shark-fin pebbles set around the tarred timbers of Prospect Cottage, and the way the sweeps of wild sea-kale and gorse merged imperceptibly with tufts of Mediterranean herbs.

Now it is one of the most famous and evocative gardens in the world, and not only as a memorial to a brilliant and brave man. On this bleak headland jutting into the Channel, against the louring bulk of a nuclear power station, Jarman created an environment that cocks a snook at the distinctions we make between the natural and the man-made.

In winter, it looks more like a bowerbird's trysting ground than a garden. It is full of *objets trouvés* and beachcombings – spirals of anti-tank fencing, rusting garden tools, necklaces of 'holey' stones, bleached ships' timbers, a collection that had the most practical of beginnings, when Jarman used a piece of driftwood to stake a transplanted dog-rose. In summer, all this happenstance sculpture becomes trellis-work, as a riotous mixture of wild species climbs up and over it. Some are plants from similar arid habitats in Europe, such as curry-plant and cotton-lavender. But they mix amicably and harmoniously with the scarce, indigenous plants of the Ness: Nottingham catchfly, prostrate blackthorn, sea pea. Seen in even this minimally gardened setting, native plants can be quite renewed. The first bunched, inky-purple shoots of sea-kale have the look of coral against the upturned flints. The 'gorse circles' echo the topography of the shingle banks.

But now Jarman's partner, Keith Collins, who has committed himself to carrying on Derek's garden, has fallen foul of English Nature (EN), which has jurisdiction over the Dungeness site of special scientific interest (SSSI). It has rapped him over the knuckles for planting more red valerian (an 'alien' naturalised in Britain for at least 500 years and already common on the Ness) and instructed him not to 'gardenise' any more (the kind of word you would expect from EN's new perception of itself as a business corporation).

Dungeness is probably the most extensive area of shingle in Europe. And it is not just a mass of randomly strewn pebbles. For the past 5,000 years sea currents have torn shingle out of beaches to the west and deposited them on the promontory. But for reasons buried in the physics of pebble movement, the sea doesn't dump shingle at a steady rate. It accumulates in slow waves, in the form of ridges. A ridge reaches its maximum size in about 12 years, and once it is stable, wave action starts building the next. There are more than 400 ridges at Dungeness, each with its own vegetation, dependent on age and exposure. From the air, the system looks like the pattern of annual rings on a tree stump.

But, like all infertile wastelands, it has been systematically abused over the past century. Large-scale gravel digging began in the 1880s, and continues apace. The nuclear power station arrived in the sixties, and every year since, 20,000 tonnes of shingle, carried east by the tide, has had to be ferried back by lorry to shore up its foundations. More recently, sections of 2,000-year-old ridges have been bulldozed into oblivion to make futile sea-defences.

Against this background of permitted vandalism, Jarman's and Collins's gentle 'gardenising' seems not only innocuous but positively benign, and in the tradition of our long search for ways of being humanly creative that go *with* nature's grain. Heaven knows what early nature bureaucrats would have done with those loutish graffitists who defaced the walls of the Lascaux caves 20,000 years ago; or with the illegal Cretan immigrants who introduced nasty weeds, such as corn poppy, in the Stone Age.

I would be wholeheartedly in favour of Dungeness being conserved as a wilderness. It is an immense memory-bank of the ways the thin, living skin of the Earth goes on evolving. But while massive institutional looting and abuse continue to be tolerated, we need Prospect Cottage as a reminder of more harmonious ways of living with wild places.

1995

GUY TAPLIN

Michael Palin, Uri Geller and the Queen all have his sculptures in their collections. One of his prototype images – the wader on a stick – has been copied by wood-whittlers in every tourist town in Britain. It's reasonable to suggest that Guy Taplin is now the best-known nature sculptor in the country. But that makes his work sound too safe, too easy on the eye. When I first saw some of his carved birds, maybe 25 years ago, what struck me was their haunting fleetingness. Carved mainly out of driftwood, his swans and divers seemed to have materialised out of the sea. Their necks arched like wave crests, they huddled in tight, sinuous flocks and seemed on the point not of flight, but of turning back into water.

I thought of his sculptures when I was walking the north Norfolk coast a few winters back, after a ferocious storm. The tideline was deep in flotsam and dead birds, and here and there, caught up among the wreckage of wood and net and fish-egg cases, was a perfectly preserved eider duck, as pink and shiny as if it had just been hatched. And that, I thought then, was how Guy Taplin's work seemed to me. As if it had been cast up by the waves, fully fledged. I imagined him seeing birds in the bits of wood he collected, releasing them from the rigid planks in which they were trapped. My image of him was pretty well trapped, too.

I visited Guy in the middle of the July heatwave, at his home in the Essex coastal town of Wivenhoe. 'Look for the two giant green buoys outside,' he'd said. When he opened the door his first words were, 'You don't look a bit like I imagined.' Both of us had preformed pictures in our minds. The house was like an ark, stuffed with bits of boats, old tools, half-decaying bird carcasses. And as we talked, my preconception of him as the introspective romantic began to dissolve, and the one-time East End Jack the Lad – and pretty much Jack of all trades – began to emerge. He told me how he had begun – the evacuation to Herefordshire during the last war, how the passion for birds had gripped him there, and later, back in Epping Forest. He had no formal art education, but an extraordinary procession of jobs: lifeguard, hairdresser, cook, street trader, which led, in the Swinging Sixties, to a brief spell of fame, making ornate belts and selling them to the fashionable. When that bubble burst, he took a job looking after the collection of waterbirds in Regent's Park. It was here that – still more the market hustler than the nature artist – he began to try his hand at carving birds, aping the decoy ducks he'd admired on Camden antique stalls. He used any distressed timber he could pick up for free: Thameside driftwood, railway sleepers, glasshouse frames. Gradually, his birds began to attract attention, and Guy began to reflect on what he was doing. He realised that the raw materials he'd chosen chiefly for convenience had a huge potential for conveying a sense of wildness and weathering, and – something that had possessed him since he was a child – the *endurance* of nature.

I asked him which comes first, the wood or the bird. It is no contest. His head is full of images of birds, and of his own feelings about them: their dignity, their exultation, their comedy. He searches for wood through which he can express these feelings. Looking at some of his pieces with him, I can see this process working. In the best sense they are caricatures, the literal shapes of the birds distorted to emphasise characteristics he feels most touched by. His *Small Old Shorebird* gazes into the distance, its plumage a lacework of bleached grain-marks. *Flying Tawny Owl* is a fantasy of an owl gazing back at a mouse it carries on its tail. Recently he has been constructing whole groups of waders, in which the mesh of bodies and bills – roosting, preening, gazing skywards – is both architecturally beautiful and suggestive of richly interdependent lives.

We travel down to his 'outdoor' studio, a ramshackle bungalow on the edge of the Blackwater Estuary. Gazing over the mudflats, he spots a common sandpiper passing through. I talk about an issue that preoccupies us nature writers: should artists aspire to be 'transparent', allowing their subjects to shine through them? He sees the question rather differently. His subject isn't the bird-in-itself, but the bird-in-his-feelings. No wonder, perhaps, that he has always been moved by stories of epic migrations. His own journey through life has been far from easy, and what he is celebrating in his sculpture is not simply birds but the challenges and triumphs common to all living things.

2006

A 'MIRROR UP TO NATURE'?

It was the first real day of summer, and a long drive and an art exhibition weren't exactly top of my list of priorities. But meandering through high Suffolk, and then the Artists for Nature in Extremadura show at Lavenham, was a journey through different visual worlds, and a true eye-opener. The exhibition opened on a day when the temperature was, providentially, the same as in central Spain, and the Suffolk villages had unfurled like magnolia buds in the sunshine. The first climbing roses were splashing the timber and plaster cottages with chrome yellow. Martins and swallows were dipping over the roads. And people walked about the streets looking bemusedly at their shadows, as if they were unfamiliar shapes.

Then, inside the Wildlife Art Gallery, these glimpses of the power of light were refracted one stage further, as the works of a group of distinguished wildlife artists showed their heads had been turned by the sun. There were patches of pure impressionist colour, surreally stretched birds, sharp cubist edges and blocks of shadow. It was like taking a crash course in why the Mediterranean had been the crucible of modern art.

To be honest, there may have been a mite of subjective bias in my reactions. With a few friends I'd spent an enchanted week in Extremadura in January. Even in the short, damp days of winter it had seemed as luminously foreign as Australia. All of us – ignobly, given what England was like outside – gazed wistfully at Robert Greenhalf's exultant picture of the medieval town of Trujillo, where we'd stayed, knowing that at that very moment its skies would be teeming with lesser kestrels, storks and hoopoes.

But the paintings were, well, metamorphic – their perspectives transformed in the way that rocks are in fierce heat. Even the more naturalistic works seemed to echo the sheer revelling in colour and form that began to erupt in southern Europe late last century. David Barker's evergreen oaks, stretching across the vast plain (Extremadura's unique *dehesa*), were like pointillist shadows against the ochre soil. In a watercolour by Lars Jonsson, a greater spotted cuckoo seemed to grow out of the impressionist dapple of olive-tree foliage. (Is camou-flage nature's impressionism?) As for hoopoes, their gypsy plumage made them every artist's favourite. One watercolour by Michael Warren was like a piece of magic realism by Rousseau. The hoopoe sits heraldic in a fig tree, against a *dehesa* changed in the sunset to the same russet and cinnamon tones.

But it was David Measures who seemed the most transformed. I've long admired David's work. He paints in the field and is used to brush-marks freezing on the paper in winter. In the heat of an Extremaduran April, another kind of solidity came into his work. In *The Last Painting Before Supper*, the olive trees were massive and sculptural, like standing stones. And 'behind the darkening triangles of the tree boles light shone on the white walls of the farmhouse, soon to become the centre of bustle over tapas and wine.' Continu-ity and vitality: how wonderful that one of the most ancient and threatened landscapes in Europe should, once again, be seen with renewing eyes.

1996

* * *

Last autumn I had the privilege of giving away the prizes at the Society of Wildlife Artists' annual exhibition. I should have been one of the judges, too, but was blocked, rather aptly, by an Act of Nature: a huge tree had fallen across the railway line to London. But I wouldn't have disagreed with the rest of the panel's choices or with their strategic decision to encourage the broadening of wildlife art's palette beyond the tradition of strict representation. It's always seemed curious to me that animal painting went down this route at almost exactly the same time as photography was developing, as if the artists saw this technological innovation as something to rival rather than bypass. In fact the existence of wildlife art as a specialism, outside mainstream painting and sculpture, is odd in itself, given the fact that it was mainstream for many centuries, and that other specialisms, such as historic art and portraiture, still are.

But there's no doubt the artists are now branching out. The show was truly spectacular, a huge advance in variety and scope and style compared with previous years. Fine representational painting was still there but joined now by impressionism, Dadaist sculpture and even a few leanings towards cubism. Top prize in the show went to Harriet Mead's *Sea Turtle*, made entirely out of scrap metal, with a tractor seat forming the basis of the shell. The gravity and power these materials gave to the piece were palpable, as was the irony suggested by the use of rubbish to portray a creature so threatened by coastal development. Kim Atkinson's underwater fantasies, *Corallines*, *Snakelocks* and various spider crabs, eelgrass and algae, were all biologically correct, but done in such deep and intense colour, and with such extraordinary perspectives, that they looked like organisms from another world – which, in a way, they are. Paul Bartlett's *Golden Plovers over Tiree*, done in cut-out scraps of paper which perfectly captured the angularity of the birds' flight, could have been an early Matisse; Matt Underwood's *Over Willowherb and Teasel* was oil and canvas laid on board, but was as luminous as stained glass and echoed the Art Nouveau paintings of Charles Rennie Mackintosh. I liked Carl Ellis's delicate, impressionist pastels of fish, and the mesmeric oils of a young newcomer, Esther Tyson. Her *Toads, the Towey*, a mysterious evocation of two muted creatures lost in a world of broad-brushed weeds and water swirls, was as close to abstraction as anything in the exhibition.

But this is far from the first time that there has been an explosion of new approaches and ideas in the portrayal of other life-forms. By coincidence, a remarkable new book came out just after the show. Diana Donald's *Picturing Animals in Britain, 1750-1850* (Yale University Press) explores how the intellectual upheavals of those hundred years – the Enlightenment's new confidence in humans' God-given superiority dashed by the geologist Charles Lyell's revelations about the age of the Earth, and then by Darwin's theory of evolution – profoundly influenced the style and subjects of animal painting.

Perhaps the most famous and unsettling painting of any kind from that period is an animal picture. Joseph Wright's *An Experiment on a Bird in the Air Pump* (1769) is like a world-turned-upside-down nativity scene. In a darkened room, a group of people are clustered around a Magus-like scientist conjuring with the life and death of a cockatoo in a vacuum pump. The bird struggles for breath, the men gaze in fascination, the girl whose pet the bird may be shields her eyes. There is ambivalence right through the picture. Is the scientist – who is looking straight out at the viewer – suffocating the bird or letting in more air to revive it? Which does the artist sympathise with, the thirst for knowledge or the compassion for 'brute creation'?

Donald's book – unusual in that it combines dazzling scholarship with real passion – shows that ambivalence (and downright double standards at times) was widespread in human attitudes towards animals, often inside the same artist. George Stubbs is best known for his exquisite celebrations of the horse and, in pictures like *A Lion Devouring a Horse*, for contrasting the 'cultured' animal with the savagery of the wild thing. Yet, a decade later, he was painting studies of leopards which portrayed them as dignified animals with independent and worthwhile lives.

Narrative animal paintings, in this 18th-century sense, are one kind of thing we're unlikely to see in a modern exhibition. I think we might find them sentimental and embarrassing, accustomed as we are to seeing such subjects covered 'authentically' in documentary photographs. Yet I confess I'd be fascinated to see artists exploring the tricky emotional territory of human-animal relationships, to see what bird-painter Robert Gillmor might make of the birds of prey in an aviary, say; or, for that matter, how Damien Hirst might see a living shark.

2008

6. WORDS

Writers on nature – the column's first subject.

GILBERT WHITE

Midsummer, 1783, Selborne: 'Great honey-dew, blue mist, rusty gleams ... The sun "shorn of his beams", appears thro' the haze like the full moon.' Gilbert White's daily notes on the turbulent weather in late 18th-century Hampshire are a caution and a consolation. Read them when you're overwhelmed by the thought of global warming, or despondent in an overdue spring, and you'll find the comfort of glimpsing continuity in change. Through his prismatic gaze, in phrases as spare and resonant as haiku, weather becomes something tangible, familiar, a drama we have all experienced, or will experience. Life goes on, and round.

The events of that June and July were the results of a massive volcanic eruption in Iceland, though White was unaware of this. What was important for him was how they were expressed in the vivid and intimate nuances of life in his home village: 'The sun, at noon ... shed a rust-coloured light on the ground, and floors of rooms ... All the time the heat was so intense that butcher's meat could hardly be eaten on the day after it was killed.'

I was down in Selborne myself this spring, helping to make a documentary on White's life with Michael Wood, and wondering if there was anything new to be said about him. His classic book, *The Natural History of Selborne,* first published in 1789, is the first and most important text in the literature of nature, and marks the true beginning of ecological thinking. On the surface, it's a guileless collection of letters about migration, the musicality of owls, the beauty of beech trees and the intricacy of insects' nests. But the setting is crucial: 'Selborne' is a whole ecosystem, a community of all beings, in which the crickets are as deserving of respect and attention as the curate. And its language is as ecologically connected as its thinking, with the metaphors and symbols constructed out of the real stuff of the community's life – just as they are in White's graphic accounts of the weather.

We'd started our filming in Selborne's hollow lanes, which are one of the central motifs in White's writing, and symbolic, I think, of his whole relationship with the local landscape. These sunken track-ways, worn deep into the sandstone by 'the traffic of ages, and the fretting of water', both defined and limited the parish. In winter they could become choked with snow, then flooded, effectively cutting the village off. Outsiders who did succeed in tunnelling their way through complained that for the last two miles they felt they were travelling underground. The sunken lanes were partly responsible for White's sense of isolation from the intellectual life of his time (he was additionally cursed with coachsickness) and for the correspon-dence he began in compensation. Yet they fascinated him, too. They were a metaphor for the vitality of nature, physical records of the past history and everyday experience of the parish. He marvelled at 'their grotesque and wild appearances, from the tangled roots that are twisted among the strata, and from the torrents rushing down their broken sides ...'

That March day, what had once been the main coach road out of the village looked much as White had described it. Six metres deep, the hollow way was a chasm, chaotic with splintered stone, ash-root stalactites and great curtains of half a dozen species of fern. And at the bottom, flowing among the first golden saxifrage flowers, was a torrent, with its own dams and miniature waterfalls. It was easy to understand how White, not able easily to get out of the village, chose instead to burrow deep into it.

I first became properly acquainted with *The Natural History* in the 1970s, and each decade since I've found some new meaning in it, some fresh allusions in the language, some unexpected glimpses of the way that White unassumingly works his own life-challenges into his descriptions of other creatures. Virginia Woolf likened the book, with its foreground setting of the village and teeming cast of char-acters of all species, to a novel. But increasingly it seems to me like a play, a drama of remarkable scenes – a raven dashed to death by a falling tree, house martins building as ingeniously as human archi-tects – of almost Shakespearean resonance.

No wonder then, as with all great drama, that every generation finds its own meanings in the text. Or that the latest tribute to White

– Verlyn Klinkenborg's brilliant and audacious *Timothy; or, Notes of an Abject Reptile* – should move on from anthropocentrism and see White through the eyes of his pet tortoise. 'I dig and dig … As deep as I can go into the warmth of the earth, carefully overlaid with autumn's debris. Anchored. Immured. Landlocked. Becalmed and buoyed in the doldrums of Selborne.'

2006

* * *

Three species of hirondelle live with us at the farmhouse. House martins nest within sight of the bath. Swifts are in the loft, just above my bedroom. Swallows use the outbuildings, especially a long shed in which there is a prime site on top of a brick column. I hope I won't offend ornithologists by grouping these disparate families together, but in any taxonomy that goes beyond pure physical structure and evolutionary history, these birds belong to a single tribe: they're summer house-guests, *Domesticus aestivalis.*

The most beautifully observed account of the hirondelles' summer lease is in Gilbert White's *The Natural History of Selborne,* and I had cause to think a lot about his four essays (he includes sand martins as well) just weeks before our own birds returned. Back in January 1990, when the 1,500-year-old yew tree in Selborne was blown down in a gale, I'd acquired a few cuttings off one of the main branches. The piece I'd kept for myself had languished in the garage for 13 years, waiting, so I told myself, for 'the right carver'. But I'd given another to my Norfolk friends David Cobham and Liza Goddard, and they found a master craftsman to make it into a bowl.

Mathew Warwick hadn't used the yew-wood for the body of the bowl, but had inlaid a collection of White's favourite creatures in exquisite yew veneer. Yew, Mathew explained, is just too shaky to accept large-scale turning or carving. So we got to talking about what he might do with my chunk, and he thought about the signature of his work – the hidden motif, the tiny acorn secreted in the oak box.

He imagined opening up the yew log like an oyster, exploring the internal landscape of splits and crevices, and how creatures might be carved *inside* this labyrinthine habitat.

Behind his vision was the sympathy he felt for White's refusal to dismiss the idea of hirondelles spending the winter in bushes or at the bottom of ponds, rather than migrating. I'd always been convinced that this seeming chink in White's scientific objectivity was an expression of the sadness he felt (and we share) at the thought of these birds leaving at the end of summer. But Mathew had a deeper view. He saw the idea of underwater hibernation as a deep common feeling, a genuine myth of shelter and dwelling.

Having studied White for 20 years, I thought I knew him, but I was brought up short by the notion that he might have been – consciously or not – writing allegories as well as sensitive natural history. Read like this, the hirondelle essays, first presented as papers before the Royal Society in 1774-5 and among the most remarkable writing of the 18th century, are transformed. White's 'minute' watching is faultless; but the essays aren't scientific in any formal sense of the word. They're disorganised, anecdotal and fanciful – and, once you're looking for it, seem absolutely like allegories of some of the great themes of all lives, and especially the life of the middle-aged bachelor, trying to maintain his flights of imagination and restless curiosity in an isolated village.

Each bird seems to highlight one of these themes for White, who writes as if they were on his mind and *focusing* the factual details. The house martin is a story of livelihood, of a proper balance between work and play. (It could have been written by William Morris.) White spends half the essay describing the work of these 'industrious artificers', who 'are at their labours in the long days before four in the morning ... by building only in the morning, and dedicating the rest of the day to food and amusement, give the nest sufficient time to dry and harden'.

The swallows' tale is of family life, the thing White never had. He talks about how the young are brought up with 'great assiduity,' of the mother's 'unwearied industry and affection' as she defends them from birds of prey, and how she feeds them on the wing: 'At a certain signal, the dam and nestling advance, rising towards each other, and meet at an angle; the young one all the while uttering such a little quick note of gratitude and complacency.' The sand martin is the unfamiliar hirondelle, 'never seen in the village ... disclaiming all domestic attachments'. It is a secret creature, terebrating deep burrows, raising its young in the dark, unvocal and unsociable. Its tale hints at the mystery of nature.

It is the swift that is White's true familiar. He celebrates its festive assemblies and life spent almost wholly on the wing. This is an allegory about another kind of 'otherness', the wildness of nature and the freedom White missed in Selborne, lacking like-minded neighbours and cursed by coachsickness. 'Just before they retire, whole groups of them assemble high in the air and squeak and shoot about with wonderful rapidity.'

The idea of the birds hibernating, which White hints at in each of the essays, is scientific nonsense. But as a myth, as a truth about our feelings for the birds, it is just as solid a fact as swifts dozing on the wing, beyond our sight.

2003

JOHN CLARE

John Clare, England's finest nature poet, has at last been admitted into the literary pantheon. On 13 June, two centuries after he was born into an agricultural labouring family in Northamptonshire, a memorial stone in his honour was laid in Westminster Abbey's Poet's Corner.

It was the kind of ceremony Clare might have enjoyed, solemn and sensuous all at once. Ronald Blythe, one of the chief champions of the memorial scheme, talked of Clare's enthralment by his tiny world of Helpston, and of his 'extraordinary ability to see furthest when the view was strictly limited'. Two pupils from the John Clare School at Helpston laid a posy of local wildflowers. Then Ted Hughes read, in an oak-bark voice that echoed round the abbey, from *The Nightingale's Nest*, Clare's minutely charted search for a 'spot of happiness', in which he becomes a creature of the copse himself:

> *All seemed as hidden as a thought unborn.*
> *And where those crimping fern-leaves ramp among*
> *The hazel's under boughs, I've nestled down,*
> *And watched her while she sung …*

The reasons behind Clare's long exile to the margins of 'serious' writing are, in a way, as revealing as the poetry itself. His contemporary patrons adored him – just so long as he played the bumpkin minstrel, and didn't stray (as he often did) into political or social comment. Even in recent years there have been patronising critics who have seen him as nothing more than an amusing primitive.

But Clare's vivid use of vernacular language and the rooting of his poems in the commonplace particulars of his native landscape – both reasons for some of the condescension he has suffered – weren't the clumsy shortcomings of a simpleton. They were a desperate last-ditch defence of the one world that he really knew, which was being destroyed by Enclosure and 'improvement' before his eyes.

Clare's prose isn't as memorable as his poetry. Yet it does show that, far from being blessed (or imprisoned) by an 'innocent eye', he was well-read, discriminating and adept at choosing *how* he wrote. His detailed critique of Elizabeth Kent's *Flora Domestica,* issued by his own publishers in 1823, is a deliciously authoritative footnote from the grass-roots. For example: '*Cardamine* this is called lilac with us as well as "ladysmock" but I never heard it called cuckoo in my life except then by books – what the common people call 'cuckoo' with us is one which is a species of "Orchis" … the vulgar are always the best glossary to such things.'

Clare gave detailed notes and locations for 16 species of orchid in Helpston, and was responsible for adding to the Northants lists 65 first county records for birds and 40 for plants. These last figures are the more remarkable when you consider that they were worked out retrospectively from his poems, and are backed up by nothing more substantial than the absolute conviction his verse carries of being based on personal experience. His work could be usefully studied by the new generation of lyricists now massing in the Green corner. Vague elegies for 'the forest', however well-meaning, are nothing beside Clare's mordant and savagely precise attacks on the despoilers of 'Langley bush … and round oaks narrow lane'.

1989

* * *

This summer marked the bicentenary of the birth of John Clare, one of the most important writers of the Romantic era. It ought, by rights, to have been the occasion for some kind of national celebration, but it passed with barely a whisper: no new biographies, no major conferences, not even a single national broadcast devoted to his work.

I don't believe there is any lingering snobbishness towards his work in the literary establishment. But it has an urgent, untidy vitality that has always challenged formal criticism. Clare fought all his life to keep his unique, indigenous voice against pressures to write 'standard' poetic English, or innocuous mummerset, both of which he saw as cages. Yet he could write reasoned, even scientific, prose when he felt it was appropriate. And, much like Gilbert White (who, by one of those odd coincidences of history, died just 17 days before Clare was born), he was fascinated by the relationship between moment and place. Both men wrestled with the problems of catching in words that relationship, and how it expressed their growing intimacy with their native spots.

For White, the answer lay chiefly in his journals, which he kept up daily for nearly 40 years. They are a model of their kind, a remarkable amalgam of scrupulous observation and inspired, imaginative insight. At least twice a day he recorded the temperature, pressure and wind direction. More casually, he noted flowerings and fruitings, and the comings and goings of migrant birds. Yet the column in his journal which was headed 'Miscellaneous Observations' was increasingly

filled with diversions, little meditations on the seasons, spare minia-
tures that could catch the flavour of a whole day in just a few words:

20 July (1778) 'Much thunder. Some people in the village were
struck down by the storm, but not hurt. The stroke seemed to them
like a violent push or shove. The ground is well soaked. Wheat much
lodged. Frogs migrate from ponds.'

29 July (1777) 'The bricklayers are much interrupted by the rains.
Much hay quite rotten. This morning more than 50 swifts sailed
slowly over the village towards the S: there were almost double the
number that belong to this place; & were probably actuated by some
tendency towards their retreat, which is now near at hand.'

Entries like these have a sense of occasion about them. They are
snatches of the kind of stories and gossip that circulate continuously
in small communities, and which, by playing the humdrum against
the exceptional, natural crisis against seasonal round, become
memorable scenes of parish drama.

Clare, when he was encouraged by his publishers to try to put
together a book like White's *Natural History of Selborne,* also kept a
journal for a while:

9 Sept 1824 'Took a pleasant walk today in the fields but felt too
weak to keep out long tis the first day of shooting with the sportsmen
& the poor hares partridges & pheasants were flying in all directions
panic struck they put me in mind of the inhabitants of a Village
flying before an invading enemy.'

Clare's journal has his customary openness and penetrating eye,
but is really just a diary, with little of the flavour of his home parish
or of the seasons. It is his poems that make up his true journal.
Jotted down as they poured into his head, on the backs of sugar
packets and old bills, in unpunctuated, present-tense phrases ramp-
ing with dialect, they have an electrifying quality of presence, of
'being' about them.

Clare walks out '& swing my stick for joy & catch at little pictures
passing bye'. He searches for a lapwing's nest in the early morning, over
'a burnt flat all bleaching brown & bare,' while 'veering overhead/ The
Pewet whirred in many whewing rings.' On Emmonsails Heath on a

winter's day he listens while 'The fieldfare chatters in the whistling thorn/ & for the awe round fields and closen rove/ & coy bumbarrels [long-tailed tits] twenty in a drove/ Flit down the hedgrows in the frozen plain/ & hang on little twigs & start again.' And he ponders on a ladybird in spring: 'In the cowslips peeps I lye/ Hidden from the buzzing fly/ While green grass beneath me lies/ Pearled wi' dew like fishes eyes/ Here I lie a Cock-a-clay/ Waiting for the time o'day.'

People write diaries for many reasons, to put a brake on time, to excuse or aggrandise themselves, to keep a kind of intellectual ledger in which they may glimpse some pattern in the normal muddle of their existence. Nature journals are perhaps more often kept as scientific and historical records, but they too can reveal – to both writer and reader – the diarist's preoccupations, and the way they interact with the natural round.

What is common to all good journals is the sense of being unexpectedly 'caught', or 'struck' (as White's storm-bound villagers were) by events. In these sharp-focused, affective moments we can indulge associations and resonances that would seem extravagant in premeditated prose. John Clare's 'Cock-a-clay' lying in 'the cowslips peeps' may be a ladybird, but it is also, of course, Clare himself, cosseted by the native landscape to which he was so passionately in thrall, and in which he still seems embedded.

1993

Clare's journals and non-fiction have been collected in The Natural History Prose Writings of John Clare, *ed Margaret Grainger (Oxford University Press,1983), and* John Clare by Himself *(Fyfield Books, 1996). [2009]*

SHAKESPEARE'S PLANTS

The end of summer makes many of us pine for that 'bank whereon the wild thyme blows' from Shakespeare's *A Midsummer Night's Dream*. It's our fantasy of a summer retreat – balmy, intoxicating, seductive. But was it ever more than wishful thinking? Seasonal stagings of the play are a legendary gauntlet thrown down at the vagaries of the English weather, which regularly responds by turning the midnight revels into a mud bath. 'Why is your cheek so pale', Lysander dares to ask Helena near the start of the play, and – I've seen it happen – the heavens open just as she answers 'Belike for want of rain'. Maybe it was ever thus. The weather during the close of the 1590s, when the *Dream* was conceived, was cold and dismal. Is the play's rhapsody of gilded evenings and flowery arbours partly our national poet's pining for 'summers like they used to be'?

I've rediscovered Shakespeare recently, helping with advice on the new production of the *Dream* at Stratford, and it's made me understand properly what a remarkable observer of nature the playwright was, and what a maker of myths. He would have learned the Elizabethan art of 'lively turning' at school, which involved taking a story, a superstition, a season's weather, a real-life place, and giving it new life with the inventiveness of your imagination.

The bank where Titania, Queen of the Fairies, sleeps is just such a 'turning'. It's a metaphor, but for what? The flowers are real English species (though the play is set in Athens) but never grow together, either in time or place. What they have in common is high, powerful scents. Wild thyme is spicy, and in Gerard's *Herbal,* published the year after the *Dream*'s first performance, is spelt 'Wild Time'. Violets are among the sweetest of all wildflowers, and are associated with both love and death. Woodbine is honeysuckle, whose flowers are most powerfully scented at night. Eglantine is the sweet-briar, the wild rose whose leaves smell enchantingly of apple, especially after rain. Musk rose speaks for itself. None of these plants was literally aphrodisiac – what Elizabethan herbalists called 'venereous' – but their seductive scents were more likely to stir Titania up than 'lull' her. She was chasing 'dances and delights' more than a good night's sleep.

Only the oxlip seems out of place, being neither scented nor symbolic. This isn't the botanist's oxlip (*Primula elatior* was not recognised in Shakespeare's day) but the widespread hybrid between the primrose and the cowslip. Might it have been a coded joke? The play was supposedly written in honour of the marriage of one of Shakespeare's patrons, and it may have been a nickname for him – or a much cruder reference to his betrothed. Yet Shakespeare was a poet, in thrall to words, and a more likely explanation is that oxlip added to the wonderful belling of Ls in his litany: wild, violet, luscious, eglantine, lull'd; the Ls of love and lust. He rounds it off with the erotic image of a shed snakeskin, lying 'enamell'd' on the bank.

The real botanical hero of the book is the wild pansy – 'love-in-idleness' in the playwright's own county of Warwickshire – whose juice, squeezed by Puck into the hapless characters' eyes to make them love the next creature they see, is the engine for all the mischief in the *Dream* – including Titania's crush on Bottom wearing his donkey's head. The pansy is also known as 'heartsease', and as 'three-faces-under-one-hood', perhaps because of the way its three lower petals suggested a woman flanked by two lovers; a flower representing frustrated, useless, 'idle' love. I suspect that Shakespeare simply made up the juice-in-eye spell as a bit of comic business. It has no roots whatever in folklore But his knowledge of the vernacular names and folklore of plants is remarkable, and he makes wonderful, layered puns with them.

What strikes me about Titania's bank is its 'otherness'. It's an enchanted land. Oberon's phrase, ' I know a bank where the wild thyme blows,' flags up its meaning. It is simply there, secret, unplanted, untended, transcending time and place, a powerful emblem of wild nature. This perhaps is one of the themes of the play: the restless, chaotic, comic energy of nature. It's set in a forest, almost always in Shakespeare a place where society's laws and conventions could be turned upside down.

In this sense Shakespeare was a 'natural' writer himself, an instinctive, allusive, unpredictable free-thinker as well as a scrupulous craftsman. Try it for yourself. Forget school English lesson prejudices, and read him as a romantic nature poet, conjuring together real, exact images of the living world with our dreams and fancies, and telling us much about our own nature in the process.

2005

KEATS'S 'ODE TO A NIGHTINGALE'

The two-hundredth anniversary of John Keats's birth occurred just a few weeks after two of his verses – *To Autumn* and *Ode to a Nightingale* – made it into the nation's top 10 poems in National Poetry Week. He was the only writer to get a double-entry, with what are both notionally 'nature' poems. But was he a nature writer in any meaningful sense of the word? John Clare, who unquestion-ably was, complained in a letter that, 'as is the case with other inhab-itants of great citys he [Keats] often described nature as she … appeared to his fancys and not as he would have described her if he had witnessed the things he describes …'

The ode isn't *about* a nightingale, in the manner of Clare's own extraordinary song of solidarity (*The Nightingale's Nest*, 1832) or Coleridge's 'conversation poem' (1798), which was the first since the medieval period to paint the bird as a symbol of freedom and joyful-ness rather than a mournful familiar of the lovesick. Keats's ode is a more complicated affair. It is one of the most penetrating poems on the *meaning* of nature to us; a meditation on mortality and continuity, and on the way the gift of consciousness can blight our experience of 'the natural' by making us too aware of its earthly limits. Yet, it was also prompted by the song of a real nightingale that had taken up resi-dence in the Hampstead garden where Keats was lodging in April 1819.

We have to understand Keats's situation that fateful year. His brother George had emigrated to America the previous summer and been ruined. His other brother Tom had died of TB before Christ-mas, aged just 19. Keats knew he was suffering from the incurable disease himself, yet had fallen in love – a hopeless, futureless love – with 18-year-old Fanny Brawne, who was living in the other half of Wentworth Place.

Then something quite mundane and wonderfully English happens: the weather changes. In the middle of April one of the great springs of the early 19th century begins, and on the last day of the month Keats goes out into the garden of Wentworth Place and sits under the plum tree. Fanny Brawne is a wall's thickness away. The nightingale is singing – that flamboyant, oratorical song, whose character relies so much on its pauses – and the pools of silence are too tempting for an introspective like Keats. Soon, he is sinking into them – and into a reverie on all that he has felt this spring.

He thinks of the nightingale's true home in the South, and yearns for that taste 'of Flora ... dance, Provencal song and sunburnt mirth' that might just save his health, and make a future possible for him and Fanny. It might have saved his brother Tom, too, who had died 'pale, and spectre-thin'. All the while, the bird carols on, a messenger from the living, from a world untouched by 'weariness ... fever and ... fret'. For a while, Keats is half-tempted by 'easeful Death ... To cease upon the midnight with no pain,/ While thou art pouring forth thy soul abroad/ In such an ecstasy.' Then, in the triumphant penultimate verse, this surrender is rejected.

This small bird has survived for millennia; its song had buoyed up countless generations of the ill, the battle weary, the displaced, back into biblical times. The poet can hardly try for less. And in its three most famous and powerful lines, Keats has a Gaian glimpse of the oneness and continuity of life: 'Perhaps the self-same song that found a path/ Through the sad heart of Ruth, when, sick for home,/ She stood in tears amid the alien corn.' Then, abruptly, he comes round. The nightingale becomes a real flesh and blood bird again, and flies off, its song fading across the Heath.

For me, it is the contrast between these last two stanzas, between the 'immortal bird', whose song has provided a chain of common experience and inspiration down through history, and the real bird, set free, as it were, from fantasy to be as vulnerable as the poet, that gives the poem its remarkable charge of honesty and courage. It is a poem which makes common cause between two species, two singers; yet which also acknowledges the essential otherness of the natural world. It could hardly be more relevant to our own predicament, seeing ourselves both as part of and 'above' nature.

1996

FUTURE NATURE

Will Self's barnstorming new novel *The Book of Dave* is the first in what's likely to become a genre of its own: fantasies fuelled by climate change. The time is about five centuries on. Most of Britain lies under water, save for a few hilly areas like Brum, Cot and Chil. All that's left of Central London is an island called Ham, where the local peasants' lives are ruled by a bizarre religion based on the jottings of Dave, a demented 21st-century cabbie. Their technology is prehistoric – subsistence farming and epic raids on the seabirds that nest in the remains of the City's skyscrapers (stacks) – the 'oilgulls' (fulmars), 'prettybeaks' (puffins) and 'blackwings' (gannets). There's a local legend that if a climber falls from a stack he'll be rescued by a formation of seabirds called a choppa.

One of the intriguing subtexts in the book is Self's vision of a posturban ecology, and the myths and namings that a traumatised population, speaking a mash of Cockney and rap, might cling to. Munchjack for muntjac deer is as good as Iain Sinclair's monkjack (in his book *London Orbital* about the M25). Blisterweed is a plausible nickname for the giant hogweed which grows in thickets around the damp edges of the settlements – and indeed may already be in currency among city kids.

Is this the way that new names for the natural world spring up, from sharp storytellers with their ears to the ground? Self uses 'fireweed' for rosebay willowherb, a tag which is presumed to have emerged in London after the German bombing raids of 1940, when it spread like a purple haze across the rubble. Yet it's been current for willowherbs in North America for at least a century before that, from their habit of springing up on the sites of forest fires.

Is there a kind of folk logic in popular names, a fittingness that joins the lingo of the people who coin them with the lifestyle of the organism and the feel of the times? I've tried spreading 'wayfrost' as an alternative to the bland and cumbersome 'Danish scurvy-grass', for the crystalline sheets of white that cover the edges and central reservation of trunk roads in spring. But it has a slight air of preciousness, of being a deliberate literary invention. The best of the names that we uncovered during the making of *Flora Britannica* had a raw, authentic edge that has given them staying power. 'The Hog' for giant hogweed has stuck, where 'cartwheel plant' hasn't. 'Grey parsons' for grape hyacinth is widely used by everyone who enjoys the self-mocking humour in East Anglian dialect. 'Lawyers' for the entangling stems of bramble is enjoying a new lease of life in litigious Britain. And 'Sally rhubarb' and 'German sausage' for Japanese knotweed in Wales (where kids munch the young shoots) whiff of gangs of sharp-eyed youngsters with an ear for language. If we need scientific names so that we can all understand what's being talked about, we also need these tribal tags to chat among ourselves.

Last year, a remarkable list of vernacular British bird names came to light, collected by the late Richard Richardson. Richard was a distinguished artist and legendary birdwatcher, at whose feet, in north Norfolk's Cley, many of today's best-known birders learned their skills. He was also a compulsive gatherer of information, and apparently built up this list from chats he had with people all over Norfolk. It's full of telling tribal touches – plays with words, witty capturings of birds' jizz, a sense of the rhythm of local languages. There's 'leg-dangler' for corn bunting, 'saw-sharpener' for great tit, 'banjo-bill' for spoonbill, 'hedge monk' for dunnock, 'Francis' for heron, 'air-goat' for snipe, 'deeve-dipper' for little grebe, 'shoeing-horn' for avocet. But the most strikingly, slangily urban is 'big razor-grinder' for the nightjar. This fits to a T the bird that took up extraordinary residence in a suburban street in Teddington, south-west London, this baking summer. It churred from the top of telegraph poles, hawked moths round street lamps and mobbed people walking the pavements. It was a nightjar hoodie, a delinquent squatter in the wrong place – or maybe an omen of changing behaviour from global warming. The backstreet big razor-grinder was only a dozen miles from Will Self's Ham, and would have fitted perfectly, name included, into his dystopian tale.

2006

ROGER DEAKIN

I owe many kinds of personal thanks to Roger Deakin: for his optimism about the world, for his passion for Suffolk, for his simple generous friendship. I wouldn't be living in his own stretch of the Waveney Valley now, with its ramshackle string of commons and fens and furze patches, if he hadn't taken me under his wing during a low moment of my life.

All of us in the natural history world owe Roger a debt, not just for two luminous books, but for an immense network of enthusiasms and initiatives, of causes championed, corporations badgered, of essays, notes, letters, beautifully crafted radio meditations, elaborate green jokes. It was more than a network, it was a kind of imaginative ecosystem, bubbling with life and inventiveness, and its energy touched people way beyond Roger's own locality.

But he wasn't some fervent missionary for the wild. He simply lived out what he believed in, in a quiet but infectious way. Central to his beliefs was a love for the common, in all senses of the word. He was a co-founder of Common Ground, the charity devoted to the celebration of the commonplace in nature and landscape. He lived on the edge of the great common of Mellis, and fought passionately to preserve its openness and ordinariness – sometimes, when necessary, against overtidy conservationists. For him commonness – the blessing of continuity and abundance – and commonality – the sharing of land between fellow humans and their fellow creatures – were inextricably entwined, and the most precious, the most rare, of qualities.

We often exchanged little news bulletins about what was happening on our home patches, 4 miles apart: seemingly mundane things, like the arrival of the cuckoo, the state of the local bees, clouds of all kinds on the horizon. Occasionally I'd become overexcited about some prodigy, such as a flush of early marsh orchids in a thistly field, and Roger would respond, with the merest hint of a raised eyebrow, with a eulogy to buttercups. Once, his corrective, his tribute to nature's connectivity, was the September calling of tawny owls, 'answering each other all round Mellis, and I guess all the way to you in Roydon'. He was exceptionally well-read and knew perfectly well he was echoing the poet Edward Thomas's 'Adlestrop', with its vision of blackbirds singing, 'Farther and farther, all the birds/ Of Oxfordshire and Gloucestershire'.

His commitment to his home countryside was uncompromising. He'd restored his 16th-century farmhouse with his own hands, and it was his epicentre, his laboratory, his museum. Dwelling properly there – he would not have approved of any description as bossy as 'managing' it – was his major project, and took precedence over (though was intimately connected to) the writing. It was full of found stones, twigs from rivers, bizarre outdoor shoes and cobwebs whose sweeping into oblivion he regarded as an act of wanton destruction. Roger saw his spiders as more anciently entitled citizens of the farm than him, the newly settled guest. Outside was a madcap arcadia: hayfields gradually recovering their cowslips, raggle-taggle hedgerows, ancient cars driven into bushes and left there to form pergolas for brambles and foxes, new woodlets planted in concentric circles, shepherds' huts in which he often wrote and slept, wild roses grown from seed gathered in the Middle East, which alas he never saw flower.

Walnut Tree Farm was Roger's home, but not his limits. One of the standing jokes among his friends was that he had apparently been everywhere, done everything: run conservation projects in Africa, trekked with nomadic shepherds in the Greek mountains, trespassed in most of the desirable private wetlands in Britain. But the joke was on us: he had done these things. One of his last trips was to Kyrgyzstan, to live rough with the local tribes who camp out in the forest for the walnut and wild apple harvest, and he somehow smuggled home a sack of walnuts bigger than his luggage. He was quite fearless in his travels, believing that most beings were benign, and would respond to the philosophy of live and let live that he applied to all species.

I think Roger had an essentially comic (certainly un-tragic) view of creation, and felt he was part of a gleeful conspiracy of wild beings – spiders, badgers, climbing roses (which he used to cover anything he didn't like, rather than destroy it) – against the forces of oppression and order. His sense of humour was extraordinary. When Polly and I came to live near Diss, he sent us a welcome card, on which were mounted two empty honesty seedheads, and the caption: '*Lunaria annua* var Diss. VN: Diss Honesty. Originally rare and locally dist. Now widespread. Identify by: missing seeds.' His mischievous insect fantasy was to make an electronic organ based on the fact that crickets vary the pitch of their stridulations according to temperature. The crickets, encased in glass tubes, would be warmed and cooled by a keyboard control. None of this was simply whimsy. Roger saw playfulness as a common ground between humans and nature, one of the places the poetic mammal could find a harmonious niche.

His travels in central Asia were for his book *Wildwood: A journey through trees,* an account of meandering through the woods of three continents. It was almost finished when he fell ill, and his editor was able to prepare the book for publication before he died. It will come out – a wry masterpiece on the entanglements of the human and the natural – in June next year. Till then, we have *Waterlog* (1999), his now famous account of swimming through Britain. *Waterlog* is partly about access to water, but also about immersion. To go wild swimming is to join the most fundamental and fluent natural entity on the planet, and to understand one's place in it: 'The next day I met an otter in the Waveney. I swam round a bend in my favourite river in Suffolk and there it was, sunning itself on a floating log near the reed-bed. I would have valued a moment face to face, but it was too quick for that. It slipped into the water on the instant, the big paddle tail following through with such stealth that it left hardly a ripple. But I saw its white bib and the unmistakable bulk of the animal and I knew I had intruded into its territory.'

2006

JOHN FOWLES

John Fowles, who died in November last year, was best known as the author of half a dozen majestic novels, books in which philosophical ideas played as big a role as the characters. Less familiar was his life as a naturalist, a description he often preferred to 'writer'. He was a brilliant field-naturalist, an expert on European orchids and the minutiae of spiders and, for a long while, the curator of the museum at Lyme Regis with its extraordinary collection of 19th-century fossils. Most importantly he was a profound writer about nature, again with a preference for exploring ideas rather than living 'characters'.

His compass was set early. His father had been traumatised by his visions of chaos in the trenches of the First World War, and ran his ordered suburban garden as if he were a drill sergeant. Fowles, already instinctively drawn by the 'otherness' of nature, drifted under the wing of his uncle, who was a biology teacher. With him he learned to hunt for lappet moth caterpillars in sloe thickets, and how to 'sugar' fences. He recalls being entrusted with the larva of a death's-head hawkmoth, and stroking it obsessively to induce it to 'peep': 'a miracle, an insect that "spoke"!' More collecting followed, then a brief passion for shooting and fishing.

But his intelligence (as much as his conscience) couldn't long accommodate the contradictions inherent in the entrapment and killing of the wild beauty he loved. In *The Blinded Eye* he describes a critical moment in his conversion: a curlew winged during a duck shoot, screaming in the mud; a clumsy attempt to club it out of its misery; the gun exploding and almost taking Fowles foot off: 'I have not intentionally killed a bird or animal since.' Some years later, dozing on a hillside in Crete, he was suddenly aware of a lammergeier hanging in the air 20 feet above him. 'It looked like an enormous falcon, its great wings feathering and flexed to the wind current, a savage hooked beak tilted down at me. I lay as still as a stone, like Sinbad under the Roc ... What passed between me and that splendid bird in the azure Cretan sky was simply this: cage me, cage yourself.'

His increasing revulsion to the appropriation of nature, the enclosure of life, emerged as the theme of his first novel *The Collector*, in which a repressed clerk and butterfly collector traps, keeps prisoner and eventually kills an art student. Elsewhere he wrote: 'Always we try to put the wild in a cage: if not a literal cage of iron, then cages of banality, of false parallels, of anthropomorphic senti-mentality, of lazy thinking and lazy observation.' He saw this as the human species' indelible flaw, the obsession that lay behind our ravaging of the planet and behind the imprisonment of our own spirits. He railed against the enclosure and confinement of nature at all levels – by list-makers, photographers, even the makers of scien-tific names. He was, I think, constitutionally pessimistic, and at times almost misanthropic.

He loved above all other places the Undercliff, the almost impen-etrable wilderness of overgrown cliff-fall that runs between his home at Lyme and Axmouth: 'It looks almost as the world might have been if man had not evolved, so pure, so unspoilt, so untouched it is scarcely credible.' In his best-known novel, *The French Lieutenant's Woman*, he makes it the location where the lovers meet to escape the straitjacket of Victorian morality, and was, I suspect, rather gratified that, during the filming of the novel, the crew wore T-shirts with the slogan 'I hate the Undercliff'.

In the end he saw even writing itself as a 'pane of smoked glass' between us and nature. In his meditation on *The Tree*, he talks of how all experience of nature 'through surrogate and replica, through selected image, gardened word, through other eyes and minds, betrays or banishes its reality ... It can be known and entered only by each, and in its now.' Fowles's intense, analytical prose sometimes seems to confirm this verdict, not always permitting the joy and consolation he felt in nature to shine through. But convincing evidence that 'gardened words' can be a portal to the wild comes throughout his work, even just a few pages earlier in *The Tree*, where he gives a haunting portrait of the ancient, goblin Wistman's Wood on Dartmoor: 'It is the silence, the waitingness of the place, that is so haunting ... a drama, but of a time-span humanity cannot conceive. A pastness, a presentness, a skill with tenses the writer in me knows he will never know ...'

2006

Some of Fowles's essays on nature are collected in Wormholes *(Jonathan Cape, 1998). [2009]*

THE NEW NATURE WRITING

There is, at last, something of a renaissance in home-grown nature writing. And – no surprise, perhaps, after decades of derring-do and feigned masculine detachment – it's women who are leading the singing. Kathleen Jamie's *Findings* includes an essay on the breeding peregrines she can see from her attic window and a meditation of piercing intelligence and poignancy on the exhibits in a medical museum. In *Tigers in Red Weather*, Ruth Padel recounts her quest for William Blake's heroic beast, 'burning bright', as she seeks her own independence at the end of a love affair. And in her forthcoming *Echo Lands*, Geraldine Taylor weaves together her sparkling explorations of the Avon Gorge woods with memories of her son.

Each of these writers would, I think, be bemused by the suggestion that it is preferable – or even possible – to write about nature as if it were some objective reality, entirely separate from one's own life. We *are* involved, like it or not, part of the same inextricable web of life. Involved emotionally, too, however creditable we may think it is to deny those emotions in seeking the 'truth'. Even scientific observation involves the most intimate engagement with the natural world.

Yet there is a sharp edge to the argument for a dispassionate natural history that isn't so easily dismissed. Is it not possible that lyrical and imaginative writing – the kind that makes connections between natural and human emotional life – marks the greater exploitation, the more cynical manipulation of nature as an object? Science does at least attempt to describe and understand the natural world on its own terms. Romantic writing, by contrast, can seem to appropriate it as little more than a vehicle for human feelings and symbols. It turns nature into an emotional puppet theatre. In that ambivalent term it 'humanises' nature. In her peregrine essay Kathleen Jamie describes the bond between the male and female bird, who 'stand upright at a distance to each other, but linked with the heightened tension, almost, of flamenco dancers. That's it – the peregrines have *duende*.' It's a startling, illuminating metaphor. But does it too glibly incorporate peregrines into human culture? Does it tell us anything about the birds themselves? I believe it does. Like all great nature writing (as distinct from crude anthropomorphism), it searches for shared roots, for common ground, for a place that is neither pure bird nor pure human, but 'bird-in-the-world'.

Ronald Blythe's new book, *Borderland*, wouldn't normally be described as 'nature writing', but it absolutely fulfils this criterion of seeing all life as part of a single creation. Since *Akenfield*, his 1969 masterpiece about East Anglian rural life, Ronald Blythe has produced what his fellow writers regard as some of the most luminous and beautiful prose in the English language. *Borderland* is volume three of *The Wormingford Trilogy*, a series of reflections on life in his Essex village, which made their first appearance as a column in the *Church Times*. Their easy elegance and discursive style belie their wisdom and immense frame of reference. His life is lived, unself-consciously, in an arena of all species. Gardening, walking, writing, he senses other lives moving past and through him. In the spinney ('like dipping into a green bath') he has a dialogue with the nettles he is about to scythe. He talks of his cat's long walks to watch hares play, and is frustrated that he cannot explain to them that he means no harm. In the garden a darter alights on his book. 'The dragonfly's wings are colourless and translucent, and I can read Binchester and Yattendon through them, so no prizes for guessing what this book is.'

His reading and deep local knowledge bridge the centuries. The book spans the period of the Iraq War and the foot and mouth outbreak, and watching spring arrive in the midst of these self-inflicted catastrophes, he recalls how birdsong and primrose profusion affected with 'surprise and heartbreak' the soldiers on the Western Front. Watching a roadman spraying weedkiller on the ancient walls that appear in John Constable's *Nayland*, he remembers how the painter, gone to live in London, had to write to a Suffolk friend for a list of flowers in bloom in July, in which he was to set *The Cornfield*.

This is not nature as an ornament, nor as the object of fastidious study, but simply as a community of fellow beings. Nothing in it is inconsequential. As he wrote about his habit of night-walking in the first volume of the trilogy: 'Everywhere, it is all so perfectly interesting one might never go to bed.'

2005

7. ISSUES

Politics and passions.

RESERVATIONS

One of the saddest experiences I've had in East Anglia was going to the Open Day, a few years back, at the Framsden fritillary meadow. Even as late as the 1960s this was a glorious site, and the owner 'Queenie' Fox used to open it to the public in early May. 'A shilling – for our local Cancer Fund – and everyone can take home a bunch of flowers.' A few years later the meadow was sprayed with weedkiller, leaving only a few dormant fritillary corms surviving. It was made a reserve in 1978, and the public were allowed in for one day a year. But as wildflower festivals go, it was a depressing one, symbolic both of the changing status of the fritillary, and of the siege mentality inevitably associated with the idea of reserves. The few surviving flowers bloomed in a tangle of rank weeds in a roped-off enclosure, round which the visitors sombrely paraded, as if they were in a botanical zoo.

The most heartening experience may be yet to come. There is talk, behind closed doors, of something dramatic happening a few miles further east, on the Suffolk coast. Not a fencing-in or roping-off this time, nor some desperate defence of some shrinking ghetto, but a great opening out. The various landowners of the tangled stretch of heath, marsh and pine forest that extends from Walberswick in the north to Minsmere in the south are thinking about what might happen if they took all their fences down, put in an assortment of half-wild grazing animals, and then let nature take its course.

What are nature reserves for? Are they principally for the sake of their wild inhabitants or to provide inspiration for human visitors? Should they batten down the hatches around species already there, or open themselves up to the dynamic processes that are always striving to pulse through living systems? We would be in a sorry state without our reserves, but they are putting out some odd and often contradictory messages at the moment.

They are compromised most of all by their defensiveness. From the understandable desire to safeguard endangered species and habitats, reserves often become little more than arks, as separated from the wild as they are from the destructive forces of farming and development that made them necessary in the first place. Round-the-clock orchid security guards, the laboratory propagation and transplantation schemes of species recovery programmes, the intensive care necessary in just about every small wetland reserve in the UK as the surrounding landscape inexorably dries out – it is all heroic stuff, but has it anything to do with *wild life*? And every choice to protect one species or habitat type, means the dismissal of another. Coppicing ensures the survival of light-loving spring flowers but drives out the shade-lovers – a crucial component of wild woodland. Keeping heaths and fens open is beginning to make scrub a newly endangered habitat, along with all those marginal ecotones in which, in a natural system, one kind of habitat mutates into another. Change, the life-blood of nature, has become the major enemy in our embattled reserves.

Nor do the visitors to reserves have much in the way of wild experiences any more. Shepherded along board walks decreed by the safety culture, and told at every turn where to go, what to look for, sometimes what to feel about it, our chances for first-hand encounters, for getting lost up to our ears in a reedbed, for exploring free-range as we did as kids, are now negligible. Is this the message we want our reserves to give, that wildlife is already an inert museum specimen, to be served up logged, labelled and utterly predictable?

But then how could it ever be different in a tiny island, where maybe less than 5 per cent of the land surface has even the remotest pretence of wildness? The problems of most nature reserves are chiefly attributable to size, to the minuteness of the token islands that they represent. But big reserves are different. They can afford to be relaxed, even to make mistakes. A big wood can accommodate coppice and high forest. A huge marsh can cope with cyclical succession, drying out and turning to wood in one corner, being flooded by the sea in another. Rare species can migrate, as habitats shift around them. Even the public can be given their heads.

With the great changes in farming that are imminent, opportunities for these large-scale reserves has suddenly become a reality. The conservation movement must seize the moment and go on the offensive. Then we might, at long last, have reserves for *naturalness* ('future naturalness' as George Peterken once called it), not just for species and specialised habitats.

2005

NATURE: THE NEW PROZAC?

There's been much discussion recently about encounters with nature being good for your health – physical and psychological. Having already become the new rock 'n' roll, nature seems poised to become the new complementary medicine. But it's not new, really. The idea that you can be mended by the healing currents of the green outdoors, by engaging with rhythms and ways of life different from your own, goes back to classical times. The Greeks had healing groves. The Romans recommended rambling as a way of resolving emotional tangles: *solvitur ambulando* – 'you can work it out by walking'. 'The country, by the gentleness and variety of its land-scapes,' wrote the 20th-century French philosopher Michel Foucault, 'wins melancholics from their single obsession, by taking them away from the places that might revive the memory of their sufferings.'

Now there are statistics to back up this ancient common sense. Jules Pretty, from Essex University, has reviewed hundreds of studies which seem to prove that the merest glimpse of a growing thing does you good ('How Nature Contributes to Mental and Physical Health', *Spirituality and Health International*, vol. 5, issue 2). A study in Michigan found that prisoners whose cells faced farmland and trees had a 24 per cent lower frequency of sickness visits than those in cells facing the prison yard. Surrogate experiences are just as effective. Patients preparing for bronchoscopies were given a landscape painting by their bedside, and tapes of birdsong. They had '50 per cent higher levels of good or excellent pain control than those who did not have the picture or sounds'. Even people commuting to work by car have measurably lower levels of stress when they drive through 'nature-dominated scenes' than when the surroundings are 'dominated by human artefacts'.

Once you are actually out and about in the green, the benefits become even more significant. 'Wilderness therapy' for disturbed young people (recently featured in a C4 reality show) has an impressive record, though it's not clear just what part of the experience does the healing. It's plainly not just 'fresh air and exercise'. One of the pioneer researchers in this field, Terry Hartig, has found that walking in a nature reserve reduces blood pressure more than walking along an urban street.

How does it work? Is it the switch in attention to something outside the self and its nagging preoccupations? A kind of subconscious regression to a simpler, ancestral way of being? The opportunity for empathy with other creatures whose problems may seem sharper and more real than our own? If so, it would be fascinating to see studies which discriminated between the effects of different kinds of 'nature experience': forest, water, hill country, city park, big birds, night-time ...

This is all exciting stuff, both for people and the natural world. It could lead to savings in health budgets and, reciprocally, to quantifiable economic value being put on natural habitats. Just one thing bothers me. There is, especially in the official utterances about 'nature therapy', a tendency to dumb-down nature, to see it as an undifferentiated green tonic (or anaesthetic, the new opium of the people), to suggest, most worryingly, that nature automatically makes you 'happy'. It does no service to our notions of health nor to our perceptions of the natural world to caricature and simplify them like this.

A full, honest experience of nature would find much in it that has little to do with happiness. The natural world is an arena of endurance, tragedy and sacrifice, as much as joy and uplift. It is about the struggle against the weather, the perils of migration, the ceaseless vigilance against predators, the loss of whole families, the brevity of existence. This spring, a mother mallard on our pond – a Jemima duck, an archetypal figure in our sentimental view of nature

– remorselessly strangled and drowned the ducklings of another brood that arrived on the pond.

Might this kind of experience of nature be debilitating or depressing – dis-easing? I don't think so. Surely a mature appreciation of all that it takes to be a living organism is a measure of true health, at least psychologically. The natural world is like a theatre, a stage beyond our own, in which the dramas which are an irreducible part of being alive are played out without hatred or envy or hypocrisy. No wonder they tell us so much about ourselves and our own frailties. I am all for nature cures. But let them be profound and mysterious and terrible at times. We will be all the better for it.

2006

YOUNG PEOPLE AND NATURE

What's to be done about young people's increasing dislocation from the natural world? The question, beginning as a flutter of concern among ageing amateur naturalists about who would carry on their great tradition of observation and celebration, has taken on a sense of national urgency. The worries of nostalgic romantics – and even of the current Education Secretary – are being echoed in an increasing volume of evidence about the behaviour and mental states of children. Only a few over the age of 11 have any direct contact with wild things, and the remainder are prone to sensory inadequacy, unworldly attitudes towards danger and death, and attention-deficit disorder. Richard Louv, the author of *Last Child in the Woods* (2007), named the whole phenomenon 'nature-deficit disorder'.

But this is a joyless, clinical view of the problem. More worrying is what it says about our whole relationship with nature. Where will delight at the living world's exuberance come from if you've never heard a real skylark or smelt a stinkhorn? Why should anyone want to solve the mystery of where house martins spend their African winters if they've never had the thrill of seeing a martlet's first flight? Who will ultimately care about the tiger's extinction when the animal's image is endlessly available on tv and the doubtlessly imminent Ecotube? A few children now begin their lives from in-vitro fertilisation. But vastly more spend the rest of their youth metaphorically 'in vitro' – glassed-in by anxious parents and litigation-fearing teachers and walls of computer screens. As our society connives in this retreat, are we really suggesting that virtual nature is as good, as meaningful, as the real thing?

The irony is that these same children are, in theoretical terms, ecologically literate. They know more about the carbon cycle and Amazonian deforestation than they know of the decline of the house sparrows in their own backyards. But, unenlivened by first-hand experience, it's a remote, unreal, mythic knowledge, and often acquired in a context of catastrophe. Nature, when you encounter it virtually, is presented as distant, unattainable, endangered. Now, its perils – largely created by us – are being visited on us in the form of Californian wildfires, Yorkshire floods and midges that carry bluetongue disease. Nature will be the death of us. The Americans, always ready with a jargon word, call this 'ecophobia', the fear of ecological disaster. And, as every psychologist knows, the cure for phobias is a gradual confrontation with the supposed demons.

To a very small child, there are no demons. Polly's two-and-a-half-year-old grandchild, Martha, is staying with us for the weekend, and demonstrating that connectivity with nature is not something we need to make children achieve, but a quality that our own paranoia and obsessions make them lose. We came back from the farmers' market listening to a *Peter and the Wolf* CD, all of us yelling the wolf's sinister tune, and me privately praying that this wasn't laying the foundations for wolf demonisation. But this was play, the process that links the virtual and the metaphorical with the real – as was what happened next, when we explored our bit of wood. Martha was impressed by our barn owl 'house' (unoccupied), less so by the extraordinary architecture of the hornets' nest (occupied) in the shed. She showed only a passing interest in the already fallen autumn leaves, even though I was taking her through the cherries, whose foliage most lived up to her ghastly preference for girlie pink. She wanted to pick *green* leaves. When I – trying to keep the action moving – pointed out she was tearing them, we embarked on a surreal rite of 'leaf-mending', which involved testing different leaves for their usefulness as plasters, a good deal of healing spit and experiments with grass to tie bandages on twigs.

I have no more worries that Martha will end up with an over-weening maternal view of nature than I have about her being scared of wolves, because her life is permeated with first-hand, physical experience. A year earlier I saw her discover seeds. Having just picked some tomatoes in the garden she toddled off with me and was trans-fixed that something comparable – ivy berries as it happened – grew on a wild bush. She spent days absorbed in them, sorting them, making them into ornaments, the real and imagined merging seam-lessly into each other, but with her perfectly aware which was which. (And for the worried among you, no, she never attempted to eat them.) Now she knows seeds as a generic idea. She's raised her own radishes and wanders the garden popping gorse pods and passion flowers, and watching the black fruits tumble to the ground.

Will she still have this blend of earthly realism and wild imagination when she hits 11? This is the age at which we begin to strangle kids' instinctive affinities with nature, erasing 'nature study' from the curriculum, forbidding them from playing outdoors. We have to find a way back from this dead end. Restoring a lifeline between the wild and children's natural curiosity and imaginative affections is not just crucial to the future of natural history, but, with-out exaggeration, to the future of the planet itself.

2008

REWILDING

'Reconnect. Restore. Rewild.' The slogan of the US Wildlands Project rumbles like an ancient incantation, sounding as if it is commanding the way forward, not just for conservation but life itself. It began improbably with Dave Foreman, former Goldwater Republican turned eco-terrorist, founder of Earth First! and general hell-raiser. In the 1980s, Foreman began absorbing the ideas of island biogeography and its message that isolated fragments of land remorselessly lose their wild species in the process known as 'ecosystem decay'. With a group of conservation biologists, he formed Wildlands with its audacious manifesto aim: 'to protect and restore the ecological richness and native biodiversity of North America through the establishment of a connected series of reserves … Our vision is simple: we live for the day when gray wolf populations are continuous from New Mexico to Greenland; when vast unbroken forests and flowing plains again thrive and support pre-Columbian populations of plants and animals; when humans dwell with respect, harmony and affection for the land.' Its map of New Green America is criss-crossed with swathes of 'connective' land that range over interstate highways, ranches, small towns. It's clearly too provocative, and in some eyes, too arrogant, ever to happen like that. But it's set up a dream to inspire more realistic action, an extreme position that's already pulling middle-of-the-road practicality in its direction. Its vision has a scope that is unfamiliar and unsettling to those of us on this side of the Atlantic, used to a modest, defensive, deferential approach to conservation. But we're beginning to take it on board.

The Dutch were first. Having spent a major portion of their national budget claiming land from the North Sea, they are now giving much of it back to the wild. In the 5,600-hectare Oostvaardersplassen reserve, the Dutch Government has created probably the largest stretch of restored wild land in Europe. It's a wet savannah of lakes, mudflats, immense reedbeds and scrub, teeming with birds – sea eagles, spoonbills, and in winter 50,000 greylag geese. There's little human intervention. The water table is allowed to fluctuate naturally, and the whole area has, as it should, large herds of herbivores: 500 'de-domesticated' heck cattle and 450 Konik horses (close relations of the last wild European tarpans). In a brave policy move that would still be unthinkable here, the animals are allowed to die out on the reserve, where their carcasses are eaten by scavengers. Soon, the reserve will be joined up via a Wildlands-style corridor with the

Veluwe, an even bigger area not unlike the New Forest, where the aim is to develop 'a major unified nature-culture preserve, with the fewest possible barriers for people and animals'.

In East Anglia, which once employed an earlier generation of Dutch land-managers to drain the wetlands away, we're making tentative steps, too. The Norfolk Wildlife Trust is joining up and restoring a group of fens and broads at Upton. The RSPB is creating brand new fenland on agricultural land at Lakenheath. In our valley, there's now a grassroots group called the Little Ouse Headwaters Project. We've a string of fragmented, embattled and declining fens that were part of a continuous chain of wetland two centuries ago, and the project's long-term aim is to 'recreate and maintain' this corridor by restoring natural river features and improving water quality. It's getting support from many grant-giving bodies, and from local volunteers. The problems, as usual, are chiefly with local farmers, who rationalise their hostility as a fear of that ancient East Anglian nightmare, flooding. The situation, of course, is almost exactly the opposite. Allowing the fen to take up more water could make it a safety-valve, a sink, for water from cultivated and inhabited areas.

The reinstatement of flood plains may be the most realistic way that Britain could take up Wildlands-style habitat restoration. There's worry in East Anglia at present about the effect of rising sea-levels on the Norfolk Broads. The sea, climate modellers warn, will drown the Broads, decimate the wildlife and have incalculable effects on the tourist trade.

The short-term and prohibitively expensive response of yet more massive sea-defences is being mooted. But there is another alternative. Some of the money that might be swallowed up by new sea-walls could be spent instead on buying up marginal agricultural land around and inland from the Broads, and allowing it to flood. And maybe digging new Broads in peat-rich areas. This would give both the water and its wildlife – not to mention humans – a chance to migrate and adapt.

Inundations are nothing new in East Anglia. The sea has been coming in and out for at least 5,000 years. The last great incursion, in the 13th century, is what created the Broads in the first place, by flooding medieval peat quarries. The bonus of inundation could be a vast wetland habitat, varying seamlessly from saltmarsh to riverine wood. Wildlands dreams of grizzlies from Chihuahua to Alaska. We can aim for cranes from Hickling to Hopton.

2004

THE HORIZONTAL WOOD

At the end of May I travelled down to Dover to 'cut the tape' at the Kent Trust's new reserve near Alkham, a site known locally as the 'Horizontal Wood'. It was a privilege to be invited and a hugely enjoyable day out in the May sunshine. But for me it was also the gratifying last act in a story whose extraordinary beginnings I had witnessed back in the winter of 1977/78, when the wood first acquired its nickname. The events at Sladden Wood that winter are now history, but are worth recalling, I think, not least for their optimistic epilogue.

In 1977 the beautiful Alkham valley was bought by a notorious intensive farmer called Hughie Bachelor, whose reputation for turning rich landscapes into arable dust was well known from elsewhere in Kent. He began work on the valley immediately, ploughing up downland and grubbing out shelter belts, and then set his sights on Sladden Wood. This was a 17-acre ancient wood, rich in plants and nightingales and much loved and walked by the local people. There were attempts by local amenity groups and the then NCC to frame some kind of protection for it, but early on the morning of 23 November, Dover County Council was alerted by phone calls from frantic villagers that Bachelor's bulldozers had already moved in. With commendable speed, the council drew up a Tree Preservation Order (TPO), and Paul Whittle sped to the site to serve it on the owner. When he got there half the wood was already flattened, the trees either crudely chainsawed or pushed over by the bulldozers. For the next few hours Mr Bachelor played a blackly comic cat-and-mouse game with Mr Whittle. He sheltered behind the avalanches of crashing trees.

He pretended to mislay his glasses. When the TPO was finally put into his hand, he read it, looked around at the now horizontal vista of Sladden and smiled. '*What* trees?' he asked innocently.

Yet the following March, when a public inquiry into Mr Bachelor's objection to the TPO was held, many of the stumps had already started to push out new shoots through the moraine of broken wood and bulldozer ruts. Fortunately the inquiry inspector had been given good ecological advice, and he ruled that the TPO was valid, because a tree remained a tree unless it was uprooted or killed, and that 'the wood will return to a woodland appearance even without recutting of the stumps.' It was a historic decision, and yet one whose wisdom is still ignored by many of those responsible for managing woodlands.

Fifteen years on, the inspector's prediction has been proved right. Sladden is an upright and lively coppice again. Lady orchids, herb paris and green hellebore are flourishing in the newly created glades and paths. But the Kent Trust has, to its great credit, resisted the urge to tidy the place up. The remains of the fallen – many defiantly and bizarrely alive – still lie under the newly sprung poles, a memorial to the great woodwreck of 1977, and a home for retiring woodland creatures into the bargain.

Sladden, now surrounded by a sympathetic organic farm, has a rosy future, and it was good to see so many local people there to celebrate its coming out. Without their vigilance and determination, a story of nature's resilience could so easily have been one of victorious human vandalism.

So *salve* Sladden, risen like Lazarus, a monument to the tenacity both of woods and of their human familiars.

1992

GREENHAM COMMON

I was last at Greenham Common during the demonstration of April 1983, when a hundred thousand people joined hands round the nuclear base in a shared gesture of opposition to cruise missiles. It was Good Friday, and I remember the little patches of daffodils people had planted close to the perimeter fence as symbols of peaceful reclamation of the land.

Whether the British peace movement had any influence on the extraordinary events that followed is a matter of conjecture. But the fact is, one Cold War is over, cruise missiles have been disarmed, and Greenham airbase is mostly decommissioned and up for sale. And for once, the conservation movement is a step ahead of commercial land-grabbers. Jonathan Spencer of English Nature, working with local people, has put together an inspired scenario for returning the base to true commonland, complete with grazing animals, blackberry-pickers and sweeps of heathland. It is a vision which has impressed the local authority, and vegetation surveys and speculative management plans are already being worked on.

So it was that this summer I found myself, in a state of some incredulity, inside the base at Greenham. There is still a small – and sensibly sceptical – peace camp at the gates, but even after not much more than a year, nature has already started to claim the ground back. The drab MoD buildings are being colonised by rosebay, and natterjack toads lurk under discarded ammo boxes. But there are still powerful ghosts here. Standing in the middle of the main runway, I suddenly felt quite chilled by memories. It is two miles long, and for a moment the dotted white line that vanishes into the heat-haze seemed to be unrolling under my feet – the nightmare cockpit's-eye-view from half a dozen doomsday films. But the feeling did not last long. There was a roe deer grazing on the heather a hundred yards away, and a family of hobbies flying exhilaratingly above, oblivious to any sinister echoes.

The vegetation between the runways is extraordinary. Much is acid grassland with heather and dwarf gorse, which was regularly mown while the base was in service. It consequently remained as open heathland and is now the biggest surviving stretch in Berkshire. It is full of crunchy stagshorn lichens and local mosses. But as you move closer to the runways themselves, it also becomes studded with chalk-loving plants. There are patches of kidney vetch, wild carrot and eyebright, and occasional plants of blue fleabane and purging flax. Even green-winged orchids flower in places in the spring. There is no natural chalk on this ridge of acid greensand, and what has made life possible for these species is calcium leached out of the massively thick concrete runways. Even before the base was shut down, it was starting to dissolve.

It is remarkable (and I can't decide whether heroically inspiring or depressing as well) how nature has tolerated the military presence here. More than that, it has exploited it, much as it did the earlier and more benign diversifying activities of 19th-century common-ers. Near the damp gullies at the edge of the base, for instance, cruise-missile lorries on training circuits have created deep ruts. These are now flooded, like the parish sand and gravel pits that were once scat-tered about the common, and are already being colonised by newts, dragonflies and aquatic plants. As for the missile bunkers themselves, Greenham's heart of darkness, they are still surrounded by impene-trable thickets of razor wire, and under the terms of the disarma-ment treaty, cannot be totally decommissioned until early next century. But they already seem to have been taken over by bats. Jonathan Spencer's vision is of the bunkers becoming picnic sites above ground, and artificial caves beneath, retreats for any shy, dark-loving creatures that care to move in.

It will be heart-warming if the place can become a common ground for humans as well as wildlife, with legally established rights and by-laws, as well as all the usual accoutrements of working commons: grazing animals, ponds and footpaths to replace the runways, which could be torn up and recycled as building materials (as has been done so successfully on another commonland airfield, Beaulieu in the New Forest). Plus, I hope, a few rusting relics to remind future generations of what this place once was.

A reclaimed Greenham could become an influential model for all those other bases, especially in East Anglia, that are due for decom-missioning. And it could become a powerful symbol, too, of the liberation of land, of the turning of the tide against the concrete, a rejection of those official, emollient arguments about the minute percentage of land being taken for development, which always forget that the original figure was itself a percentage just a short while back … From now on, an acre back for an acre lost.

1993

FLOOD

It has become the new condition of England. After years of baked soils and hose bans we are now awash, with more water falling from the skies and spilling over the land than has been seen for a generation. Nine months of downpour have transformed landscapes across much of southern Britain. Country roads have turned into waterlogged ruts. Miniature ghylls have been carved out in the woods by flood-races. Even the Chiltern chalk streams are in spate again. The Chess Valley, where I often go to banish winter stodginess and sniff for an early spring breeze, now feels closer to the Everglades than the south coast. The field oaks, roots swathed in new moss and lichen, are standing in pools of water. Herons lurk *inside* woods, probing tongues of flood water that have found gaps in the wood-banks. The River Chess itself is a torrent, smeared jade and murky white with pulverised chalk and algae, and almost effervescent as gales whip at the surface and pump oxygen back.

'We told you so,' relieved water and river authorities are no doubt longing to say, as most of southern England's lost streams and rivers reappear. But how long will it all last? Is this real, resident water we are seeing, or just flash-floods running off the surface of compacted fields and out of overburdened drainage ditches? The whole of the modern rural landscape is designed to move water on as fast as possible. It gathers in under-field drainage pipes, seeps into sheer-sided ditches, pours into canalised rivers and rushes eventually down to the sea, out of sight and out of mind. This suits our cultural attitudes very well. We enjoy water when it behaves like a liquid arable crop, and are happiest when it is tamed, uniform, pure and reliable, and is 'harvested' and moved on as briskly as possible. As long as it keeps to its own domain – or what we have decreed to be its domain – we see it as a benign ally, inexhaustible and cleansing, a universal solvent.

The images and metaphors of 'washing away' dirt and corruption – be it from hands or souls – reach very deep in our culture, and may have something to do with our cavalier attitude towards water. The emphasis has always been on what is to be cleansed, never on the agency of cleansing. That, laden with its cargo of several sorts of sin (including these days PCBs, human sewage, pesticides, radio-active isotopes, jettisoned oil and abandoned drift-nets), runs off into the distance – and forgetfulness. Only when water breaks out of its straitjacket and washes some of this repressed material back are we reminded that it simply moves dirt around, it doesn't necessarily destroy it.

1992

* * *

Anyone who has been birding on the north Norfolk coast will remember Cley Coastguards – the rickety observation tower, the greasy spoon, the little snug with its bird log and bizarre library. Well, this much-loved retreat from East Anglia's capricious weather has vanished, courtesy of the same forces of nature it was designed to be proof against. The structure was badly mangled during the storm tides and floods that ransacked parts of England last autumn, and which wiped out all freshwater life in Cley and Salthouse nature reserves for a season. A short while later it was put out of its misery and razed to the ground. It's one of the first buildings to be voluntarily surrendered to the sea, a rehearsal of the ritual submission that is now government policy along the east coast.

The phrase 'managed retreat' is now regarded locally as a kind of diabolic curse. But it's not a new idea, being first mooted in the National Strategy for Flood and Coastal Defence in 1992. Climate change has already pushed the annual rise in sea level to more than 6mm, and doubled the frequency of storm surges, so the government decided that it was not economically feasible to defend the whole of the east coast. Progressively, as the sea walls that protect nature reserves, grazing marshes and villages are breached, they will not be repaired.

The economics are certainly jaw-dropping. It costs £10,000 a metre to build a new sea wall. The bill for keeping the sea out along the whole eastern coastline, from Ramsgate to Hull, for another two or three decades, has been estimated at £10–20 billion. And even that would be no guarantee, as no one has any idea where the repulsed sea would go, or what it would do.

East of Cley Coastguards the Environment Agency had already tried a progressive approach to sea defence, creating broad shingle banks to try to take the energy out of the waves. After the storm of 9 November 2007, they looked like chewed fish. The sea had gnawed through in dozens of places and sprayed tongues of shingle hundreds of metres into the freshwater marshes where bitterns and harriers breed. Along the Blythe Estuary in Suffolk, the sea water is still lying in the meadows, and nature reserves from the Ouse Washes to the Deben Estuary have all lost breeding birds because of flooding, high rainfall, tidal incursion and raised river levels.

But the real storm in Norfolk happened in May, when a supposed plan by Natural England (NE) to withdraw the sea defences some 4 miles inland and create a huge saline lagoon was leaked to the press. To be fair to NE it was just a desk exercise, one of a number of options as to how to respond ecologically to rising sea levels. But as it involved the surrender of 25 square miles, including the two best known Norfolk Broads, Hickling and Horsey, all their surrounding reed-marsh (where the cranes breed) and six far-from-derelict villages, it didn't go down well with the public.

Natural England fielded their climate change scientist Dr David Viner to quieten the uproar, but his politically naive explanations made things worse – especially his insistence that the 'social side' was none of NE's concern but was the responsibility of 'other parts of government'. The admission that, even in this time of supposed 'joined-up government', politicians, economists and eco-logists are each developing responses to climate change in isolation is shocking. But so is the Government's ruling about which bits of the coastline are to be saved: their policy appears to be based on an index of short-term political convenience, rather than long-term ecolo-gical necessity.

Some kind of retreat is inevitable, sooner or later. The rising sea can't be kept out indefinitely without bankrupting the nation. But it can be done intelligently, with benefits both to wildlife and human communities. In the Blackwater Estuary the Essex Wildlife Trust has experimentally breached the sea walls around 200 acres of derelict farmland, where no human settlements are involved. In just five years, the results have been remarkable. Saltmarsh is already form-ing and waders have started to move in. The wide saltings are prov-ing far more effective at buffering tidal energy than abrupt sea walls, and better sinks for water, too – saltmarsh and flood-plain grass-land can soak up more than six times the volume of water that arable land can.

By working with natural processes rather than against them, it might be possible to achieve a compromise: embank human settle-ments, but allow the rising sea much deeper into the estuaries and river systems to form new saltmarsh, and create flood-plain 'washes' and rain-absorbent freshwater habitats further upstream. Buying the land for this would be far cheaper than the cost of 'holding the line' everywhere. At the moment we are preoccupied with trying to 'prevent' climate change. But it is already happening, lapping at our doorsteps, and we must learn to adapt, too.

2008

GHOST HABITATS

So how was 2008 for you? In East Anglia at least, the spring and summer were a washout. We had, so the meteorologists say, the wettest summer for 300 years. Also, though I haven't seen this quantified, probably the windiest. The impact on wildlife still needs to be assessed, too, but it's pretty clear that it was calamitous for many groups, especially flying insects and everything that depends on them, and anything that breeds on low-lying floodable land. So, to take just a few examples, butterflies, bees, house martins, lapwings and marsh harriers all look as if they had a grim year. For the Ouse Washes, the internationally important wetland site in Cambridge-shire, the results are already terminally filed away. This spring, 1,500 pairs of waders and ducks had their nests and eggs washed away by floods. The irony is that the Washes were created as a flood-water sink, to protect nearby towns and agricultural land. Now, they need their own overflow lands.

Is this going to be the shape of summers to come? Not the droughts and heatwaves that climate change was expected to bring, not colonies of hoopoes nesting in Sussex olive groves, but years of warm grey rain, where the seasons have been ironed out? It's too soon to tell, of course. Weather is not the same as climate, and three wet summers in a row don't constitute a trend. And when I mention our local losses to friends in other parts of the UK they're bemused. Their house-martin colonies are expanding and their dragonflies having a bonanza. Down in Milford Haven last winter, a group of swallows overwintered at the oil refinery. Britain is too intricate a region to make generalisations about, too full of niches that break the rules. 'Every now and again,' wrote Roger Deakin in his post-humously-published journals, *Notes from Walnut Tree Farm*, 'you find yourself slipping into a little pocket, a little envelope, of country that is unknown to anyone else, which feels as though it is your own secret land.'

I go to my own little envelopes in bad weather and troubling times, though few of them are personal secrets. I go for reassurance that life goes on, I suppose, and to try to recapture moments from less anxious days. I slip this time down to a remote corner of Suffolk that I haven't visited for 25 years. It's in the small parish of Shelley, but I can't find the lane I'm looking for in this flat and often hedge-less country. Then suddenly I'm in an arching tunnel of trees, and have got my bearings. They're native small-leaved lime trees, and they range along this lane for more than 600 metres. The atmosphere is extraordinary: sinewy trunks of old pollards and coppice stubs, and clouds of tan-tinged autumn leaves, like tiny lozenges of stained glass. It is, I suspect, the only hedge formed from this native woodland tree in England, and when it was discovered three decades ago the reason for its existence was a mystery. The solution came from an old map. The lime hedge coincided exactly with the northern edge of the ancient Withers Wood, the rest of which was cleared in the 19th century. It was the ghost of a wood.

I don't know who first coined this term, but there are ghost habitats everywhere: sheets of bluebells among the bracken, marking the site of vanished woods, gorse on a roadside where a common once was. The concept of habitat ghosts is a poignant one, reminding you that there was once a much more lively presence. But I also find it a pleasingly mischievous notion, suggesting the possibility of hauntings, of apparently deceased habitats rising up and getting about again … Certainly the Shelley ghost is far from dead, though it will take a radical warm-up in the climate for the limes to start regenerating from seed once more.

And in improbable corners all over the country, enterprising wild spirits are surfacing from their mausoleums and taking bodily form again. A few miles east of the Ouse Washes is another great wetland site, the RSPB's Lakenheath Fen. Ten years ago it was an intensive carrot farm. Now, deliberately reflooded and planted up with reeds, it's become one of the most exciting watery places in East Anglia. And it's not just birds like bearded tits and bitterns that have returned. Springing up quite spontaneously, from a seed bank that's been dormant under the fields for centuries, are whole new suites of scarce fenland plants.

Wildlife is more resilient and more actively adaptable to environmental change than we often give it credit for. A good resolution for 2009 would be to have more faith in its poltergeist's stubbornness.

2009

ALIEN NATIONS

The ruddy duck was the first seriously rare duck species I ever saw. I watched one on Tring Reservoirs in the mid-1960s, a decade after a few had escaped from Peter Scott's Slimbridge sanctuary (it was originally from North America), and long before the species was added to the official British list in 1971. I thought it was a hugely likeable creature, with its bright blue bill and cocky flag-pole tail, and was delighted when it began to spread to lakes and gravel pits throughout Britain.

Ironically, the ruddy duck's adaptability and success look like proving its undoing. It has now reached southern Spain, and local ornithologists have discovered occasional hybrids between it and the local race of its close relative, the white-headed duck – the symbol of Andalusia, but reduced by hunting and wetland development to an embattled population of about 350 pairs.

Keen, I imagine, to divert attention from their own role in the white-headed duck's near-demise, the Spanish authorities have set their sights on the transatlantic species, and prophesied that it will before long interbreed its scarce and genetically unique European cousin out of existence. Last year they persuaded the EC to order the extermination of the ruddy duck throughout Europe. The directive has been endorsed by British conservation agencies and, with a rather bitter irony, by both the RSPB and Sir Peter Scott's own Wildfowl and Wetlands Trust.

Trials to find 'humane' ways of eradicating the birds began on Anglesey this May. It is always unpleasant to hear of coldly planned massacres of this kind, especially when they are based (as here) on flimsy evidence and thinly veiled nationalism, and when the hapless victims seem to be doing no more harm than blurring a few tidy-minded scientists' maps of the world. By no criteria could they be described as pests.

But there is a rising tide of hostility among scientists towards all immigrant and introduced species. Warrants are out on Canada geese and Roman dormice. Commercial foresters have commissioned research into the spread of Chinese muntjac deer. Even botanists have begun to hoist apologetic quarantine flags. A recent report for Plantlife warns against the dangers of 'non-native plant material' finding its way into wildflower seed mixtures. Foreign strains may, Dr John Akeroyd argues, compete and cross with native plants of the same species, leading eventually to the extinction of 'native forms,' and 'confusing the complex and ancient patterns of our landscape'.

I am not for a moment minimising what can go wrong when an alien species, freed from all its usual predators, gets loose in a new country. The devastating effects of, for example, Dutch elm fungus (from Canada, actually) in Europe, and rats in the Pacific should be warnings enough. But I sense something deep-rooted behind the current wave of obsessive vigilance. It is absurd to compare it with the obscenities of 'ethnic cleansing' as some writers have suggested (though I suspect they spring from a shared legacy of territorial and ecological insecurity). It is not even a loathing of foreignness, but a mixture of worry about the expansiveness of immigrants, and something akin to the nostalgic devotion to tradition and 'authenticity' shown by fans of folk music and real ale. 'What if it was our robin that was being eradicated by an introduced species?' supporters of the ruddy duck cull have argued. Indeed. But do they mean the robins that breed here, or the Scandinavian ones that come for Christmas? And what if they had chosen some other 'British' symbol to bolster their argument – brown hare, horse chestnut, corn poppy, for instance, all ancient introductions to these islands? The fact is, there is no absolutely clear line between native and introduced species, or between their effects. Most exotics aren't especially pushy, and prosper only if they find a vacant niche – as did, for instance, the little owl (introduced from the Continent in the 1870s) and the collared dove (arrived under its own steam from south-east Europe in the 1950s).

What is disturbing is an ideological opposition to introductions simply because they are foreign; and a conviction that conserving biodiversity means fossilising species, turning habitats into isolation wards, ecological theme parks. Biological diversity evolved by exactly the opposite process, by species mutating, developing, cross-breeding, and radiating out. E O Wilson has described this in his new book *The Diversity of Life*, and also how almost all habitats on Earth, from an English copse or a Spanish marsh marooned in farmland to whole sea-bound kingdoms, now behave ecologically like islands. Species become extinct on islands continuously, even without human pressure, and unless they are replaced by new species from outside, the community will be on the long slope towards biological degradation. In an unstable world, the ruddy duck hybrid might be the best chance of saving some of the white-headed duck's genes.

Maybe we should try celebrating these instances of evolution in action. It is surely only the churlish whose hearts aren't gladdened by the thought of African ring-necked parakeets trapezing round south London cemeteries; by the feral wallaby colony that has somehow survived 50 winters in the Peak District; by Chinese buddleia delighting butterflies and commuters in every city centre. These intruders are the resilient, magnanimous face of nature, and maybe its insurance policy, too.

1993

* * *

At the risk of being deported as an undesirable myself, I want to return, very gingerly, to a subject I dipped my toe in a few years ago: immigrant species and how we perceive and cope with them. Like it or not, we already have large numbers of exotic settlers, plants especially, and the list will increase. It's a process inseparable from our own territorially unbounded expansion across the planet, and we need to find a sensible perspective on it.

I'm attracted to the idea of 'naturalisation' as a rough-and-ready index of the acceptability of an immigrant species, though this, too, is a debatable concept. Norman Tebbitt once notoriously suggested that the test of successful naturalisation for West Indians was that they should support the English cricket team. I don't know what the equivalent would be for, say, a Caribbean willow, but I'm sure it should be more generous.

In scientific terms, naturalisation simply means that an exotic species has become viable in its new habitat. It's a definition that passes no judgement. But the cultural meanings have more helpful undertones. To become naturalised is 'to be admitted to the rights and privileges of a native-born subject or citizen', or 'to settle down in a natural manner'. 'We, by act of Assembly,' they pronounced during the French Revolution, '"naturalise" the chief Foreign Friends of Humanity.' In all these definitions there is a sense of give and take, of the foreigner giving something to its adopted culture, but blending in with it, too.

I wondered how a handful of 'aliens' established round my Norfolk village would look under such scrutiny. Winter heliotrope, first flower of the year, crystallises the problems. A pot of it was brought to this country in 1806, after being gathered from a French stream-bank, and it has since spread through southern Britain, though staying pretty well confined to damp, disturbed roadsides. In its favour are its Christmas-flowering lilac tassels and a gorgeous honey and vanilla scent. But it's highly aggressive. It can build up large clonal patches, and its saucer-like leaves, which persist throughout the summer, shade out everything beneath them.

The starry-white blossom of the cherry-plum overlaps with the winter heliotrope. It's the first real sign of spring in the hedgerows, and has so successfully 'settled down in a natural manner' that it's taken to be early-flowering blackthorn. But it was probably brought from the Middle East (as the myrobalan) by returning Crusaders, for its fruit. Crossed with blackthorn, it is the precursor of the domestic plum, and it was one such chance hybrid, found in a Sussex wood in 1840, which was brought into cultivation as the Victoria. So cherry-plum emerges as a beautiful and useful intruder, but one with the habit of breeding with the natives, and whose fertile offspring can occasionally penetrate ancient woods. This puts it in an ambivalent position in the excellent and pragmatic new document 'Plant Diversity Challenge: The UK's response to the

Global Strategy for Plant Conservation', qualifying both as an 'invasive non-native species' that 'can hybridise with close relatives', and a component of 'useful plant diversity'.

Almost nothing uncomplimentary could be said of ivy-leaved toadflax. It came from Italy, so the story goes, 'by means of its seeds having been brought in some marble sculptures from that country to Oxford' in the 17th century. It was an aptly elegant entry. The neat purple and yellow snapdragons made it popular as an ornament for the vast number of elegant stone walls and buildings created over the next two centuries. It went on to colonise old stonework throughout Britain, displacing no indigenous plants in the process and never straying into natural habitats. By contrast, it is hard to think of a good word for parrot's-feather *Myriophyllum aquaticum* – an aquarium throw-out from South America that can become overwhelming in pools or slow rivers. Here, in south Norfolk it's rather ominously spreading on to summer-dry land in heaths and carr.

So which species should get their naturalisation papers? All but the last in my book. Most exotics live in (and do nothing but improve) artificial habitats such as roadsides and railway lines that are cosmopolitan by their very nature. They are, in that obsolete word, commensals, species which live as our tenants. (There is a close parallel with arable weeds here. Many of the species which are now on Biodiversity Action Plan priority lists – eg, pheasant's-eye, shepherd's-needle, corncockle – are themselves anciently naturalised aliens from southern Europe, rarely seen outside man-made habitats.) Indeed, remaining a commensal might be a good test of acceptability for an immigrant plant, were it not for species such as the sweet chestnut, which is respected for precisely the opposite reason – because it has become inextricably intermingled with the natives. Sweet chestnut has been spread so much that there is no longer an indisputably wild stand in Europe. It was probably brought by the Romans, but it grows here so well, so naturally, that it may well have arrived much earlier. It is unquestionably an 'honorary' native, in our wild landscapes, our folklore, our culture.

The bigger question-mark hangs over the species that introduced it. How do we – another invasive, habitat-destroying colonist from southern Europe – rate in terms of naturalisation? Do we deserve 'to be admitted to the rights and privileges of a native-born subject or citizen' by the rest of the ecosystem?

2004

MICROBES AS WILDLIFE

It used to be said that once humans had gone the way of the dinosaurs, the insects would inherit the Earth. On recent evidence neither of us stands a chance against the great nation of microorganisms. Increasing numbers of infections that we thought we had vanquished for ever are returning in newly virulent forms. Tuberculosis is back among the poor. A common throat bug, slightly mutated, is causing rampant gangrene of a kind common in the First World War. Every month there are new revelations of the ubiquity and adaptability of microbes: the existence of infectious proteins ('prions'); the possibility that viruses are involved in afflictions as different as asbestosis and motor neurone disease; an Australian doctor's remarkable discovery that gastric ulcers are due to a bacterium that can survive in the inimically acid conditions of the stomach. All of which makes the Natural Environment Research Council's recent spraying of a caterpillar-infested Oxfordshire cabbage field with a genetically-engineered moth virus, boosted with scorpion venom and untested on other species, seem a tad irresponsible.

The dramatic successes of antibiotics mean that we have never bothered, as a culture, to work out the ecological and ethical status of these 'little animalcules' that van Leeuwenhoek began glimpsing through his microscope three centuries ago. As part of the living scheme of things, are they included when we make grand statements about conserving biodiversity? Do we want flu and 'flesh-eating bacteria' off the planet, or just out of our systems?

These aren't just academic debating points, as the kind of answers we feel inclined to give will shape the compromises we make between our own and other species' well-being, the risks we are prepared to take. It would take a degree of holistic belief verging on self-destructive insanity to view one's body as the bacteriological equivalent of an oak tree, a vital host to an immense variety of predators and parasites. Yet it is worth remembering that we could barely even survive without many of our fellow-travelling micro-organisms. They digest our food and clean up the debris on our skin. They almost certainly played a crucial role in evolution, bacteria and protozoa combining to form new kinds of complex cell, early viruses introducing new genetic material.

When he was in solitary confinement in a Greek prison, George Mangakis fed three mosquitoes off his own blood, for company and solidarity. I doubt that one could summon up the same fellow-feeling for a TB bacterium. Yet maybe his story is a parable about the need for at least some respect and caution in our attitudes towards the ancient and resilient pestilences of the Earth.

1994

VERMIN

You may have seen that splendid story of the London vixen that sauntered into a fashionable Portobello Road shoe boutique in broad daylight last October. It generated a wildlife photo of Spitting Image resonance: a very foxy fox padding over a gleaming white floor past a collection of impossibly trendy footwear. It also generated a farcical commotion in the shop. 'We had lots of people in the middle of trying on shoes,' the manager explained, 'who started shrieking and ran out into the street in their socks ... We shut the shop because we couldn't tell if it would make our customers sick.'

This is one of the less offensive examples of a worrying new development: the New Vermin Panic. With a sense of disgust and outrage that seems borrowed from the Dark Ages, wildlife is increasingly being demonised for the slightest intrusion into human affairs. And this isn't a matter of threats to life or limb, but to comfort and convenience. 'Swallows Bring on My Allergy!' 'Ladybird Invasion Threatens Ice-cream Sellers' Livelihoods!' 'Herons Steal My Koi Carp!' 'Biodiversity Wrecks Our Biodiversity Action Targets!' Even the conservation business has got on the bandwagon, blaming impeccably native species for intervening in the lives of rarities. Hedgehogs are culled and exiled for raiding waders' nests. Common toads – common, alas, no more – are cleared out of their ancestral breeding grounds for the sake of the rarer natterjack toad. And there are whispers that the Government may soon cave in to the powerful game-shooting lobby and make some relaxation in the absolute protection currently given to birds of prey – long regarded as vermin, of course, by estate managers with rich syndicate shoots to keep happy. It is as if the very success of nature conservation has revealed an awful truth: wildlife is prolific, untidy, inventive and in our backyard.

Roger Lovegrove's fascinating trawl through the parish records of routine wildlife slaughter, *Silent Fields,* shows just how deep-rooted the vermin reflex is in our culture. But I was disappointed by his sitting-on-the fence conclusions. He abhors what he calls 'sentiment' over these issues, and says that conservationists must be prepared to make compromises with 'legitimate human interests'. I disagree. I'm afraid that the evidence of history is all too clear about what happens when compromises are made: humans don't make sacrifices, nature does – or rather becomes a sacrifice, a scapegoat. I believe that without sentiment and feeling and a strong dose of ethics, and a sense of reparation for what we've done to wildlife in the past, we could easily slip back to the bad old days documented in Lovegrove's book. These are some actual examples I've collected over the past few years of what can happen when the 'rational' approach is adopted and wildlife is treated as an inanimate inconvenience, to be dealt with as if it were so much litter.

House martins: widely persecuted because they spoil the look of the pebbledash. In Tring, Herts, the council tried to keep their town hall exterior civically neat by putting up pigeon-wire under the eaves.

Unfortunately, the newly hatched martins were inside the wire and their frantic parents outside. (Martins, alas, do not always seem in tune with the Neighbourhood Watch mentality: I once saw a nest slung under a jeweller's burglar alarm.) Cormorants: already legally killed to keep coarse fishermen happy. A Norfolk landowner recently applied for a licence to have a colony on his land destroyed because they were spoiling his ornamental conifers. Brown long-eared bats: Norfolk again. A local vicar is trying to get the law changed so that he can destroy the colony in his church because their droppings (just about the least offensive in the animal kingdom) make the interior of the church appear 'unholy'. Yew trees: last year Bristol City Council grubbed up 100 yew trees round a children's playground because it thought the children might poison themselves by eating the foliage. It would need handfuls of nauseous foliage to cause any trouble, and I have been unable to trace a single case of human poisoning from yew leaves in the past 100 years.

Real threats to life and health are one thing. Nuisance, mess, missed targets and minor loss of income are another, and not legitimate excuses for wildlife pogroms. A better response would be to accept these intrusions into our comfort zones as a kind of tithe, a voluntary sacrifice for the privilege of living on a planet rich with life.

2007

BIG ANIMALS

The medieval town of Trujillo, south-west of Madrid, is guaranteed to overturn any prejudices you might have about Spanish attitudes towards wildlife. It's a town in a state of permanent occupation by birds. More than 100 pairs of lesser kestrels scythe about above the battlements, chatter from tv aerials and terrorise the local sparrows. Hoopoes set up squats in unrepaired back walls. Pallid swifts scream between the groups of tourists in the Plaza Mayor, flying so close to the ground that you can, for once, see their paler backs. And posing heraldically among them all, are the town's storks. They build their bed-sized nests on ducal palace roofs, in the bell towers of Gothic churches, on arched gateways and ornamental balconies. They have colonised electricity pylons and satellite aerials on the edge of town. In the breeding season bits of nests, sticks and old rags drop down into the streets. And with a satisfying poetic justice, stork guano blotches the statue of local conquistador Francisco Pizarro, the man who, above all others, exported Europe's nastier attitudes towards the wild to South America. But modern Trujillans are a gentler lot. The nest debris is swept up nightly, the statues cleaned, and the town lives on entirely amicably with its avian citizens.

Gazing at this Eden-like scene, I wondered how a heritage-proud British city would cope with such a colonisation. Despite the magisterial beauty of storks (and their history as symbols of fertility), would they be tolerated on Canterbury Cathedral or the Brighton Dome? How would the citizens of Bath react to them soiling their historic spa? This isn't just a fantasy. Although storks are declining generally across Europe because of wetland loss, they're thriving where they have been reintroduced in the Low Countries. It's an easy flight from there to Stodmarsh or the Pevensey Levels in south-east England, and one that a changing climate might induce the birds to make. Would they be welcome?

The precedents aren't encouraging. Our national paranoia towards any creature that is big and predatory, or which intrudes into our sense of domestic quiet and tidiness, is obstructing the return of a whole range of indisputably native species, especially ones high up the food chain. Recently the wild boar has been up before the courts for anti-social behaviour. Boars lived wild in Britain no more than four centuries ago, and have reintroduced themselves by escaping from farms. The population, scattered about southern England, the Welsh Borders and the Peak District, may now number several hundred, and the boars have been found guilty of rootling in gardens and, allegedly, peering over primary-school walls. So a committee has been appointed to consider their fate – a decision greeted with disbelief by friends in France, where communities live satisfactorily with hundreds of thousands of the animals.

Wild boars are, of course, big and potentially aggressive (though only when they're provoked) and we would need to work out a *modus vivendi* with them. The bonus – as well as the restoration of a magnificent animal to its rightful place – might be a better under-standing of our human place in the natural scheme of things.

If we genuinely hope to restore big, wild landscapes in Britain, we need to welcome every species in the food chain, from the lowli-est, ugliest fungus to the top predator – and that includes the ones that crap on monuments, rootle in allotments and snatch the odd piglet. If we only want the well-behaved, the thoroughly controlled, the picture-postcard species, then we might as well keep our animals in zoos.

2008

CONSERVATION AND
THE ENGLISH LANGUAGE

George Orwell's celebrated essay 'Politics and the English Language' should be pinned up on the wall of every policy-maker in these jargon-ridden, slippery-tongued times. 'If thought corrupts language,' he wrote in 1946, 'language can also corrupt thought. A bad usage can spread by tradition and imitation, even among people who should and do know better.' Things have got even worse in the 60 years since. In the conservation world, as in many others, language is now cyni-cally manipulated for political effect, or to plaster over real differences of opinion, or to disguise value judgements as statements of fact.

A short while back I heard an environment minister explaining on the radio why the Government was no longer going to support Village Design Statements. For some years now it's been encourag-ing communities to discuss and log their local landscapes and wildlife, and produce statements that would be given consideration in planning matters. But now, the minister said testily, the whole business had become silly. People were trying to save the most triv-ial features. Their affections were subjective and out of proportion, and stood in the way of 'the national interest'. The Government was responsible for deciding what places and things were really important, and the rest of us must just grow up and accept this. We must, he said, pulling out his green calling-card, 'learn to be holistic'.

It's worth dismembering this arrogant nonsense, and its topsy-turvy conclusion. What the Government is saying is that if you think your village green-patch, with its clumps of cowslips and bramble bushes, is important because villagers like walking there and swallows like hawking over it, you are wrong. Value and importance are matters for higher authorities (scientists, governments, etc) to rule on, not humble commoners. Parochial attachments, by any species, must be surrendered to the Greater Good. This is what the minister, thinking it would show him to be ecologically sensitive and aware, described as being 'holistic'.

This, needless to say, is a travesty, as is the minister's top-down model of the workings of an ecosystem. Holism is not about the supremacy of the whole over the parts, but, precisely, about the importance of all the parts to the workings of the whole. It is about the connectivity of life, about the value of the seemingly insignificant, about the necessity of intricacy and detail. In an ecosystem (and a society for that matter) all members are equally and intrinsically valuable. If choices appear to be necessary because of human value judgements, then politicians should have the guts to say so, instead of hiding behind misused and apparently 'objective' technical terms.

In this case, it wasn't long before the Greater Good was revealed. It was the 'imperative of housing' – a 'need' which must take precedence over all other uses of the land, as if Britain were already like some Sudanese refugee camp. But it would be all right – and here the minister produced his second, and more familiar, green sweetener – because it would be 'sustainable' housing. Now, however socially desirable and environmentally sensitive a housing development is, the one thing it can never be is sustainable. Unless, that is, it is built entirely from renewable resources (eg wood and grass), is self-sufficient in energy production and waste disposal, provided with no new service roads and, for every unit in it, one existing house is demolished and the land given back to nature. But that, of course, the minister would protest, is not what he meant by 'sustainable' at all. He was talking about road-carrying capacities and available policing, not all that airy-fairy nonsense about non-renewable materials and green space.

I'm afraid the conservation movement has created a Trojan Horse with its indiscriminate use of this concept. 'Sustainability' once had a precise meaning. You harvest from a natural system no more than it can naturally recoup, indefinitely. But it's degenerated into a meaningless buzzword. Institutions as far apart as Forum for the Future and the World Bank use the term as cynically as 'natural' is used in the food industry. Charities crowbar it into their programmes to help them get grants. Businesses wave it like a passport – or a credit card. Governments indulge in the delusion of 'sustainable development', and John Prescott euphemises his housing estates as 'sustainable communities'. What on Earth is a sustainable community? A castle built in the air and living on salad and solar energy?

When words are abused like this, it's often illuminating to explore their roots. The earliest meaning of sustainable was 'capable of being borne or endured', an inflection which saw things from the point of view of the suffering person, or object. But at the time of the Industrial Revolution it came to mean 'capable of being upheld or defended', subtly switching the centre of attention to the protagonist or oppressor – or developer. These days sustainable means what you can get away with for the next 20 years.

Language use reflects the politics of the language user. Jargon is propaganda by another name. It's an attempt to avoid – or suppress – critical thinking. And, as Orwell so damningly pointed out, its parading of an aura of expert, privileged knowledge is the sure mark of an authoritarian institution trying to smother dissent and argument. A radical green movement should have no truck with it.

2006

CONSERVATION AND BUSINESS

The love affair between conservation and business – which grows more avid by the day – has already produced at least one good fable: The Worm Turned, or how green stopped being the shade of innocence and became the colour of money.

About four years ago a group of enterprising alternative technologists devised a small plant in which earthworms can be used to turn rubbish into compost. Under controlled conditions the worms will tackle anything, from abattoir refuse to pickled-onion factory waste. In a matter of weeks they multiply prodigiously and reduce the garbage to a dark and fertile loam. Up to this point it sounds an almost perfectly benign process. But customers won't accept compost containing live worms, and so the thankless creatures have to be separated out in a centrifuge. More high-energy input follows to satisfy the requirements of the market: sterilisation in a flame-chamber, electronic sealing in plastic bags.

On balance, the process is such an improvement on chemical waste-treatment that its disadvantages are outweighed by its benefits. The same might be said for two of the principles underlying the new *rapprochement:* the conservation movement's willingness to compromise with the real world, and industry's understanding that producing goods which 'press more lightly on the planet' may be in its own interest as well as the Earth's.

Yet I have a feeling that something more ominous than compromise is taking place, and that the conservation movement is allowing its ecological principles to be replaced by those of the market. Increasingly ethics are regarded as being irrelevant, market forces relied upon to produce 'values', and distant costs and effects disregarded.

This is most obvious in the greening of industry itself. At the Green Designer exhibition in 1986, John Elkington of SustainAbility talked, encouragingly, of moves towards 'designing problems out of products'. Where this has happened (with Body Shop products, for example) it represents a real advance. But too often greening is simply a cosmetic exercise in damage limitation (pesticide applicators that reduce wind-drift, for example) which, far from challenging the central problem, accommodates and legitimises it.

Again, the flourishing new business of pollution-control engineering needs a continuing high level of pollution as its basic raw material, and therefore has an economic interest in encouraging processes which have not had the problems 'designed out'. The most notorious example of this occurred in the 1970s, when the big oil companies fought long legal battles against the patenting of a cheap biological oil-slick dispersant, as this would undermine their profitable, sideline marketing of detergents to disperse their own slicks.

Too often, conservation bodies seem reluctant to enquire into the motives and backgrounds of the firms they are collaborating with and into the possibility that they may be being used. Are all those working on research projects financed by the British agrochemical industry – into a chemical spray alert for beekeepers, for instance, and the wildlife of drainage ditches – sure that the money is coming out of the research, and not the publicity, budget? Is the Hawk Trust, which has received a substantial donation for barn owl conservation from a multinational mining firm with strong South African links, confident that it is not saving British birds at the expense of greater ecological and human damage in other continents? Does any of this matter? Should we accept money from, do business with, anyone – just so long as the natural environment seems to benefit in the short term?

This is the argument normally used to justify links between conservation and field sports' bodies. The latter – a rich and influential lobby – raises another aspect of the market, that is by no means free, but favours the most powerful. By the time this article appears, the Nature Conservancy Council (NCC) will have published a policy statement on its attitudes towards field sports in 'creating and maintaining habitats for wildlife'. More surprising is a clause which states that, in considering grant-aid for the purchase of land for conservation purposes, the NCC will want to know the purchaser's proposed policy as regards field sports, and that the 'curtailment of traditional rights and practices could affect our ability to offer a grant'. This condition – which could lead to the irony of the NCC being the first body to give state support to field sports – was introduced by the direct request of the Secretary of State for the Environment, who was dismayed to find that wildfowling had been restricted in the Solway Firth.

It is to be earnestly hoped that the NCC – which seems to be under more political pressure by the day – will honour its promise to apply this clause fairly. It has a statutory duty to have regard for the social and economic rights and practices – which include what the French have christened 'les droits de non-chasseurs' – of the whole community, not just those who have the money and clout to bag grouse.

Yet even the grouse are being increasingly perceived as products, to be streamlined for the market. The Game Conservancy has been researching the annual fluctuations in grouse populations, and has concluded that the birds are not fit enough, chiefly as a result of internal parasites. So the grouse will have to change to a more healthy lifestyle. They will have medicated grit put out at their feeding stations. Predator control will be stepped up. This kind of intensive care was not the reason the grouse was able to adapt and survive as a British native for hundreds of thousands of years. 'Improving the stock' is risky as well as morally dubious (as Bernard Shaw observed, when Isadora Duncan said what an exceptional child they could have together, given his brain and her beauty. 'Yes,' he replied, 'the snag would be if it had your brain and my beauty.') Nothing better demonstrates the fact that the interests of the two sides in the concordat do not exactly coincide than these images of two sorts of grouse: wild, unpredictable, and occasionally a little sickly – or pampered and programmed.

None of this means that the conservation movement should cease to deal with other bodies, however partisan they may be. But there is a world of difference between proper bargaining and swallowing the market ethic wholesale. Real negotiation, for instance, would make a conservation 'seal of approval' dependent on genuine improvements in industry's standards or processes, not just on a donation from the publicity department's expense account.

Conservation, industry and recreation have been horse-trading for more than a century, and during that time almost everyone has been relieved to leave behind the Victorians' mawkish adulation of the natural world. But if I had to choose between a society which designed the Crystal Palace with the help of a reverent wonder at the structure of giant water-lily leaves, and one that does the exact opposite – modelling a relationship with the environment on the mores of Wall Street, I know which I would take.

1988

THE RIGHTS OF NON-HUNTERS

August is here, and the sound of the twelve-bore is heard again in the land. Britain's killing fields are open for another season. I have tended to keep my head down in the acrimonious debate about field sports, but not because I don't have strong feelings about them. I find the whole lot odious and incomprehensible, and am saddened at the way some conservationists shrug off the moral issues simply for the sake of gaining another apparent ally in habitat protection. But I know and like some of their practitioners. We live in the same parishes, sit on the same committees. I acknowledge their enthusiasm and their desire to carry on a hobby that, for many of them, is the focus of their lives, and have felt that the argument was better carried on quietly, person to person.

What has shaken me out of this silence is a campaign of unprecedented selfishness and extremism by the field sports lobby. No doubt the election and fear of possible legislation lay behind it originally; but it has now acquired a momentum of its own, and has two so-called 'Country' columns in the Saturday papers as its mouthpieces. Much of their argument is a familiar brew: the supercilious jibes at the ignorance of 'townies'; the assumption that anyone who lives in the countryside must agree with them, otherwise they are cracked, treacherous and probably politically suspect; the attacks on anthropomorphism and the crediting of animals with human feelings, which never acknowledge that leisure hunters themselves practise what we might call zoomorphism – the fallacious crediting of humans with untameable animal urges.

But it is not these arguments I want to discuss here, nor the philosophically tricky issues of animal suffering and rights. What I want to talk about is *human* rights. This is the new plank in the field sports lobby, and their manifesto closes with the ringing phrases: 'We must beware that the State doesn't encroach on what is rightfully the province of morality and choice. If it does encroach, it takes away the individual's right of choice.' What I want to know is what about *my* right of choice? Has it never occurred to the hunting lobby that every time they kill an animal they also destroy the rights and freedoms of those who choose to enjoy it alive?

This isn't some abstract philosophical point. It happens daily in the countryside. It happened recently to Eric Ashby, when the New Forest foxhounds invaded his garden and caused his famous badgers to desert their sett. It happened to me a few years ago in Norfolk, when wildfowlers shot a short-eared owl we had been watching all winter. Most outrageously it happened on a national nature reserve while I was showing round a party of primary schoolchildren.

The estate was holding a 'courtesy' shoot for its staff that day – a reckless arrangement that was reflected in the accuracy of the shooting. The official bag was 60 birds, but a friend who was ill in bed and amused himself counting the shots, recorded in excess of 500 firings. The misses rained down on the children's dormobile and on any other living things that happened to be in the way. By lunchtime we were faced with a lake covered with dead and wounded birds, and a group of frightened and distressed children, bewildered at what right these men had to kill birds on a nature reserve *and* take away their freedom to enjoy birds peaceably.

It may be argued that these are untypical examples, illegal or 'bad form'. Yet, historically, the law as regards the killing of animals has tended to safeguard neither the animals themselves nor the public, but the sectional interest of the hunters. The worst privileges and impertinences of the 19th-century Game Laws may have been replaced, but the hunting lobby was still able, in 1985, to get the House of Lords to block greater protection for badgers on the grounds that it might lead to innocent foxhunters and earth blockers being heinously charged.

Even the basic common law on animals is biased in favour of vested sporting and landed interests. English law recognises no *absolute* right of property in a wild animal. While it is still free and alive an animal belongs to nobody – or everybody. But it can become property by being – it is a sickly euphemism – 'rendered into possession'. That is by being caught or killed. And from this moment it belongs to the owner of the land on which it is taken.

This finders-keepers principle might be all right for a hunter-gatherer economy. In a society trying to work out a more equitable way of sharing its natural resources and a better relationship with its fellow creatures, it is cynical and antiquated. If wild creatures can be said to 'belong' to anybody, they belong to the whole planet.

Members of the sporting lobby would reply that they are acting in the common interest, since they help conserve habitats, and that they only hunt creatures which are 'either edible, or pests, or both'. If so, why are they not trying to extend their activities closer to those of their colleagues in *la chasse*? Why not go for house martins, say, wretched pests that ruin the look of the Dulux? Or nightingales, a great delicacy in most of the Mediterranean, and no doubt excellent sport when they are hiding in their favourite thickets?

I would like to believe that English sportspersons have not gone this far because they do feel some of the emotions they despise in the opposition. But it is also because they recognise that the social consensus would be overwhelmingly against them. Rights – especially those that determine the fates of living things – cannot be claimed unilaterally. They are freedoms which human beings grant to each other. And freedoms which ride roughshod over the liberties and wishes of the majority of citizens are not freedoms at all. They are what the upright sections of the press call 'licence'.

1987

FILTHY IMAGES

No one could have anticipated the power of those first images of the Gulf oil-slick on 26 January 1991. After 10 days in which the reality of the war had blurred into a series of firework displays and ambiguous statistics, this terrible, seeping collision between life and matter was like the surfacing of a suppressed nightmare. It won't be easy to forget the eyes of those stricken cormorants; nor the lapping of waves on the shoreline – once the oldest, brightest sound on Earth – muffled to the dull beat of a funeral drum. Even ministers of state and hardened war correspondents, skilled in giving blandishments about human tragedies, found themselves choking over the pictures.

Perhaps it is not so surprising. In a far-off war fought by computers, sanitised by censors and the guardians of media taste, cormorants dying on camera are about the only casualties we have been allowed to see. But I believe there is more to it than that. Animals have always become symbols at moments of human crisis, and it would be hard to imagine a more pointed metaphor for this war than a cormorant drowning in oil. A native of the open seas, feathered and tarred, forced into the final humiliation of trying to crawl on to the concrete highways to escape. A bird, smothered by ancient waste products that the Earth wisely seals up beneath its skin.

Animals caught up in human conflicts are true neutrals. Their suffering hasn't been chosen or voted for. It is not given for the sake of aggrandisement or abstract values. It is stripped of propaganda, obfuscation, religious cant and political hedging. It is a stark mirror of what war means to us as fellow living creatures, which is why we are so shriven by the sight of it.

For Edward Thomas, in the First World War, the chastening came from an English owl. He heard it in Hampshire one cold February night in 1915, two months before he left for France:

No merry note, nor cause of merriment,
But one telling me plain what I escaped
And others could not, that night, as in I went ...

Speaking for all who lay under the stars
Soldiers and poor, unable to rejoice.

Time and again, animals seem able to focus and clarify the complicated and fuzzy entanglements of human affairs. Remember the
cranes returning to Vietnam in 1986, the first signs of the healing of
a landscape ravaged by 10 years of war? Or the release of the two grey
whales trapped in the Alaska ice in 1988? This frantic, inspiring rescue
mission by Eskimo, Russian and American teams was watched around
the world, and seemed to presage not just the thawing of the Cold
War, but a new phase in our respect for other species.

I don't believe that finding moral or metaphorical meanings in
animals has anything to do with sentimentalising them or imbuing
them with human characteristics. Mostly it is exactly the opposite, a
momentary glimpse of their one inalienable and unarguable right, to
be themselves, or simply to *be*. It is not always a reassuring vision.
No one who watched *The Trials of Life*, for instance, with its harrow-
ing sequences of killer whale and chimpanzee hunting sprees, can
harbour any illusions about gratuitous violence (or so it appears)
being confined to the human species.

Yet perhaps, like military strategists, we have been duped by a
surfeit of unconsidered information. We know about tactics for
ambushing prey, about territorial defence and group bonding, and
persuade ourselves that we therefore 'understand' animals. We do
not, of course, and the labyrinth of their inner lives remains a
mystery to us. In the late thirties, Colette wrote an extraordinary
essay, inspired by her horror of zoos, in which she argued that we
had intruded too far into animals' 'real' lives:

We are no longer free even to remain ignorant of how a boa
constrictor chokes a gazelle, or how a panther … rips open the
throat of a goat which – since the combat must be spiced and
the cinema has no use for passive victims – has a kid to defend.
It is high time I said good-bye to reality … I shall dream, far
from these wild creatures, that we could do without them, that

we could leave them to live where they were born. We should
forget their true shapes then, and our imagination would
flourish again. Our great-nephews would once more invent
an indestructible fauna, which they would describe as they
beheld it in their dreams, with dazzling intrepidity, as our
forefathers used to do.

Colette was not arguing that humans and nature should be separate, but that animals can be imprisoned, limited by literalness and scientific presumption as well as by cages. In other essays – on listening to her dog's heart, on watching the motion of a python ('it liquefies, flows along the branch, and on the other side, becomes rigid – it is creating a tension within itself, presaging some emergence I cannot guess at …') – she identified what common ground and what fellow feeling lie between us. We share universal, irreducible needs for space, freedom, nourishment, affection and the flow of the seasons. But as humans we also have a unique imaginative insight into the whole intertwined variety of creation, in which individual creatures – the returning swallow, the oiled seabird – have meanings for us as well as flesh and blood existence.

I do not know what new horrors will have occurred by the time you read this column. But I doubt if there will be a more chastening image of this war, and the current condition of humanity, than the accusing glare in a cormorant's eye, and that vision through the wrong end of history's telescope, of the glint of life slipping back into the slime.

1991

PATRIOTISM

In our fleeting spells of fine weather this summer I found myself drawn more and more into the deep Chilterns south of my home, for my money now the most sublime patch of hill country in England. The pubs and walks are unbeatable, the tumbling beechwoods are edging further down the hills, the skies are full of birds of prey. One especially halcyon day, I saw in a thermal four red kites, three buzzards and a darting hobby, itself surrounded by a boiling mass of swifts that seemed to have descended from the heavens. I had not seen anything like it in England before, and it reminded me that there was much in this inspiriting landscape that wasn't home-grown. The red kites had been introduced from Spain, the swifts were brief summer visitors from Africa, the hobby may be from north-west India. Even the beechwoods had probably been planted up from French or German stock.

It was a salutary lesson. We have been stuffed to the gorge with overheated patriotism this summer. Euro '96, the 'beef wars' and the endlessly festering rows about Europe have shown that an ugly jingo-ism still lurks in corners of Fleet Street and Westminster. This kind of brainless nationalism is a dangerous anachronism, and certainly has no place in a world trying to face up to its environmental crises. Pollution, big money and wild creatures all move about the planet without any heed to national boundaries.

Yet real patriotism – a love of one's own place that bears no hostil-ity to others – is a profound and positive emotion. It is one of the roots of environmental concern, and the context in which the great slogan 'Think globally, act locally' is acted out. It is also, I believe, an ecological emotion. Most living things are loyal to their own patch without being disrespectful of others' territories. Birds can sing from self-assertion not aggression. Plants can cling on to their favoured spots for millennia, simply because that is the place in which they live. The things that inspire our own territorial attachments – the sounds of a home accent, a glint of heather, brass bands, the wood we made dens in as children – are more complicated but not so different. They are not about winning but belonging. And the sight of birds that have travelled from three continents, enjoying the summer over one corner of an English field, is not a bad symbol of that.

1996

THE FREE MARKET

You could say that the English language has biodiversity. It prospers because of its complexity and richness, and the fact that so many words have, as it were, multiple subspecies of meaning. But the cost is a kind of fuzziness, as is the case with Charles Darwin's two best-known phrases – 'the struggle for existence' and 'the survival of the fittest'. They're like psychologists' ink-blot tests: how you interpret them depends on your own beliefs. Having at various times been used as excuses for communist revolution, slavery and the persecution of the Jews, they're now being quoted by apologists of the ruthless greed that has brought the world's economic system to its knees. 'The free market is a force of nature,' one banker recently proclaimed. I don't know what is saddest about this, the spectacle of supposedly sophisticated humans denying they are in control of their own affairs, or the belief that ecosystems are as crude and inelegant as the global financial machine.

Darwin saw these ideas more subtly. Take 'fitness', for example. Although he does employ the word in the modern sense of healthiness and vigour, in the theory of evolution it also means 'fitting in': those organisms survive that are best adapted – most fitted to – their environments, and so are able to reproduce successfully. And though this means privation and possible extinction for those organisms that aren't, this rarely happens through the bloody combat of popular myth.

The evolution of the 13 species of finch that Darwin studied in the Galapagos is a classic case. Tiny mutations in the genes that govern the shape and size of beaks eventually produced subtly different species, which exploit different food sources. Some are cactus finches. They drink cactus nectar, eat cactus seeds, even nest in cacti. Others strip bark or chew leaves or prise ticks from the backs of iguanas. The process of species' 'radiation' is still going on. During a drought on the island of Daphne Major in 1976–77, the average beak size of the larger finches increased by half a millimetre. Variations too small to see with the naked eye had given those birds the edge in breaking into the last, sun-baked seeds of the caltrops bushes.

These may yet become the 14th species of finch. All Darwin's genotypes still survive. They've struggled with a merciless environment, but not often with each other, continuing to prosper in parallel by sidestepping into different habitats and behaviours. Increasingly, Darwin realised that the most successful organisms were those that had evolved ways of avoiding the energy-expensive and risky business of direct physical conflict. Birds do sometimes fight, but the defence of territory by song is a much more efficient way of resolving competition. Many snakes wrestle, but don't use their fangs, and rutting mule deer won't attack when their opponents expose their unprotected flanks. In the 1970s the biologists John Maynard Smith and George Price worked out a 'games-theory' explanation for this which didn't assume altruism in animals. They worked out the profits and losses for creatures genetically programmed to use different strategies: the Hawk (which invariably is an outright aggressor), the Mouse (which never is), the Bully (which uses dangerous tactics against cautious ones) and the Retaliator (eventually refined as 'tit for tat': it starts by cooperating, then copies its opponent's previous move). Only the Retaliator was, in Maynard Smith's words, 'evolutionarily stable' – the only strategy which, if used by all members of a population, couldn't be supplanted by any other kind of conflict resolution.

Given the peculiar nature of our consciousness and culture I think it's foolish to try to draw human political lessons from the workings of evolution. But the bloodier side of the struggle for survival has been stressed so much that it's no bad thing to realise that negotiation and cooperation have also been powerful ingredients, albeit from self-interest. Many recent discoveries inside the tradition of Darwinism have reinforced this point. Darwin knew about symbiosis, and would have been pleased to learn that the majority of life-forms in the rainforest live in this kind of arrangement with their neighbours; that symbiosis can result in new species by a kind of cellular fusion; and that viruses have had an important role in creating new species by ferrying genetic material about.

Supporters of the unregulated financial markets like to believe that they work 'naturally', creating myriads of new business species and economic habitats. In reality, as we now know, human ambition and greed give the Hawks and Bullies a free hand, and the economy becomes dominated by immense, predatory super-species.

Evolution's contrary process – the ceaseless generation of diversity – does have one profound and unequivocal political message, vividly captured in Darwin's famous sketch of the Tree of Life: every single living thing on the planet is biologically related to every other. It's also a message of great beauty, as the father of modern biology expressed in the heart-stirring last sentence of *On the Origin of Species:* 'Whilst this planet has gone cycling on according to the fixed law of gravity, from so simple a beginning endless forms most beautiful and wonderful have been, and are being, evolved.'

2009

INDEX

Passionate about wildlife?

BBC Wildlife Magazine is your essential guide to the natural world. Every issue showcases the **wonder and beauty of wildlife** and helps you to understand, experience and enjoy nature more. The magazine is packed full of **breathtaking images**, informative features, practical advice and much more.

Try it today
5 issues for only £5*

Order online
www.subscribeonline.co.uk
/wildlifemagazine PLEASE QUOTE BWNBK10

Telephone hotline
0844 844 0251 PLEASE QUOTE BWNBK10

Calls to this number from a BT landline will cost no more than 5p per minute. Calls from any other providers may vary.

 Magazines